T
the Wi
Nit

By

Ed Barnes

Here to There,

and Back,

Again

Dedication:

**To Mirjam, to Sue, but
Above All,
To Pops**

Travel: the Witty (Shitty) Nitty Gritty © 2020 Ed Barnes

First Published 2020

The moral rights of the author have been asserted.

All rights reserved. No part of this publication may be reproduced, distributed, or transmitted in any form or by any means, including photocopying, recording, or other electronic or mechanical methods, without the prior written permission of the author, except in the case of brief quotations embodied in critical reviews and certain other non-commercial uses permitted by copyright law. For permission requests, please contact the author at: edbarnes99@hotmail.com

Author's note: Whilst this is book a work of factual content, please note that all names have been changed.

In-Flight Menu

Introduction

Author's Note

Aperitif – Blackcurrant Coulis 10

PART ONE

1. Welcome to India! 19
2. Gulliver's Travels. 28
3. As If by Magic, a Man Appears. 38
4. Are You Sitting Uncomfortably, Then We'll Begin......48
5. A Holler from a *Wallah*. 54
6. Darling, I Want You, But Not So Fast. 58
7. Taken In. 66
8. That's Some Numb Bum. 81

Drinks Break

9. Wherever I Leh My Hat. 92
10. Bash, Smash, Crash. 113
11. Having the Last Laugh. 125
12. Lord of the Flies *vs* Gandhi. 143
13. What a Wimpey. 145
14. Bhanged by the Lassie. 148

PART TWO

15. Just Shout 'Jim!' Really Loudly. 161
16. Don't Chicken Out Now. 180

4

17. Free at Last? 190

18. That Man Jim. 197

PART THREE

19. The Shitty Shits. 205

20. Enough, Already! 211

21. The Last Hoorah. 216

22. Suffering, so Much Suffering. 224

23. Cairo, or Bust. 229

24. Play Your Cards Right. 238

Inter-Course – *Amuse Bouche* 244

PART FOUR

25. In the Beginning. 248

26. The Rag 24-Hour Hitch. 261

27. Trucking Hell. 273

28. Adroit, or *A Droite*? 281

29. Sneaking a Peek Behind the Curtain. 288

30. Short Cut to Heaven. 299

31. Ios. 314

32. Homeward Bound, How I Wish I Were. 317

33. Egg on Face. 324

PART FIVE

34. What Were The Odds of That? 328

PART SIX

35. The Unbearable Randomness of Being. 332

36. You Lucky Cow! 348
37. A Sinking Feeling. 355
Dessert – Daft Pudding 359
Epilogue 365

Introduction

1988.

I am impoverished 19-year old university student in urgent need of an inexpensive means of reaching Greece to holiday with my old school chums. The affordability of Low-Cost Airlines is still, sadly, far off in the Unknowable Future.

The solution?

To travel by lorry, from Battersea Park, in London, to Piraeus, in Athens, down through Belgium, West Germany, East Germany, Czechoslovakia, Hungary, Yugoslavia, and finally into Greece, a 4-day adventure providing a fascinating (if brief) peek into life behind the Iron Curtain.

Through Bruges town centre (unintentionally), along the incorrect side of a Hungarian motorway, for 10 miles (intentionally, very much, surprisingly), we rolled along, at a steady 56mph, witnessing the last year of separation between East and West before the Wall came crashing down, and the nature of Europe was forever changed.

A curiosity of the Wider World had been sparked.

1992.

I set off from Heathrow on a 12-month adventure, off to Australia via Hong Kong, then home, by way of Indonesia, Singapore, Malaysia, Thailand, Nepal, India, and Egypt.

At least, that was the Plan.

At the outset, all seemed so simple.

The internet, mobile phones, Wi-Fi and ATMs were, in '92, mere twinkles in their creators' eyes.

Saying 'Goodbye' to your friends and family, 'see you in a Year' really did mean, 'Goodbye' – no FB, no emails, no updates, no news.

Alone: Out there, the Dark.

A Stranger in very Strange Lands indeed.

In the 30 years since, I have travelled to more than 80 countries, to all Four Corners of the Globe, and many of the parts in between. Along the way, it's fair to say some Stuff has happened, either to me, or to the incredible mix of people I have been fortunate to have encountered.

During this peripatetic period, friends and family have constantly cajoled, badgered and hectored me to commit to paper an Account of My Travels.

Until now, I have resisted, doubting many – *any*? - would wish to read of *my* Tales.

For sure, they are remarkable to *me*; but to *others*, who can say?

Travel: The Witty (Shitty) Nitty Gritty.

As anyone who has spent serious Time on the Road will attest, Travelling is not always a Bed of Roses.

Shit Happens. All sorts of Weird Shit. All sorts of Weird *Shits*.

Sometimes, the Poop even impacts the Oscillating Air-Circulatory Device.

At Times such as these, the choice is either: Laugh, or Cry.

There really is only one option to choose...

Author's Note:

Unless *explicitly* stated otherwise, all views and opinions contained herein, on Cultural Attitudes and Beliefs, or on Geo-Political issues, relate *specifically* to the time periods the travels in this book covers (1988/ 1993).

Time marches on. Geo-Political situations change, sometimes for the better, often times for the worse. Societal Attitudes and Beliefs shift, too; just what Attitudes and Beliefs on the issues discussed are currently – *exactly* - well, you'd have to make the same journeys all over again, asking *exactly* the same questions, to be able to determine properly.

Omniscient as the Internet believes itself to be, sitting in your dirty underpants - laptop open, typing questions into standard Search Engines - is no substitute for getting up off your (possibly) spotty bum, out into the Wider World, and gleaning your information straight from the Horse's Mouth.

Go on – what's the worst that could happen?

Aperitif

Blackcurrant Coulis

June 1992.

I am currently in gainful Wine Merchanting employment in Barnes, SW London.

Barnes: a leafy, sleepy suburb, nestling serenely beside the Thames.

A name carrying a certain *cachet*.

Home to a smorgasbord of A-C Listers – the likes of (previous) Dr Who incarnations, Dad's Army combatants (*Don't panic*, I won't tell him, *LCpl* Jones!), Brian May & Roger Taylor (Queen), Pete Tong, Stanley Tucci, and, er, Gary Lineker - plus a plethora of high-rolling bankers, accountants, lawyers, and other eminently successful middle-class professionals for whom the Common, its duck-filled Pond, and nearby Riverside Walks are the primary allures.

Wine Merchanting is a job I find surprisingly enjoyable, especially when such luminaries as Catherine Zeta-Jones and (now Sir) Trevor McDonald pop in to sample our latest oenological delights, and chat about all things Grape.

The only downside is the relentless weekend work, thrice out of four, on strict rotation, an encumbrance severely denting my fledgling social life.

I am in my early twenties.

Having a day off in the middle of the week doesn't chime with anyone I know.

This job, I fear, will not evolve into my *metier*.

I am restless. I feel the need for change. I am currently considering my options.

An old school friend, Bob, is presently progressing through the SKB Graduate Training Programme. Bob has been assigned to cut his teeth, if that is the correct use of the phrase, on the Ribena brand. Ribena, a sugary blackcurrant squash marketed at the younger generations, might, I fear, do a little more than simply *cut* one's teeth.

Bob asks if I would like to earn £50 for a morning's work, at a children's charity event in Battersea Park.

£50 for a morning's work does indeed seem child's play.

I ask what is required in order to earn said £50.

'Dress up as a Ribena Berry,' I am told.

A costume will be provided. I will simply need to wear said costume and stand around for a few hours.

Nothing difficult in that, eh?

'It'll be a doddle', Bob says.

It is precisely for high-skilled jobs such as this that I have spent nine of my young, formative years, through Primary and Secondary Schools, studying vigorously and religiously, sacrificing evenings and weekends to slavishly swot for forthcoming exams, achieving a veritable smorgasbord of high grade 'O', 'A' and 'S' levels.

But 50 quid is 50 quid.

I console myself with the thought that at least none of my contemporaries will ever know it is me inside the Berry costume.

The day arrives.

At the venue, I am introduced to the costume.

The ensemble comes in four parts:

Purple leggings, that rise to just above belly-button height, held in place with elasticated shoulder straps.

Over-sized, darker purple felt shoes, that surprisingly dwarf my already over-sized Size 12 feet.

Over-sized, darker purple felt hands, which also surprisingly dwarf my own already over-sized clown hands.

And to finish this snazzy outfit off, a purple, berry-shaped top-half that comes all the way down below my groin, its face complete with eyes, nose, mouth and eyebrows, and crowned with a trio of browned leaves, a configuration not unlike the most foppish of hairstyles.

The Berry possesses a fixed, cheesy grin, a look easily confused with the silent delight one gets from peeing inside a wet suit. The eyes are no less distracting, seemingly staring directly at you, in whichever direction you go; worse, the frowned brow appears to signify the presence of worryingly impious thoughts.

I have no idea what effect this costume will have on the children.

I presume the Berry has passed all mandated Criminal Background Checks.

He (could be *she*, it's tricky to 'sex' a Berry) looks decidedly dodgy to me.

I am helped into the costume by my friend. I realise, once everything is in place, that I cannot see much, if anything, out of the eye holes. As a result, I will need to be guided around by the hand, all morning, wherever I go.

This would be somewhat humiliating if I hadn't already checked my dignity in at the door.

There is no turning back now.

It is a warm, sunny day. I mention this because despite technically being summer, this warmth is still rather unusual for England. Thankfully, in the decades to come, Climate Change will alter our tepid English summers for the better, although not everyone will consider this Warming a 'Good Thing'.

My friend leads me around the Park, to meeting after meeting with all manner of Grand Dignitaries and Youthful Attendees, but I am completely none the wiser as to the identity of any of the people I (sort of) meet. I cannot hear much out of the costume, either; some vaguely familiar voices make utterances in my near vicinity, but I'll be damned if I can ascertain precisely to whom these voices belong. I am told later that some are – *were* - quite famous, although this presumes (Soap Opera) EastEnders actors and actresses are actually 'quite famous' people.

Inside the costume, I am counting the seconds until this ordeal is over.

Celebrities?

Hoo-flippin'-rah!

This news matters to me not one jot.

An hour and a half passes, although not quite in the blink of an eye.

I am asked if I'd like to take a break.

I mumble a 'Yes' as best I can from beneath my costume; nodding the affirmative doesn't quite register with those around me.

My friend leads me round to the back of the large marquee tents being used by all the marketing bods who've also given up their Saturday morning for this charity shindig.

The top half of the costume is removed.

I am back in the world of daylight, of 360-degree vistas.

I can see again. This is wonderful.

I can breathe again, too, which is also wonderful.

I ruffle the sweat out of my hair, plonking my arse down on the nearest flat surface, relieved to be able to take the weight off my over-sized feet for a few minutes.

I am passed a lit cigarette, which I most gratefully accept, taking a long, deep pull of its therapeutic vapours, before exhaling the smoke with an equally long *Ahhhhh* of reinvigorated relaxation. With propitious timing, at the very moment of this exhale a young boy, of no more than six or seven, who's obviously just seen the Ribena Berry being led around the back of the marquees and has decided to go see what Ribena Berry does on his lunch break, pokes his head around the side of the tent.

His facial expression is one of wild excitement blended with hopeful anticipation; eyes wide, mouth contorted into a cheery grin, joy unbound.

This look suddenly morphs into one of extreme horror, of wild panic, as I exhale another long draw of smoke, blowing smoke rings as I do.

The Terror!

The Ribena Berry smokes!

Da da **DAAA**!

'Something is not quite right here', the boy is probably thinking, overwrought as he must be with bewildered confusion.

In a flash, the lad turns heel and runs off, well before any of the other zoned-out lunch-breakers around me can react and give chase. I still have those damn clown shoes on so am in no fit state to be running anywhere, let along chasing after a young boy now in tears – in any case, just how would that scene look to the outside world, a semi-naked Ribena Berry chasing frantically after an obviously distraught child?

The erroneous conclusions people might jump to?

Imagine *that* image appearing in the Press the next day.

No such thing as Bad Publicity, eh? This might be the Exception that Proves the Rule.

The boy disappears out of sight, no doubt off to look for his mother.

'Mummy, mummy, you won't believe what I just saw!! Ribena Berry, smoking a cigarette!!'

His mother will, most likely, tell him off for fibbing, for making up tales, for letting his imagination run away with him, for trying to stir up trouble. The young boy's persistent protestations will doubtless be met with, 'Enough Already!', threats that, 'We'll have to go home if you don't stop this nonsense', ringing in his ears. He will most likely require several thousand pounds of therapy to restore him to his previous state of equilibrium. This one event may even have caused him to turn rogue, setting him off on the path to the Dark Side.

On such small details can futures be fixed.

Back at lunch break camp, I am not sure whether to laugh or be somewhat concerned. Those around me simply shrug it off. I decide to defer to their greater marketing acumen and take the same approach.

All too soon, the top half of the costume is returned to its previous position. Once again, I am virtually blind to the world outside, needing to be guided by the hand towards my next appointment. I am *so* glad there is no one else I know here to witness this humiliation.

We are slowly making our way out from our half-time position when a male voice near me proclaims, with rather too much glee if I am being honest, 'Last week, I drank your cousin.'

I peer as best I can through the costume's eye holes, making out the shape of Clifford, the Listerine Dragon, standing beside me.

If you're not familiar with Clifford and his series of commercials back in the '80s, let me elaborate.

Please now picture in your mind an 8-foot tall Green Dragon, with red spines running down its back, a long green tail protruding out several feet behind him.

This is Clifford.

Listerine is a bacteria-killing, refreshing Mouth-Wash-Gargle.

Quite why anyone would think of advertising a bacteria-killing, refreshing Mouth-Wash-Gargle via the medium of a large green dragon called Clifford is beyond me, but then again, I am no Marketing Guru earning £200k a year. The surreptitious subtleties of Marketing are a Dark Art indeed.

So here we are. Inside this Clifford costume, some insensitive and evidently callous sociopath has, without provocation or preamble, declared war on me and my Ribena kin. Clifford has made what he presumably believes to be a humorous quip, whilst simultaneously declaring that he has committed, without incitement, murderous fratricide.

In my mind, I scroll down a list of possible responses *à la Terminator*.

'Fuck you, asshole,' seems a tad too harsh.

'Please come back later,' too random.

I decide to wing it, selecting, 'I hope you choked,' as my best all-round, impudent-but-pithy comeback.

I detect a sharp, audible intake of breath from the direction of the Dragon.

An imminent blast of fire might, I fear, be about to wend my way.

Instinctively, I turn to avoid being burnt to a crisp.

Quick Wit is often followed by Quick Reflexes, or so the saying goes.

There is no jet of fire. No scorched earth. No burnt to a crisp.

'I thought this was supposed to be a charity event', Clifford instead whines, before scampering off to lick his wounds, whilst I presume mulling over the toxic impertinence of this large purple Berry.

Clifford's elocution and accent remind me of a north-London Guardian reader. Possibly someone who teaches, 'The Evolution of Human Form & Movement within a Neo-Classical Context'; someone who, without hesitation, would – willingly - slit the throat of anyone unseemly enough to pronounce, '*Quinoa*' - 'Kin-O-Ah'.

This realisation hits me like a joyous bolt from the blue.

'Oh My,' I suddenly think, 'here is someone plumbing the Depths even more than me.'

This man may even consider his turn as Clifford *the Performance of His Life*.

My mood is restored to a thousand times its previous level.

The second half is suddenly looking up.

I am led forth by my captor, back, or so I am informed, towards the fray.

The 50 quid is so nearly mine. So close, I can taste it; the wondrous bottles of Spain's finest *Gran Reserva* the moolah will afford me.

After a few minutes' walk to who knows where, I am requested to stand still so the photographers can take their shots. I sense someone to my left, someone whose voice is ever-so-slightly recognisable, someone evidently older than the high-pitched, overly-excited, squeaky-voiced kid to my right, a kid who is right now repeatedly trying to squeeze the fingers in my right hand as hard as he can whilst simultaneously digging his left heel repeatedly into my right foot with all the force his slight frame can muster.

The Little Shit.

Thankfully, the Little Shit is unaware he is merely squeezing on and digging into the felt costume. My *actual* fingers and toes are nowhere near his puny digits. I am then led away from this tableau, all the while considering whether to dob this kid in for being *such* a Little Shit.

As my mind is pondering a suitable response to the kid's shittyness, I receive some rather disturbing news. It is news I am sure anyone would find hard to take.

For I am informed that I have just had my photo taken with none other than Jeremy Beadle. The photo is, I am told, set for distribution amongst the local rags covering this event, as well as for use in SKB Ribena marketing brochures.

The shock of this news completely breaks my chain of thought.

Jeremy Beadle. Beadle's About.

Watch Out! Watch Out!

Oh, dear God.

The horror!!

I try to calm myself.

Deep breaths.

It'll be fine. My secret is surely safe.

No one will ever know it is *me* inside *that* costume.

My honour and dignity can rest easy.

Nope. Not so.

My now so-called friend Bob feels it is far too funny an image not to share with our peers.

Infamy. Infamy. You know the rest.

Time, possibly, to Leave the Country?

PART ONE

Chapter 1

Welcome to India!

June 1993.

The emotional farewells of the raucous leaving party nine months back are but a blur within a faint memory inside a dream; the parting cry, 'So long, folks, see y'all in a year', a faint, muffled whisper lost in distant ether. I can still recall the image of me as the young man uttering those words, but only just; I see myself - my shape, my form, my features – but, in truth, I no longer recognise *that* version of me.

It *is* me, sure enough; it *looks* like me, but a mere facsimile of a *me* that once was.

Maybe I haven't really changed so much on the outside. Maybe to look at, you wouldn't immediately grasp the truth that the man inside is now a completely different person.

That was Then.

This is Now.

Between Then and Now, a few Things have been witnessed, some Stuff has been experienced. Several incidents have occurred, too.

Nine months.

Time to gestate a new human form. Time to gestate a newer version of oneself.

How Time flies.

Where *does* it all go?

I'll fill the gaps in later, presuming we have enough Time.

Maybe, I'll have to make Time, but I have yet to figure out how one *makes* Time.

Time flows; Time ebbs; Time races.

Time always *is*; Time always *was*; Time always *has been*.

Time never starts; Time never stops; Time never *will* stop.

Rather than *make* Time, maybe instead I should figure out how to *hold on* to Time; after all, Time is all we've got.

Time.

Time to head into *Terra Incognita*.

Time to enter the Twilight Zone.

Time to step beyond the boundary of my Known World.

Time, once again, to Extend my Horizons, to Push the Envelope, to Stretch the Bubble, to take a long stride off the sanctity of solid ground onto swampy sods, sods that might possibly swallow me whole, down in one, my very existence erased in a single gulp should I stray too far from the path, sinking down into its dark, dank morass.

Time, even, to stretch the metaphor well past all reasonable, acceptable limits.

It is Time to leave all sense of Logic, of Reason, of Normalcy, far behind.

All those things you *think* you know, they don't count for shit anymore; all those Societal Norms, those Customs, those Values and Beliefs, that sense of order, of fair play, of trust, gone, vanished, faint will-o'-the-wisps floating off into the air.

You're on your own, young lad, a Stranger in a very Strange Land.

I am indeed alone.

It hasn't always been thus.

At first, we were two.

Lately, many.

But Time passed; it is, once more, 'Me *vs* The World'.

More precisely, 'Me *vs* India'.

After a month in Nepal, a month being regaled by tales from recent escapees, repeatedly, tales of Incomprehensible Mayhem and Unimaginable Muddle, tales which, with each passing day, became wilder, crazier, scarier, it is fair to say I am more than a tad apprehensive.

For India, from information freshly gleaned, is a vast country like no other: a country of Complex Simplicities; of Baffling Logic; of Staggering Disparities; of Organised Chaos; a land which fascinates and repulses in equal measure; where Up is Down, Day is Night, and 2 + 2 might just = 5.

To write so fervently of India risks accusations of excessive hyperbole; fear not, dear scribe, for no matter how extreme the picture your words might paint, the Reality far transcends in outlandishness.

Overstating India is an impossibility.

I don't claim to be Blazing a Trail; I do not consider my quest *Heroic*; I am not endeavouring to discover, uncover, nor *recover* Ancient Mystical Truths mislaid aeons ago when Civilisation came crashing into this vast land; I am not retracing the History of Empire; this is no lament to a bygone Golden Age.

No.

I have taken a Gap Year, back when taking a Gap Year was more of a Rite of Passage than the year-long jolly it seems to have morphed into for many of today's whimsical youth (Care to Discuss?).

I have Gone to See the World.

I have Gone to Find Stuff Out (exactly what kind of Stuff I have frankly not a clue).

I might even have Gone to Find *Myself*, ever trusting that if successful in this quest, He and I will be sufficiently lucid to remember to swap numbers.

****

Outskirts of Birgunj, Bihar state.

It is an ungodly hour of day, one better suited to still being tucked up in bed, rather than standing forlornly in an inhospitable land with the fuggiest of heads wondering what the hell is going on. A smattering of people mills around, local people, people I could ask for enlightenment, but they don't strike me as the types whose answers would help elucidate this fug. The handful of Westerners nearby, some sitting motionless on their rucksacks, others focussed on rolling their first fags of the day, might have the answers, but none seems keen to make eye contact, such is the intent of their focus, or the parlous state of their own particular fug.

I could go forth in search of answers.

Or, I could take their lead, plonk my arse down on my rucksack, and hope instead the answers might come to me.

So very passive.

So *very* India.

These are the last muffled moments before dawn. The sky's tinge attains a crisp, rose pink; the sun readying to re-emerge over the horizon. Wispy mist banks hover over the countryside, soon to be burnt away, providing an atmospheric dampener to the sounds I can now hear. A panoply of birds sings their merry morning songs, the sounds punctuated by the occasional clamour of a peacock proudly announcing his presence to potential suitors, or maybe simply to whoever might now be in earshot.

'Look here at *me*, why don't you?' he cries.

Scantily clad young women walk by barefoot, small bundles of firewood for their daily kitchen balanced skill-fully atop their heads. Dotted all around, small cliques squat silently beside still smouldering fires, the older folk wrapped in thick blankets, patiently anticipating the sun's warmth once more.

I am shattered. It has been a gruelling 12-hour overnight journey from Kathmandu.

On the plus side, I have just learnt a lesson. It is a valuable lesson, one to file in the memory banks for years to come. Like many lessons that stick over time, it is a lesson learnt the hard way.

For I have just learnt that Assumptions really *are* the Mother of all F-ups.

I have learnt more questions should be asked prior to rushing in headfirst, prior to presumptuously presuming the word *Sleeper* - in reference to a mode of carriage - has *precisely* the same meaning out here as it does back at home.

I have learnt that the lexicon of language can both aid and hinder, for the Nepalese *Sleeper* bus which has just deposited me here afforded the bare minimum of sleep.

The bumpy, twisty roads didn't help. The jolting forwards, backwards, upwards, downwards, side-to-side-to-sidewards, and all the way back again, weren't ideal, either. The thinly padded, not-nearly-clean seats, seats that declined to recline past the standard 90-degree angle were possibly the tipping point, no pun intended.

True, most everyone else on the bus slept like babies, locals well-practised in the art of making the most out of nothing.

So, yes, *technically* it was a *Sleeper*.

But not for this weary traveller.

Welcome to India.

Although, not quite.

The border crossing does not re-open until 6am, a long forty-five minutes from now. Sure, you could simply pass straight through the frontier post – there is no one to challenge your progress, no fence nor barrier to stop you from wandering between the two countries – but to continue on your way now would be unwise. Should this approach be chosen, you won't subsequently possess the passport entrance stamp you so desperately require for your existence in country to be *official* – no *official* hotel accommodation; no *official* transportation access; no *official* money changing facilities. Certainly, attempting to depart through any of the recognised frontier posts without an authentic entrance stamp would create considerable concerns, questions surely raised, no doubt hauled off to the nearest police station, to be processed as an Illegal. Vast sums of baksheesh would need to be waved in the police officers' direction to smooth your path back onto an even keel of legitimacy from *that* particular issue.

The travellers smoke their wonky roll ups, picking small, errant pieces of tobacco from the tips of their tongues, rubbing their bleary, sleep-crusted eyes, endeavouring to remove the final vestiges of last night's restless coach-ride.

Nothing to do but wait.

Learning to wait.

An Indian prerequisite.

Learning to wait *patiently*.

Eventually, the guards emerge from their bungalowed offices, rubbing their quaggy guts over the tops of their poorly fitting uniforms, the front buttons appearing overly burdened with the task of keeping the Officials' beige uniforms fastened shut. The movement in front of the office spurs us travellers into action. The weary group shuffles forwards, passports readied in hand, hoping the not inconsiderable hassle of the Visa Application Process back in Kathmandu has indeed ordained us with the correct paperwork to now enable our unhindered passage through these entrance formalities.

Indian Immigration Services, we have been warned, are sticklers for exactitude. Not a dotted '*i*' nor crossed '*t*' can be out of place, the details on your passport matching *exactly* those on your Visa, no two letters reversed, no digit(s) missing nor miss-scribed. Not an iota of a nanometre can be out of place. Immigration officials are not permitted any laxity, nor endowed with common sense, when it comes to permitting entrance to their fine country should any detail in your paperwork contain even the teeniest degree of in-exactitude. No amount of protestation that the error is *obviously clerical*, that the person the paperwork refers to and you are *obviously one and the same*, that this tiny mistake should clearly *not* prohibit your admittance into India, will result in them changing their minds (at least, not without considerable fiscal lubrication).

I cross fingers and toes, smiling meekly at the uniformed officer as he holds out his grubby fingers to take hold of my passport.

The official looks pensively at my Visa particulars, at the details shown inside my passport, then at my passport photo, then up at me.

Then back at my photo.

The back at me.

Then back at my photo.

The man frowns.

Or is it a scowl?

This might not be going so well.

With theatrical hesitation, the official reaches for the entrance stamp, checks the date configuration on the bottom, before donking the stamp into the ink blot, and then forcibly onto my passport adjacent to my Visa.

Phew!

Success!

I am *Official*.

In India, it is always best to be *official*.

Without further dawdling or dillydally, I find the bus for Gorakhpur. I climb the shiny, somewhat slippery ladder at its rear, to deposit my rucksack onto its roof rack. I remove a sturdy chain from my pack's side-pocket, weaving the chain around my rucksack's straps and the rack's bars, so the straps and the bus are most definitely interlocked as one, before closing the chain in place with a solid, heavy padlock purchased for this very purpose, heeding the many warnings told by sad, sorry travellers about the dangers posed to your personal effects in this land. Sad tales from unfortunate guys who'd lost all their possessions - everything, except for the clothes then on their backs - when their rucksacks had, mysteriously, disappeared from the roof of the buses in which they had been travelling.

Accident or foul play?

Hmmm...

Unless you want to be sitting up top, or be shoving your head out of the window, watching what the porters are throwing off, at each and every stop – and on a 6-hour journey there might be literally hundreds of stops - a padlock and chain is the best solution to this otherwise irksome issue.

Cheers for the heads up, guys; sorry you had to learn the hardest of ways.

I take a seat inside the bus, acknowledging the handful of other travellers dotted around the otherwise empty interior.

I can now relax.

The hard part of the day has been successfully surmounted.

I sit. And wait.

Despite being told we are to leave 'soon', the bus does not budge.

An age passes.

'Soon', in reference to a departure time, does not, I fear, mean as 'soon' as one might think.

'Soon', it soon transpires, actually means, 'eventually'.

We all sit and wait.

Sitting and waiting *patiently*.

A young, moustachioed Indian comes inside the bus, berating us Western travellers verbally for some unknown reason, then demanding money for the bags we have all placed onto the roof. We Westerners glance at one another, unsure whether this fee is indeed payable, or whether this man is simply trying it on. We are all still in a state of early-morning shock. No one has the faintest idea whether the demands are real. The man is being very insistent, and rather threatening. We all sit there in silence, refusing to hand over any money, as he stands over each of us in turn, with an air of nervous menace, getting down closer and closer into our faces, trying to spook us into coughing up a few *rupees*.

None of us flinches.

None of us hands over any cash.

Eventually the man relents, his face turning from deep scowl to broad grin; he says something in Hindi to the guys lurking beside him, laughs a haughty laugh, and then rapidly exits the bus.

We have all past the first test; we have just survived our first scam.

Welcome, indeed, to India.

Chapter 2

Gulliver's Travails

What follows is a six-hour ride in a rickety, boneshaker bus whose seat pitch would have created issues for even the most gravitationally challenged amongst us.

Me, I measure 6-foot 3" from heal to hair.

192cm in new money.

Between the seats I simply do not fit.

Squeezed, squished and squashed inside what at departure is a dangerously over-packed bus, barely able to breath, no wiggle room in which to stretch out, for six long hours, awakens me to challenging levels of cramped claustrophobia and distressed discomfort I have hitherto not known. India may be an oversized country, but it is designed, or so it would appear from this first fleeting glance, for undersized people who are considerably more compact than me. I tower above the average, the more-than-average, even the extremely-more-than-average Indian.

I wonder if I should change my name to Gulliver.

Finally, thankfully, the bus reaches Gorakhpur, a sprawling, bustling city of more 20 *lakh* people (one *lakh* = 1,00,000, written thus), a city whose grounds for existence at this specific geographical location are unclear, a city the likes of which can be found a hundredfold around this vast country.

I alight from the bus, sore, stiff, numb.

Never again will be too soon.

I make a mental note to refrain from using such sardine cans for anything other than short durations.

This may prove tricky. In India, there may be few short duration journeys.

Did I mention, India is a *vast* country?

There are, I will soon discover, *no* short duration journeys.

It is a blisteringly bright sunny day. Not a cloud in this vast canvas of a sky. It is a large, rondure beast of a sun, larger - or it seems, as its intense heat beats down - than the average English sun. I squint upwards to study its form as best I can. I understand it is impossible for the sun to be larger – this must be an optical illusion – but it dominates the sky, looming large, beating its rays down onto the parched, scorched earth with all the power it can muster, torching the soil to a deep orange-tinged-with-pink hue.

It is a sun on steroids.

A sun squared.

A sun *cubed*.

It is just past noon as I leave the mêlée of the bus terminal, setting off, on foot, to the train station. It is a journey of less than a mile, or so says my Guidebook. Having been cooped up for so long, I have decided a short leg-stretch is in order. Get the blood flowing. Put some colour back into my cheeks. Despite their doggedly persistent attempts to persuade me otherwise, the taxi-*wallahs* will not be getting my custom this afternoon.

To a man, they insist the train station is *very far* from here.

I tell them, 'Not so, it is but half a mile'.

Half a mile, according my Book.

According to my Bible (*aka* my trusty, well-thumbed Lonely Planet).

As one, they all laugh at this statement. It is not exactly clear what they are laughing *at*.

Are they laughing because the distance is much more than a mile?

Are they laughing at the thought of my wanting to walk?

At just who might *want* to walk?

Their laughter fills me with unease.

No matter. I choose to ignore them, to not believe their claims.

Not for me your taxis.

No, Sirs. No, Thank You.

It only takes a couple of minutes to realise walking might not have been the wisest of decisions.

Stubbornness and a strong independent streak can be useful traits.

Alas, not here.

It is hot. It is more than hot. It is *more than* more than hot.

Mad dogs. And this Englishman.

All around, as far as the eye can see - and my eyes can see far, given that I am the highest point in this vicinity, buildings notwithstanding - I spy hordes of people, milling around, standing still, bustling about, shouting, gesticulating, staring, pondering, squatting, or lying flat out on their backs.

So many people.

Thousands. Tens of thousands. Many *lakh*.

They decline to stand still long enough for me to count. I have never before seen so many people all just going randomly about their days.

The bustle is immediately overwhelming. My eyes dart left and right, left and right, taking it all in.

I double-take.

Some of these people appear to be - no, they most definitely *are* - defecating right there at the side of the street, an act others find totally unremarkable, as they walk on by without even the faintest glimmer of recognition or acknowledgment. As I witness these acts, the smell of rotting faeces creeps uninvitedly into my nostrils, pong-wiffery of the highest order, a most unwelcome olfactory intruder.

My eyes start to stream.

Sweat is pouring down my face, my neck, my back.

This absurd heat is melting my mind.

Then come the flies. Hundreds of little critters, dive bombing me, tormenting me with their Doppler-hewn sound effects, down past my ears, constantly, left to right, up to down, over and over and over, like an electric drill burrowing through my skull. The pesky flies land on whichever piece of exposed skin they can find - arms, legs, nose, neck - darting off again just in time to avoid my pathetically slow attempts at swatting them away. I swear I can hear them laughing as they go. Attempting to swat them away is a waste of energy, an exercise in futility.

I must learn which battles to fight. I want to scream at the world.

There are so many things wrong with this scene.

I search my mind for the reset button.

Maybe I should click my heels.

Three times.

There's no Place like Home.

And this is no Place like Home.

****

I reach what I hope is the sanctuary of the train station. I am now a soggy sheaf of sweat from top to toe. This new look is evidently quite the sight as several of the locals, who wouldn't, it seems, bat an eyelid to someone dropping their trousers and crapping right in front of them, now pay more attention than I consider strictly necessary to this stranger in their midst.

I cannot decipher their looks.

Pity? Disgust? Fear? Intrigue?

They stare without shame, without blinking, heads fixed in position, their eyes running up and down, from toe to head, and back again, before suddenly deciding to continue on their way, their unspoken thoughts a mystery I will never solve.

A riddle I will never decode.

OK.

Gather yourself.

You can do this.

After several wrong turns, I eventually locate the ticket office, and begin waiting patiently for my turn. Waiting patiently for your turn does not actually help you progress in the line. There is no line. No line to speak of as we might understand the words *orderly queue*. I squeeze forwards towards the man in front, who appears to know what to do, who appears to be heading in the same direction as me, namely the small hole in the ticket office counter through which people at the front are passing money.

This man and I join forces under a silent, unspoken Non-Aggression Pact. Collectively, we repel any dodgy insurgents and sly interlopers who attempt to push in front of our position.

Finally, I reach the ticket office window. It is some small success.

I am resigned to learn from the ticket attendant that the next train to Delhi is not for another four hours.

'Assuming the train is on time'.

Which might not be an assumption you'd want to put any money on.

Unless it's money you're happy to lose.

I purchase a ticket, Sleeper class, Second class.

The train, the attendant tells me, is scheduled to arrive in Delhi just before 9am tomorrow morning.

'Assuming the train is on time'. A *caveat* oft repeated in India.

So, what to do here for the next four long hours?

I doubt I can survive the heat. The madness.

The What-the-Fuckery.

I must rest my feet. Create some sort of base. Establish some sanctuary from the Craziness.

I look around the station concourse. There are, alas, no available seats. Sitting directly on the ground is a somewhat unappealing proposition. What detritus or expectorated body fluids have created the Pollockian tapestry currently underfoot I have (currently) no idea. There are light brown stains in abundance. I presume this to be human faecal waste, although I am no less disgusted to later discover this particular brand of effluent to in fact be Paan spittle, the end result of chewing a mixture of Betel leaves and Areca nuts, a practice widely followed in this part of the world for the mild euphoric buzz this concoction provides. See someone with heavily stained, dark brown teeth (and wild, bug eyes), it's a sure, safe bet they're a user.

I find a vantage point standing at the back of the platform, leaning up against an almost clean, heavily pitted wall. Paan spit is thankfully gracing only the lower levels of this chunk of concrete.

I glance around, people watching, to pass the time. The platform is packed, three, maybe four hundred individuals, a few standing but most sitting, on their haunches rather than bum down, a position that looks remarkably uncomfortable, difficult to maintain and woefully bad for your knees, although preferable I guess to letting any part of your person make contact with the ground.

Forty-or-so yards in front of me, at the platform edge, I notice a dusty maiden, a young infant lying on her lap. This youthful woman suddenly, and hurriedly, picks up her child, raising it upwards, lifting it higher, like an offering to the Gods, so that the baby is now held - a little precariously if truth be told - one-handed, under its arms, directly over the tracks. With her spare hand, the young woman then whips off the child's white linen loin cloth, just in the nick of time, for as she completes this manoeuvre the baby, with a surprising degree of power, then proceeds to emit a forceful stream of light-beige effluent from its nethers, straight down onto the tracks.

Thirty long seconds pass.

All done, still holding the child one-handedly, the mother manages to tip a few drops of water into her cupped left hand from a bottle placed precariously between her knees, water she then applies in between the baby's wee legs.

Up and down. Up and down. Up and down.

There, there, my child.

Concluding this splattering of liquid to have thus rendered the infant suitably sanitised, the mother rewraps her progeny into its white – well, more *off-white* - loin cloth, returning to her sedentary position, baby cradled under one arm.

I look around to see if anyone else has also witnessed this scene.

No. I am alone.

I am alone, alone with my overly sensitive English sensibilities, alone with being more than a little disgusted at how that scene just played out, right there, for the whole world to see.

Here the remarkable appears unremarkable.

Something triggers deep in my subconscious. I suddenly have the feeling I should acquaint myself with the whereabouts of the nearest facilities, not because I have current need for their services, having excreted several bladder-fulls of sweat in the last half-hour alone, but because it is an indelibly sensible idea to establish the quickest route between your current location and the nearest loo, should an urgent call of nature suddenly come through, the type of call requiring of an answer well before the second ring. Nine months on the road has taught me many things; putting such call on 'hold' is never a viable option. Secret Agents study how to enter a room and instinctively clock all potential threats, all safe exit points; travellers learn to interact with their surroundings far more practically.

I pass the Ladies', its door wide open. There is an overwhelming aroma I can't, at first, quite make out.

Ah, yes, *that's* what it is.

A one-inch lake of urine covers the floor from door to lavatory, twenty feet inside the dimly lit, poorly maintained room. There are no dividing walls between the individual loos. Instead, three white porcelain toilets just sit there, on a raised platform, waiting expectantly, forlornly even, for their next desperate clients. These are all Western-style sit-on loos, rather than the squat holes you would usually expect to find in an Indian public convenience. It appears the locals have yet to be adequately schooled on the use of these sit-on loos. Rather than simply resting their nethers on the loo seats, the ladies instead have, for reasons unknown, decided to climb up directly onto the seats, squatting their haunches precariously on the narrow rims, from which decidedly awkward and ungainly stance they loosen their bladders.

And then pee all over the floor.

Evidently, there is an inherent design flaw within this system.

Is it the Hardware? The Software? Or the End User?

I locate the Gents fifty feet down from the Ladies. A hammer blow of ammonia smacks me square on the chops as I enter the darkened room.

Oh, dear Lord.

The stench is too much for my delicate system to take. I am forced to beat a hasty retreat outside, to take a deep, much-needed breath of fresh, uncontaminated air.

I take stock of the situation. I look around, watching others entering the room without so much as a flicker of recognition towards the burning reek of ammonia contained inside.

'How can this be?' I wonder.

How can anyone walk nonchalantly into this room, without reacting, as if everything inside smells rosy, without even the slightest flicker of acknowledgement that something is significantly remiss?

How can olfactory receptors become desensitised to this blast of thick ammonia stew?

I am completely at a loss.

The aged attendant, squatting low on her haunches beside the entrance, has her hand held out, palm faced upwards. It appears she expects some form of payment for my aborted trip into her facility. I study her, wondering whether, or not, she is indeed the toilet attendant, or someone simply hoping to palm a few *rupees* off unsuspecting passers-by. I see no signage stating this a Paid Loo. Equally, no overt indication readily leaps out to confirm, even were the monies she requests to indeed be payment for these facilities, any *rupees* she purloins are thence invested in furthering the cause of cleanliness inside this decrepit facility.

I decline this payment request, on the grounds that I haven't actually, you know, *used* the toilets. The lady seems quite adamant that payment is still required, even for my abortive excursion inside, thrusting her palm forwards towards me, repeatedly, doggedly.

I wave *Goodbye* as I leave.

Thankfully, she does not follow.

I look at my watch.

Three hours and forty-five minutes remain.

I am not sure if I can do this.

I feel like I'm drowning.

****

I must learn how to swim in these turbulent Indian waters. I must learn fast.

I don't count the hours. I don't even count the minutes.

I make peace with the sights and smells.

The train pulls into the station at its allotted hour. I should be thankful for this small mercy.

Next morning, after another fitful night's sleep, I make it to Delhi.

It is already Hotter than Hell in a Heatwave.

This time I take the taxi.

See, I am learning fast.

I am still a sweaty mess, though.

Chapter 3

As If By Magic, a Man Appears

I check in to a hotel, a raggedy, run-down property whose star-rating I surmise, after quick initial inspection, cannot in all honesty be a positively stated integer. The hotel is situated in the tourist part of town, a few narrow, dirty streets away from the hubbub of Connaught Place. I have been recommended this lodging by another traveller, being described as 'OK'. 'OK' is quite the recommendation, given the wealth of absolute shit holes I have so far encountered, from Denpasar to KL to Kathmandu.

The receptionist, a man in his late-forties, I guess, suggests I might like to pay a few *rupees* extra to upgrade from their Standard room with Shared Bathroom, to a slightly better Standard room, with *en suite* Bathroom (he might even have called the room '*deluxe*').

This *deluxe en suite* Bathroom, I am informed, includes a stand-alone, *power* shower.

With that, the receptionist has my undivided attention.

A shower!

Cold water!

Any water!

Did I mention it is freekingly hot?

Not just hot, but pre-monsoon, clingingly, stickily, humidly hot.

Mid-40s C.

Given my sweaty mess of a condition and the extreme heat, I agree to this not unreasonable upsell suggestion, gladly paying the extra few *rupees*. I climb fitfully up three flights of stairs (no lift, no luggage-*wallah*), finally reaching my room, sweatier than a fully clothed man in a sauna - which is, to all intents and purposes, what this heat and humidity resemble.

I dump my bags down triumphantly, performing a quick, flitting survey of my new surroundings. The room is less than spartanly furnished, no mod cons, and nothing to suggest a woman's touch has been employed to smooth over the rough edges of stark design with which the evidently predominantly male portion of the design team has imbued this place.

This is not the time for critical decor appraisal, though.

There are four walls.

Windows, one of which can be seen out of.

A bed. With a mattress. Of sorts.

Best not to inspect the sheets or pillowcases too closely.

But no obvious signs of bed bug infestation.

All boxes therefore ticked for the Hardened Traveller.

Instead of critiquing my new surroundings, what I really need right now, right this very minute - this very *second* - is a blast of wonderfully wet water.

A shower.

Oh, the bliss. The eagerly anticipated Bliss.

I strip out of my soaking, clingy t-shirt and shorts, being quietly impressed with the *splat* they make as they hit the cracked porcelain tiled floor, turn the shower knob clockwise, standing there with my hand under the showerhead - expectantly, excitedly - ready to receive the fresh torrent of water the plumbing is intended to provide.

After all, the piping has been installed but for one job: Water Delivery.

Hmm.

How.

Odd.

Nothing is emerging from the shower head.

I turn the knob further clockwise.

Still nothing.

And further.

Still nothing.

Yet further.

There is now an alarming looseness to the knob.

No, no, no!

Say it ain't so, Jo! Say it ain't so!

By all that is sacred, this cannot be.

Noooooooo!

The sound of deep existential despair echoes around the empty chamber of the bathroom, bouncing off its four stark walls with never decreasing acoustic resonance. Outside, flocks of birds suddenly take flight; wild dogs howl uncontrollably; record styluses mysteriously scratch out from their grooves; cows look up from their perpetual cud chewing, sensing a Tremor, a tearing in the very Fabric of the Universe.

I stand there, motionless, still with the misguided expectation that a river of water will disembogue suddenly from the shower head.

No. This is not an illusion.

There really is no chuffing water.

Nada. Zip. Zilch.

Not even the tiniest of drips, the weeist of drops.

Nothing.

But.

Air.

And not even the freshest of air, from the mephitic pong greeting my nose as I venture too close to the showerhead to inspect.

Poo-Wee!

OK.

This is How It Is.

I have been on the move for the better part of 36 hours.

I have suffered two fitful nights' sleep.

I have endured all manner of weird shit India has so far decided to throw my way, in the space of this seemingly never-ending day.

I am more than bedraggled.

I am dangerously dishevelled.

My patience has dwindled.

And, right now, I am completely out of sympathetic understanding.

Right here, right now, at this particular moment in time, I don't think I am asking too much for just a teensy-weensy dribble of water to flow out the shower for which I have just paid good *rupees* to have exclusive use of in my supposedly Better than Standard *en suite* room.

Am I?

Am I *really*?

My basic Balneal Rights must be respected!

OK. Deep breath: in-2-3, out-2-3, in-2-3, out-2-3.

My mood lessens ever so slightly, from Nuclear Armageddon down to mere Pitiless Indignation. Resigned to having to go sort this farce out, I scrape my wet shorts and clingingly wet t-shirt off the floor, slowly – wincingly - pulling them back on. The door slams loudly behind me as I stomp angrily back down the three flights of stairs to Reception, a rage welling inside, to complain in *no uncertain terms* to Management about this rather critical Lack of Water.

I am sure I am quite a sight. With as much tempered restraint as I can muster, hampered by an inner rage boiling feverishly just beneath the surface, I avail the Receptionist of the current state of water, or *lack of*, flowing, or rather *not flowing*, from my shower head.

The Receptionist laughs.

Ha Ha Ha.

I am unaware I have just made a joke.

'Of course, there is being no water, Sir. In your room the water is not being working. The water is indeed not being working in *any* of the rooms.'

I give him a steely-eyed look, a look everyone back home would know to mean, 'Seriously, Buddy?'. My scowl, alas, falls on deaf eyes.

I sense my control faltering.

I take more deep breaths – in-2-3; out-2-3; in-2-3; out-2-3 - to slow my excessively pounding heart rate.

Calmly, I ask the Receptionist why on earth he suggested I upgrade to a *deluxe en suite* room?

'Why,' I *really* need to know, 'have I paid additional *rupees* only to have this shower that is currently *not being working*?'

The Receptionist smiles some more. He asks which country I am from.

I tell him, 'England', hopefully with an air of, 'What the hell has that got to do with anything?' thrown freely into the mix.

He nods, several times, still smiling. 'Ah, yes. Yes of course'.

It appears my being from England explains everything.

That's it.

There is no water *because I am from England.*

I am still standing there in front of him, like a prize lemon, waiting for a proper answer, when the Receptionist calmly moves away to one side to speak to another guest - I presume, or maybe a paid decoy - who has suddenly materialised at the reception desk.

That is the end of the Receptionist's interest in resolving my problem.

I realise this is not a battle I am ever going to win.

There is much to learn in India.

I must learn even faster.

****

Shower-less but now sporting a new ensemble comprised of wonderfully dry - and clean - clothes, with a quick spray of underarm deodorant to hopefully mask my redolence, not that there aren't a thousand and one objects, persons and animals in my near vicinity that aren't also in a somewhat rude state of pungency, I head out from the hotel in search of a bottle of drinking water. Still seething from my previous encounter, I am not currently holding the locals in much regard.

Their collective stock rises, however, when I find that the enterprising street vendors are selling not just chilled bottles of water, but completely *frozen* bottles of water. The coldness to the touch is divine.

Heaven.

I run a bottle down from my forehead, my cheeks, the back of my neck, along my arms, down my thighs.

Heaven indeed.

Less than half an hour later, what's left in the bottle is too warm to be considered suitable for consumption and is discarded.

This heat is crazy.

I realise I won't survive here in Delhi longer than a day. Two max.

I need to do as the Brits of Empire did during the blisteringly hot summer months.

Head for the Hills.

I take a stroll up the main tourist drag, lined with the ubiquitous smattering of tour operators and guest houses, restaurants and handicraft shops that litter tourist quarters the world over, searching for ideas and options.

As I peruse one shop window in which a poster-sized notice describes the offer of a Trip to Kashmir, as if by magic, a man suddenly appears.

I tell him I my name is not 'Benn'.

He does not understand. He evidently has not had the pleasure of children's TV in the UK back in the early '70s.

His loss.

For some years visiting Kashmir has been top of my Wish List, having heard so many wondrous things about the region from my sister who visited in '87. Now, however, in '93, the conflict in Kashmir has been stewing nicely pretty much ever since, having erupted with a bang from a twenty-year slumber following the Soviet withdrawal from Afghanistan at the end of the 1980s (those underemployed militants and leftover weapons have to go somewhere). The Merits *vs* the Safety issues of visiting the Region now are not immediately clear, or easily evaluated.

The man asks whether I am interested in visiting Kashmir.

I tell him I am so inclined.

He says he can accompany me up to Srinagar tomorrow, to a houseboat on Dal Lake.

Like a crazy, stupid, impetuous fool, I agree to go with this man I have only just met and know absolutely diddly squat about all the way to a houseboat in Kashmir.

'Don't tell anyone you are going to Kashmir,' he tells me.

I consider this comment most odd, but this is India after all. I am getting inured to odd comments.

Maybe this comment is not really that odd.

For India.

I should probably be far more concerned than I am, but I haven't checked the up-to-date Foreign Office travel advice for the region so am blissfully unaware of any potential risk I might be undertaking.

I still need to learn. The bullet-proofed ignorance of youth might only get me so far.

Getting me back again may be asking too much.

That evening, I bump into small gaggle of lads I had met briefly on Koh Phangan in Thailand. They suggest I come back to their hotel room for a smoke. I gladly accept their kind offer. They are a raggedy raddled collection, although to be fair they only require a thirty-minute Barber's Shop visit, a long hot shower with a vast vat of shower gel, and a set of clean, pressed clothes to once again be presentable back in the Real World.

'Never Judge a Book by its Cover', or so they say; in the World of Travelling, it is certainly never correct to judge someone by the state of, nor their choice of, attire, for it does not pay to be too clean or manicured in these decidedly dodgy parts. Only the rich present themselves in spotless, freshly pressed clothes, or so the shopkeepers believe.

Why mark yourself out as an easy target for elevated *ferengi* prices?

You are already considered 'rich' in that you can afford to take a holiday, even if you've barely two farthings to rub together, and are scrimping along on the meagrest of budgets.

Lie low, blend in, don't wash, don't shave, let nature takes its course, and before you can say, 'Stinking like a wet dog', you'll fit in just fine.

One of the lads rolls a large, long, well-packed spliff. He is proud of his creation, and not without reason. It is quite the Monster.

'This,' he informs us, with some satisfaction, 'is called a Camberwell Carrot'.

He asks whether we know why it's called a *Camberwell Carrot*?

I do, but allow him his moment nonetheless.

'It is called a *Camberwell Carrot*, he continues, 'because I first rolled one in Camberwell, and it looks like a Carrot'.

It is a line from a film.

I tell him I'd like the Finest Wines known to Humanity, I'd like them Here, and I'd like them Now.

He looks at me blankly.

Unperturbed, I demand to have some Booze.

He looks around the room, I guess for something to offer me to drink. There is nothing to hand.

His face is still blank. I'm guessing he passed out during the film. He wouldn't be the first to have prematurely over-cooked the goose if that's the case.

I ask him if he has ever been Truly Medicined but fear I have taken the *Withnail & I* references as far as they can go.

The roller takes another long tug on his spliff, its sweat-smelling smoke wafting gloriously, filling the room with wondrous aroma. How heavenly is this scent after the day's prior effluvial olfactory offerings. The joint is passed – clockwise - according to the Law. Each drag is truly treasured. There is no rush to receive, for this is an Ariston of joints, one which will go on and on (and on and on...).

I tell my buddies of my plans for Kashmir, thence to Ladakh. They tell me they are heading to Manali. Manali is to where most pot-heads head, for its marijuana resin is the stuff of legend. Days, weeks, then months can all too easily be lost in the happy haze and foggy fug of being completely and utterly stoned out of your gourd from dawn until dusk, until dawn comes round yet again.

Happy Haze!

Happy *Daze*!

Happy **Days**!

From Manali, the lads stress quite ardently, they plan to then head up to Ladakh.

I think they doth protest too much.

I tell them they'll never leave Manali once they settle in.

I am given the Look. It is the Look that says I have spoken a Truth That Must Not be Uttered, for who doesn't want to live a life of Self-Deception?

I mutter that I hope I am wrong.

'You'll *See*', they say.

They must have the Sight, for it is indeed True that I will *See*.

Chapter 4

Are You Sitting Uncomfortably? Then We'll Begin

Purchasing a ticket for an Indian long-distance sleeper train is, as I am soon to discover, a monumentally Herculean challenge.

The system back in 1993 is this.

Firstly, you must head to **Window A** to collect a **Travel Requirements Form**.

Secondly, you must then hand the completed **Form** detailing which train number(s), date(s) and class(es) of travel you require to **Window B**, for approval.

Lastly, you must visit **Window C** with your officially approved **Form**, where the ticket will be issued. You will then be required to pay the appropriate sum.

On paper, and as with so much in India, this all sounds perfectly straight forward and simple.

How hard can it be?

And how long should this simple process take?

I hope you, too, are learning.

Nothing in India is ever as simple or as straight forward as it should be.

At the Booking Hall, I discover a throng of people all simultaneously trying to get to **Window A**. There is no orderly queue to speak of. You need sharpened elbows and a stern resolve to protect your position inside the mêlée as you slowly nudge, bump, grind and push your way forwards towards your goal.

I reach **Window A** in thirty long minutes.

It is a relief to finally have this piece of paper in my hand.

Oh, I can hear what you are thinking.

Might there possibly be a better way for this **Form** to be made available?

Why not simply have the **Form** stacked in multiple points around the Booking Hall so anyone can grab one should they so require?

That, alas, is the key to this quandary, for a piece of paper such as this **Form** is a commodity for barter or trade, a commodity exploitable as the basis for some unscrupulous entrepreneur's business model.

Were the **Forms** simply left stacked in suitable positions around the Booking Hall they would all disappear in the blink of an eye, creating a profit-making racket for enterprising individuals keen to let no business opportunity go untapped.

'Sure, you *can* queue for the **Form**, Sir, but if you want to save at the very least 30 minutes, why not purchase one of *my* **Forms**, Sir? Only *Rs5* each.'

I enter my requirements onto the **Form**, then start my quest to reach **Window B**. The swarm of people here is greater than for **Window A**. Getting to **Window B** seems an impossible task. I decide to seek an alternative, easier route to success, heading up to **Window C** where, oddly, there is no queue at all.

No one.

I show my **Form** to the ticket clerk seated behind **Window C**, asking whether, seeing as he's not actually *doing* anything right now, he'd mind approving and issuing me with the ticket as stated on my **Form**.

'No, no, Sir', the clerk tells me, with that nodding of the head motion Indians are want to do whenever they really mean 'no'. 'Approval of the **Form** is being only at **Window B**'.

I point out again that he's not actually doing anything right now, so it shouldn't be too much of a strain for him to approve this **Form**.

'No, no, Sir', the clerk says again, smiling at the obvious absurdity of what I have just suggested. 'You must be going to **Window B**'.

The man then turns around, showing me his back, a clear indication our conversation is now over.

I restart my quest for **Window B**. Rucking and mauling skills formulated and honed on the rugby pitch prove most handy. I may be several times larger and carrying significantly more mass than the slightly built locals, but they play a dirty game with no discernible Rules and absolutely no shame in being underhand and cheating, even if there *were* Rules, which there appear not to be. I resolutely stand my ground, giving as good as I get. This is no time to worry about being *nice*. My fellow strugglers and I reach a level of mutual respect. They quickly understand that I will not suffer any argy-bargy nor sleight of hand. After another 60+ minutes of warfare I reach the hallowed ground of **Window B**.

I am exhausted. The clerk examines my request, then selects a large, A1-sized ledger from behind him, writing something down on the vast page where there is already much written down in tiny scrawled handwriting, both in columns and rows. He inks his stamp, and with a forceful 'donk' approves my request. The **Form** is then handed back to me.

I am now free to advance to **Window C**, where, thankfully, there is still no queue. I am confused as to why this should be the case, after the swarms of people heading for the other two windows, but there is no one suitable to ask, and I don't think the clerk from **Window C** will be very forthcoming.

I try my luck anyway.

'Oh no, there wouldn't be,' he replies to my query concerning the lack of queue.

'Wouldn't be?' I ask back.

'No, no, there wouldn't be.'

He is smiling, a broad, brown-stained grin wider than the Panama Canal. His smile is tainted with confusion, confusion at what to him is the obvious absurdity of my question.

I decide to park the question, not wishing to push my luck and have him refuse to issue me with my ticket.

I hand over a small sum of *rupees*. I am returned my formally approved Rail Transit Permit.

It is with much relief that my hard graft has resulted in me now being the proud owner of one 3rd class 3-tier Sleeper rail ticket to Jammu for the following afternoon's departure.

The following afternoon.

I am waiting patiently alone on the platform for my overnight train to Jammu, the winter capital of Kashmir. I say *alone*, but in India you are never *really* alone. I am a curiosity interest to the swarms who pass by my stationary figure, rucksacks resting by my feet. The people stare at me, look me up and down, say something in Hindi, to which their friends all giggle and snigger, before rushing onwards, places to go.

My eyes dart around the platform, observing the strange habits of the station workers. A couple of loin clothed men draw a thick, heavy hose around in the deep recesses between the platforms and the tracks. I wished I hadn't looked closer, for I see in better detail the detritus in which they are standing, barefoot: crumpled cardboard boxes; soggy, torn newspapers; discarded paper plates; small metal food trays containing gloopy currified remnants; and numerous beige patties of human waste. The hose is turned on, the force of its stream encouraging this mess to congregate to one side, out from under the tracks, into the darker recesses at the base of the platforms. A couple of over-sized rats scurry for cover from the invading force of the jets. I wonder what other horrors might be lurking down there, too.

At last, my train pulls slowly into the platform. There is a mad rush, hundreds of people all trying desperately to embark as one, even before the train has come to a complete stop, and even though our scheduled departure time is not for another half an hour, *'presuming punctuality is preserved'*.

I push my way forwards, forwards, through the mêlée, and finally in through the tight carriage door.

I find my allotted carriage; my allotted compartment; my allotted seat. I am, it appears, the first of our compartment to arrive.

The train, according to the signs on the platform, seems currently to still be 'on schedule'.

I am reminded of a tale of another Englishman travelling around India, in the age of the Raj, who is surprised to see his train pull into the station at exactly the correct hour, an almost unheard-of occurrence in India.

'This is most unusual', he thinks, but is not about to complain about his train arriving dead on time. He climbs aboard, searching for his carriage, his compartment, his seat.

To his surprise and confusion, he finds someone already sitting in his seat. He rechecks the carriage number, the compartment number, the seat number. All match the information on his ticket. The man gently remarks to the person sitting in this seat that they might like to move aside - There's a Good Chap - for *they* are sitting in *his* allocated seat.

'Ah yes,' the person sitting in this seat says, 'you do have the correct carriage, the correct compartment, the correct seat. But this, in fact, is *yesterday's* train'.

I plonk myself down on the bottom bunk. I have been allocated the topmost of the three tiers but have no desire to be sitting up at roof level right now, given how roastingly hot the compartment currently is, even at ground level. I wrap a chain through the straps of my rucksack, through the metal struts supporting the seat, padlocking the ends together, my hopefully fool-proof bid to deter stray hands from giving in to temptation.

I take stock of my situation. I prepare to defend my space.

The wait begins.

More waiting.

Always waiting.

Waiting *patiently*.

This is not easy.

The carriage is as hot as a sauna, from having sat in the sidings, under the baking sun, windows closed, for about a year, or so it seems. The oven-like blast that engulfed me on entering virtually knocked me backwards. The windows are now open, but sadly not a breath of cool air is currently passing through, into the carriage and to my aid. All too soon, I once again resemble someone daft enough to sit fully clothed in a sauna.

I am a drenched, dripping, drowning man.

In the blink of a sweaty eye, I have drunk the three large bottles of water I brought with me for the entirety of this 14-hour trip. Foolishly, it would appear, I considered three bottles would more than suffice. I dare not now leave my seat to restock, for fear of being overrun, or of losing my prized spot. The downside of travelling on your own.

My compartment fills up fast. I eye my new compartment compatriots with both wonder and suspicion. This is possibly how they eye me, for they are all staring intently at me without an iota of embarrassment.

I smile.

They smile back.

I wave.

They wave back.

Not exactly the most in-depth discussion, but it's a start.

More waiting.

Still waiting.

To loud screams and hollered shouts emanating from the platform, and the clatter of dozens of doors slamming shut one swiftly after another, like the rapid retorts of artillery fire, the train suddenly jolts sharply, inching its way forwards, slowly, ever so slowly. I worry there has been an incident, a passenger - or two - gravely wounded, a last-second attempt to board the moving train disastrously unsuccessful, such is the commotion and brouhaha outside. Nobody in my compartment seems even in the slightest bit concerned.

Our departure is only a few minutes past the scheduled time. The train's pace increases with a juddering lack of urgency.

Finally, the compartment starts to fill with fresh, cooler air that streams in through the blessedly large windows.

I can relax a little. We are finally under way.

Chapter 5

A Holler from A *Wallah*

I am seated in a 3-Tier, 3rd Class Sleeper carriage. The benches are comprised five, 5-inch-wide wooden slats, with half an inch or so's gap between each slat. After only thirty minutes I am already fidgety, shifting my weight from one cheek to the other, leaning forwards, backwards, and sideways, trying in vain to locate the sweet spot, or at least the point of minimal discomfort, lacking as these seats are in the comfort stakes. My compartment companions all appear to be taking the rigours of these pews in their stride.

They smile at me some more.

It is a smile that says, 'Yes, these seats are Totally Terrible. Welcome *very much* to India'.

I try to count our number. We are too numerous for me to finalise an accurate tally. Above and in front of me, the middle and upper bunks are each home to four on each level, their occupants' short legs dangling precariously just over the heads of those on the bunks beneath. I cannot make out just how many are perched on the two bunks over my head. There appears to be an odd number of legs, which can't be right (or left).

I have been allocated the upper bunk in this compartment. From 6pm, each allocated bunk becomes your own personal space, for you, and you alone. If you wish to take possession of your allotted space this means, most likely, having to shoo any current incumbents off when the designated hour arrives. It is a daunting prospect. I am unsure how seriously this requirement is taken. I am unsure how willingly these men will comply. I am unsure if anyone will come to my aid should I need to act with any degree of persuasiveness to ensure they all *do* ultimately comply.

There is nothing to do but stare out of the window.

Villages and farmland rush by.

Well, potter by.

Just like the *Sleeper* bus, this is *Express* in name only.

The sound of the wheels on the track is hypnotic.

Tickety-tock. Tickety-tock. Tickety-tock.

The combination of the constantly changing scenery and the wheels clicking over the tracks sends me into a trance-link state.

I stare out the window for hours.

I look but don't see.

My mind is elsewhere.

****

With a start, the clocks chime 6pm. Time for action.

I rise and show the men on (what is now) *my* top bunk my ticket, pointing rather exaggeratedly at the compartment and the seat number, and then, for yet more emphasis, at my watch.

You know what I mean. You will almost certainly have done the same sort of thing at some point during your own travels (with greater or lesser success).

The men on my bunk all smile, nodding back at me, but nothing happens; none of them budges, not an inch, not in any direction.

I show them my ticket again, pointing at them, then pointing to the floor.

You, onto the Floor (there's a Good Chap).

You – floor; You - floor.

The men all smile, and all nod some more.

Nope. Still zero action.

I try again.

You – floor; You - floor.

More smiling. More nodding.

And again.

YOU – any of YOU – floor; YOU – any of YOU - floor.

More smiling. More nodding.

Smiling. Nodding.

Smiling. Nodding.

We are getting nowhere.

I take in a deep, exasperated breath. I put on my widest, fakest grin, attempting to mimic their facial expressions, then grab the nearest fellow by the lapels, forcibly, but not roughly or overly aggressively, pulling him down from his - but technically now *my* - lofty perch.

Firmly gripped, the slight man makes a controlled descent. His feet hit *terra firma*. He is now standing next to me. I tower over him by at least two feet. He nods at me, as if to say, well, who knows what – 'Well played, Sir. Thought I had you there' - smiles some more, then disappears out of the compartment, into the corridor, off to who knows where.

Hopefully not to gather reinforcements. I may have just won the Battle but be about to lose the War.

Thankfully, the remaining three lads on my bed get the unsubtle hint, deciding to climb down of their own accord, thence disappearing off into the corridor in hot pursuit, possibly, of the previous fellow to depart. Without pausing for a second, I climb up the side of the seats to reassert my claim on *my* space. It has been a hard-fought gain. I now dare not move to search for the still much needed refreshments in case squatters move in and retake my spot.

This bunk is now my sanctuary.

This spot is mine. *All* mine.

Decidedly, definitively, and now dangerously dehydrated, I need to whet my whistle.

Right on cue, there comes a holler from along the carriage corridor.

'Chai, chai, chai!! Chai, chai, chai!!'

It is a holler from a *wallah*. The chai-*wallah*.

I stick my head out into the corridor, halting the young man in his tracks, and negotiate the purchase a couple of mugs of this fine brew he is offering for sale. Two small tumblers are passed up to my lofty position.

I survey my purchases intently.

I am unsure, exactly, what *Chai* is. I know it is a drink. But exactly what type or flavour of drink I am currently none the wiser.

I take a sniff. And another.

I take a small sip. And another.

The liquid is a light brown, sickly sweet, luke-warm, milky tea, with a dash of cinnamon sprinkled into the mix.

I am not a tea drinker.

At all.

Probably this is nothing *like* tea.

At all.

But the liquid is just what my system needs.

I chuck these two mug-fulls down without the liquid hitting the sides, and await impatiently the chai-*wallah's* next passing. I take two more on his next voyage down the corridor. The chai-*wallah*, being a man with obviously sophisticated business acumen, realises I am a customer offering good repeat trade, for he passes my spot with increased frequency throughout the night.

The taste does not improve the more I drink. But my whistle is wetted. I think I will survive.

Chapter 6

Darling, I Want You, But Not So Fast

The train pulls into Jammu early next morning, barely an hour after its scheduled arrival time. There is no bunting to celebrate this almighty achievement, no brass band to play us in.

It has not been the best of nights, I must admit. I have slept fitfully, hampered both by the irregular churning, bumping, grinding, jolting motion of the train, and the unforgiving hardness of the wooden bunk. Getting comfortable in one position was simply not possible; within only a few minutes, whichever side I was on was crying out for relief, necessitating the need to rotate - side, back, side, front - round and round and round and round, like a slowly barbecuing piece of meat.

It would seem the Hardened Traveller I wish to consider myself is still under construction.

Sleep Comfort Ratings the world over are given in measurements relative to Concrete and Air. An **SCR** of '100' represents the unforgiving hardness of lying on a concrete slab; an **SCR** of '0', the serene softness of floating on air.

The mattresses in Vietnam all score in the high 90s – you make the mistake of falling onto one from any sort of height, expecting to be gracefully subsumed into the mattress's soft springs, only the once. That the population seems to think nothing of sleeping on the virtual equivalent of concrete might be the reason for the Vietnamese people's tough resilience. Maybe it is no wonder the American Army (and the French Colonial Forces) were so roundly vanquished.

This Indian 3rd Class 3-Tier wooden-slatted offering of a bed had a **SCR** in the mid-80s. I make a mental note not to be such a spend-thrift the next time I venture on an overnight railway journey in this vast land.

Outside the station, I relocate the man from the agency in Delhi, who also travelled up on this train but in a separate compartment. His fresh appearance makes me think he's had a far better experience overnight than I. The experiential benefits of local knowledge, I guess.

There is no time to stop and gather myself. My guide negotiates a shared taxi ride to take us on what I learn will be a twelve-hour drive, from Jammu up to Srinagar, a journey of only 300km, but on a twisty, poorly maintained, mountainous road.

In many countries, the 'How far to X?' question is answered not in distance, but in time, for knowing the distance tells you little; you need to factor in the current state of the road - is it smooth, straight and flat, or is the road heavily rutted, with more twists and turns than an Agatha Christie novel? – to be able to make an accurate assessment of *How Far*.

Our taxi is a white Ambassador, a classic Indian automobile based on the Morris Oxford Mark 3. The car has a fixed bench front seat able to accommodate three people up front, two plus the driver, plus three more - four at a push, five if you're *really* pushing - in the back. Our driver was *merely* pushing with his backseat fares; we are now seven for this next leg of the journey. My fellow passengers give me the now standard series of looks up and down - and up and down once more for luck - their thoughts betrayed by facial expressions and twitches I think I am starting to understand.

'Look at this man,' they seem to be saying. 'He is very high'.

I am given one of the front seats, as it offers slightly more in the way of legroom.

Who as a kid didn't always want to be the one sitting up front?

Who didn't fight their siblings continuously over whose turn it was to ride 'shotgun'?

This vantage point proves to not necessarily be the most ideal spot from which to survey the Forthcoming.

****

It is a long, windy, precipitous mountain road up to Srinagar, the summer capital of Kashmir, up through dense Alpine pine forests, down amongst deep valley floors. It quickly transpires that our taxi is not operating optimally. Second gear has ceased to be a selectable option. In order to compensate for this deficiency, whilst in First Gear the driver must over-accelerate the car, then, with a flurry of revs, change straight up to Third. If the driver must perforce veer onto the wrong side of the road in order to overtake, whilst possibly rounding a blind bend, to maintain our momentum, then so be it. No matter that anything could be coming at us in the opposite direction.

Anything. Quite literally.

Massive, heavily laden trucks heading back down to Jammu pass us every 30 seconds or so. Instinctively, I turn my head to one side, holding my breath during each crazy overtake. I give the driver beside me a long, hard stare each time we return to the correct side of the road, and (relative) safety. I suggest making such wild manoeuvres with such regularity might not, you know, be the wisest course of action, especially when he has no idea *whatsoever* what might be coming down the road in the opposite direction, heading straight for us.

The driver shrugs. 'All is being well if Karma permits,' his simple reply.

Our old friend Karma.

I wonder exactly how this system of Karmic reckoning works.

Is the outcome based solely on whether the driver has lived a life of Virtue and Goodness, or otherwise?

Or should we take an average Karmic score of the seven people riding this vehicle?

Or maybe we should deduct the highest and lowest Karma scores, and *then* take the average?

Then again, is it the *Sanchita* Karma to which he is referring?

Or the *Parabdha*?

Or even the *Agami*?

The Universal, the Sudden, the Reincarnation?

The accumulated total of our past actions, or the net worth of our lifetime's deeds?

I need to know. I *really* do.

Our driver's attitude to road safety is no different to many Indians' attitudes to their decision-making paradigms, in that their decision-making paradigms appear to be of a somewhat passive, rather too *laissez faire* nature for my liking. It seems many appear to struggle with the concept of Cause and Effect – the Scientific Method - that doing (or not doing) **X** might be directly associated with the likelihood of **Y** occurring (or otherwise). The concept that the choices they make shape their future outcomes appears alien to most.

Take obeying road laws. A sensible, rational person would most likely not choose to push a vegetable cart into oncoming traffic in the outside lane of a 3-lane highway; a sensible, rational person would surely not open the driver's door whilst speeding along at 90kph, to expectorate his mouthful of Paan spittle, lest he desires to add to the already horrific road traffic tallies.

How about observing strict hygiene routines. Most sensible, rational people would not choose to deposit human waste right in the middle of the street, rather in standard, toilet-shaped receptacles; most sensible, rational people would choose to wipe down their food preparation surfaces with disinfection or bleach rather than, say, tap water and a tatty, stained newspaper, lest you desire to catch some horrific bacterial or viral disease and die a slow - or rapid - painful death.

Such evidence-based, scientifically mandated advice is, as far as many Indians are concerned, piffle and nonsense. This form of Reasoning acts merely to provide false comfort to those wishing to believe their Life's Direction *is* indeed Controllable. Instead, for Indians, the most commonly held belief is that the Universe has already decided what Fate has in store for them (and everyone else), that they are mere passengers in the crazy, twisting courses of their Existence in their current - human - form of Being. They are but actors in the pre-scripted Shows of their Lives. To suggest that altering your style of driving will reduce the likelihood of an accident is simply outside of their comprehension.

To them, this implies you feel *you* control the Universe, you control your Destiny, that *you* orchestrate the Course your Life.

For many, this is utmost arrogance, for how can one person ever conceive of the notion of *controlling* the Universe; one small, insignificant person, against the size and might of the Infinite?

At the time of your conception, your Fate has already been decided; your Future, already decreed. There is nothing that can be done to alter this, neither by you, nor by some outside Agent or Agency.

Your sole life's task: to learn to Go with the Flow; to happily submit the *desire* to control; thence to live *in* the Moment and *for* the Moment; to respect and pay tribute to the Graces; to revere the Deities; to submit suitable *Diya* offerings to the Gods on all the most auspicious calendrical dates, accepting the Inevitability of your Fate and the Status of your Position with good Grace (see *The Unbearable Randomness of Being* & *You Lucky Cow!*).

What might, to unseeing outsiders, resemble a society engaged in Chaotic Machinations is simply the unfolding of a billion+ Predestined Outcomes.

Welcome, once again, to India.

I sit back, watch and wonder.

I am struggling to unpick the Secret Intricacies hidden within the Tessellations.

I am endeavouring to see beyond the Poop and the Noise and the Chaos.

I am striving to comprehend the Beauty inside this Disorder.

No wonder many travellers to this fine country spend most of their time here stoned out of their gourds, for to be too lucid, too hurried, too hasty, is to fail to notice the underlying rhythm inside the Chaos. To be able to unpluck the Chaos, one must first reduce the pace of one's gaze, and really look.

And then look some more. And then *more* still.

Indian Time, from first glance, appears to elapse under its own unique schedule.

I have not partaken of the herbal cigarette.

I am seeing our lives flashing before our eyes as lorries miss us by mere whiskers.

I am experiencing this Madness in Real Time.

Our driver, despite my persistent protestations, continues his erratic manner of car/ road management. At several spots along the way, we pass groups of men and machinery clustered at the roadside, all staring ponderously down the mountainside from their elevated positions. As we meander further along the road, I look back down the mountain to where they all were standing, noticing a burnt-out wreck of a truck, a bus, a car, the remnants of a recent parting of some poor souls from their mortal coils. Our driver seems not to recognise our own proximity to deathly disaster.

Reckless driving, it appears, is a common problem on this snake of a road, and not limited to our own vehicle.

We pass a vast rectangular sign at the roadside, writ in large letters.

'Darling, I Want You, but Not So Fast' it reads.

Well, indeed.

Wise words.

There is no one with whom to share this glorious *double entendre* delight. I am fairly certain the sign is referring to the male road-using contingent's driving skills, and not something else. In any case, its hidden meaning is well worth a chuckle. There have been precious few opportunities for laughter recently in any case.

Well, unless the laughter has been directed *at* me.

No one, it seems, wants to laugh *with* me.

The manner in which Indian English uses my mother tongue is a delight, as if the English language were shipwrecked and abandoned all those years ago, in 1947, since failing to evolve, stuck in a bygone era our grandparents would recognise with misty-eyed nostalgia. Indian English uses the language far more florally, more poetically, more prosaically than our harsh modern British vernacular.

'Smoking is Injurious to Health', says the Indian Ministry of Health.

A turn of phrase less exacting than our own: 'Smoking Kills'.

We pass another sign at the side of the road.

'Is it Food that You are Looking for?' is the question it poses for all.

I presume nearby there is a restaurant, desperate for Business.

'Hungry?' might appear a more concise sign, better, maybe, at stating its aim; better, maybe, at allowing it to have been fully read before you've sped on past.

So, better *all-round*, really.

Unless you happen to be a Sign-Writer paid by the letter.

Chapter 7

Taken In

We reach the Jawahar road tunnel separating the northern and southern parts of Kashmir. Named after the first Prime Minister of India – Jawaharial Nehru - this is an old, single-lane piece of rudimentary engineering, completed in 1956, considered past its sell-by date even in 1993. The single lane means the subterranean passage can only be used in one direction at a time along its 3km length. We must therefore await our turn; the flow is scheduled to be reversed from 1pm onwards.

Waiting.

More waiting.

More waiting *patiently*.

In India, patience is indeed a virtue.

I take stock of my surroundings.

A large military presence has been deployed here; this tunnel is a strategic link into the heart of Kashmir, my taxi companions tell me.

A trio of tanks.

Several squads of soldiers.

Quite the show of military might.

It is hard to know whether this military presence is a reassurance, or a concern. Any blockage to this artery would seriously affect trade and commerce, and the ability of the Indian Army to race reinforcements into the area should the need arise, or so I am informed. We have been passing large convoys of army trucks laden with hundreds, nee thousands, of Indian soldiers, all heading up to Srinagar, pretty much since we left Jammu.

Tensions are currently high, I learn, between the Islamic guerrilla soldiers from the Pakistan side of Kashmir, and the Indian government. Many Kashmiris in India want the two halves of the

State unified, under an independent Muslim Rule of Law. Back in 1947, when partition was decreed by the British at the end of Empire, the Hindu Maharaja of Kashmir, with its predominantly Muslim population, wavered in his decision over whether to cede the State to the new, mainly Hindu India, or to Pakistan, with its vast majority of Muslims. This hesitation resulted in others taking the matter into their own hands, with fierce fighting breaking out between rebel forces from the two new countries, fighting that continued on and off in many different forms during the following two decades, until a ceasefire was finally agreed in 1971 - after the Indo-Pakistan War which led to the creation of Bangladesh (formerly East Pakistan) - the relative positions of the two armies thenceforth being known as the Line of Control (LoC), which then become the new *de facto* border between India and Pakistan.

Since the late '80s, there have been numerous incidents instigated by both sides of this never-ending conflict. Who did what, to whom, and exactly how many were affected, will vary depending on whose side of the argument you find yourself situated. In 1990, a massacre of possibly as many as 280 people by Indian government troops occurred near the Gawkadal bridge. Many more are alleged to have been killed by Indian Government forces in the protests that followed this tragic event. In October 1993, a few months after my departure, another alleged massacre by Indian Government forces of up to fifty protesters will occur in the village of Bijbehara. Like any playground spat, 'who started it & why' gets lost as the retaliations ramp up, tit for tat, for tit for tat.

Ariston, and on, and on...

'Enough already!', you feel like shouting.

The simple truth, I will discover from the many locals with whom I discuss the issue during my time in Kashmir, is that the Indian government has invested such huge resources into Kashmir – both militarily and financially - it is highly unlikely to ever seriously countenance surrendering the State to Pakistan, nor to granting the State its own Independence.

It is a complex situation. For sure, those who devised Partition in 1947 most likely did not foresee this particular outcome. At the time, there were many outspoken voices who opposed the creation of a separate Muslim country being sliced from the former Hindustan, the intention for this new creation thenceforth called India to be a secular State, home to those of all Faiths. Even when those with the final say acceded to the request for the creation of the Muslim majority West and East Pakistan, there were some States for whom the choice of 'sides' was no simple decision, split as their populations were 50/50 on religious grounds.

So, 36 years later, here we are. The decision over whose 'side' to be on continues. As a result, Kashmir is no longer the affluent playground for the scores of Rich and Famous who used to consider the region a must-visit for their annual vacations. Times here have been hard for far too long. Money is scarce. Many people are suffering badly. Peaceful resolution (still) needs to be achieved.

Finally, our waiting ends. We are on the move again, through the dimly lit tunnel. Our progress is slow, bumper to bumper in convoy with the trucks ahead that can barely squeeze through the tunnel's narrow entrance. Our passage through takes an age.

Suddenly, daylight.

The exit from the northern end of the road tunnel provides a most spectacular entrance to this Region. From the tunnel's seemingly never-ending dank darkness, we exit like a rebirth, thrust out into the light, into a new world, a dream world, a landscape whose beauty words are but redundant to describe.

I shall endeavour in any case. The land to our front drops away dramatically, providing a vast vista over lush, fertile fields, to far off snowy-capped mountain ranges that glisten in the sunlight, taking up the entirety of the horizon. The sky is an uninterrupted wall of deep azure. Not a cloud blots the sky. The sun beats down, its rays' brilliance and potency increased by the elevation of this altitude.

The rigours of this seemingly never-ending journey evaporate in a flash. It is not much further now to Srinagar, just another 50 miles or so. We reach town, continuing on through, the substantial military presence marked by regular clusters of soldiers on foot patrol, and heavily armed vehicles standing sentinel at all major road junctions. There is an eerie sense of a town under siege.

The streets are virtually deserted. There is hardly a soul around. This would be out of the ordinary in most cities (at this time of day), but here in India, where I have so far always been surrounded by people in their hundreds and thousands, it is something else, something rather eerie.

We drive on.

We do not stop, not once, instead continuing to our destination, a houseboat on Dal Lake, 3km out on the far side of town.

The end is near.

Thankfully, not *the* End. Just the end of our long journey here.

I step out of the taxi, relieved Mother Karma had nothing negative hidden up her sleeves.

I am looking forward now to some time alone, to gather myself after such a long journey.

No such luck.

I am immediately enveloped by my host, Gupta.

Mr Gupta.

What a character. 6-foot 6", broad as an ox, larger than life.

'Mr Edward! Mr Edward! Welcome, welcome, welcome! I am already feeling you are my Brother. Come! Come!'

Gupta beckons me follow him inside the boat, up the internal steps, and out onto the roof's viewing platform.

The panorama over Dal Lake is stupendous. Smooth, ripple-free, crystal-clear, pristine waters are dotted with a smattering of flat-topped, reed-hewn *Shikara* skiffs; distant snowy-capped mountains glisten like beads of diamonds in the sunshine; luxurious, neck-high rows of reeds line the lake's banks, swaying gracefully in the gentle early evening breeze; squawks and cackles fill the air, emanating from a plethora of unfamiliar aquatic avian wildlife.

This is a mighty fine spot. No wonder this place is being fought over.

Gupta orders tea be served. Nothing can be discussed or decided here in India without a serving of tea. This most British of rituals, whilst originating from China, was first introduced by the Empire makers who recognised India's climate and geology as being perfect for its cultivations, an enduring legacy of the Raj many Indians of a certain age still cling to as a vestige of an Era they were in some ways sad to see come to an end. The pros and cons of the British Empire can be argued extensively, and in depth, with valid theses on both sides of the discussion – it is a complex discussion that would for sure fill a whole library - but there are, surprisingly maybe, many Indians who lament aspects of its passing.

Who else, *these Indians* argue, could have organised the general population in the efficient and effective manner the British-Indian Civil Service was able to achieve?

Who else, *these Indians* state, could construct a wealth of bridges and buildings, still to be standing a hundred+ years later?

The Rabble who currently call themselves 'the Government', or so *these Indians* believe, are only really in it for their own personal aggrandisement.

The population certainly are now 'free' from the oppressive British rule, but *many openly state* they do not feel the quality of their lives has necessarily improved as a result. These same people have not forgotten that prior to British Rule, the country formerly known as Hindustan suffered numerous invasions from far less benign invading forces (of course, it can be argued that *no* invading force can ever be considered *benign* to any degree).

I am *not here to take sides in the debate*, nor to offer my own opinion.

I am here to listen, to learn, to understand better, to comprehend more fully.

It is a complex, multi-layered, nuanced issue for sure

I do not discuss such intricacies with Gupta. At least, not now; certainly, it is not a topic for discussion for this stage of our acquaintance. Instead, we make plans for my four-day stay.

Gupta says it is unsafe for me to travel around alone.

It is hard to know whether this statement is factually accurate, or whether I am being hoodwinked into purchasing additional services unnecessarily.

There is no way to verify this contention for sure. There are some things you just have to let others be the judge of, I guess.

Gupta insists that I must have not only a driver with me wherever I go, but also a *passe-partout* - a fixer, a helper, someone to smooth the way, someone to ward against who knows what perils that might lie in wait for the unsuspecting traveller.

I am introduced to Anil for the first time. He is a short, dark haired man, mid-thirties, with a wispy, pencil-thin moustache. He has a rather annoying habit, or so I will soon learn, of licking his lips at the end of each sentence, and of frequently sticking out his tongue to pick something forever invisible off it with his fingers.

Just what my own particularly annoying habits are I will leave for others to describe.

'I speak English very bad', or so Anil tells me.

I smile as I shake his hand. Our conversations will, I fear, not contain much in the way of in-depth analysis of the current geo-political situation in Kashmir. This may turn out to be a Good Thing.

After a decent night's sleep on the most comfortable bed I have experienced for the better part of a week now, with just the faint sound of water lapping at the hull to lull me to into a much-needed deep unconsciousness, the following day is spent floating serenely around the lake, propelled by a haggard, octogenarian boatman whose forward rate of progress is satisfactorily slow.

Anil sits opposite me, describing to me the scene in an English I cannot quite understand, apart from the odd snippet here and there, but have not the heart to tell him.

Under clear blue skies, warmed to perfection by the sun's brilliant rays, we potter slowly along the huge lake's occasional narrow waterways, channels created by floating gardens and vast banks of reeds, reeds that sway and ripple in the ever-present breeze.

We see fisherman casting their lead-rimmed nets, searching, Anil says, for carp; farmers trawling the lakebed for algae, both for animal feed, and to be used as fertiliser on the land; and long boats converted into floating grocers' shops, overladen with all manner of essentials: rice sacks; hessian sacks; pots and pans; fruit and vegetables, all brought straight to the door of your watery abode.

Lake life.

So calm, so tranquil, despite the heightened strains just a few kilometres away in town.

We camp overnight in a quiet spot by the waterway. It is a bitterly cold night under canvas. Anil, bless his soul, awakens me just before dawn to witness the sunrise. There is a light, crisp frost where the dew has formed and then frozen along the grassy banks of the waterway.

A thin fog rises around us. Bird song can be heard.

I really do see why they are fighting over this place.

Were it mine, I would not want to give it up, either.

What a place to call Home.

****

Time in Kashmir flies hurriedly by, despite the languid pace of life. The days pass seemingly in the blink of an eye, much of the time spent sitting in wonderment on the houseboat's rooftop platform, getting lost in the scope of the scenery, beguiled by the beauty all around. I am lost in the scope and beguiled by the beauty just so long as I am not being harangued by the near-constant stream of hawkers and craftsmen Gupta has invited onto the boat to ply their trades for my private personal perusal. The stream of sellers peddling their wares appears virtually endless. It is almost impossible to relax as yet another desperate trader looks pleadingly into my eyes, hoping, praying, that I will buy something, anything, from them.

I realise money is scarce, that sources of income have dried up since the Troubles flared up again four years ago.

I realise their needs are many. However, my own means are not exactly unlimited.

It becomes harder and harder to say, 'It's Beautiful, but I don't want to Buy One' as the river of salesmen and women tallies higher and higher, one, after the other, after the other.

'Enough already!' I feel like crying.

I try explaining to Gupta that I am not *actually* made of money, that my funds cannot support the whole town, or even a small sector of town.

My entreaties fall on deaf ears. Each time a sale is agreed – for a rug/ a throw/ a carving – instead of sating these merchants and drawing a line under the whole hawking business, it seems instead to feed the beast, to make the salesmen hungrier for even more.

'Another success!', they all think. 'And if we continue pushing, we can squeeze still more out from him. There is still plenty left to wring from this poor sucker'.

'Next!!'

I am *of course* not unsympathetic to their plight. I am *of course* not unsympathetic to their predicament, to the current state of play here in Kashmir, to their urgent need for financial support from anyone, no matter whom. However, this constant barrage is seriously affecting my sympathy, which seems now to be on the ebb; my compassion dwindling to near zero with their never-ending attempts to extract yet more money from me.

I spent a four-figure pound sterling sum on a bulk order of their local handicrafts just the previous day. Is *that* not enough?

I am reminded of a (possibly apocryphal) story concerning the car maker Henry Ford, who, back in the early 1900s, was asked to make a charitable donation whilst visiting the Republic of Ireland, the land of his forefathers. He offered most generously to contribute £5,000, quite a sum then, towards the cost of building a new hospital. The next morning's Press, however, announced Ford's largesse with a headline that had mysteriously added an extra 'zero' to this already not-insubstantial figure. The hospital trustees were quick to contact Ford and offer their sincerest apologies for this unfortunate error; the newspaper would, they said, gladly correct the headline the following day.

Ford, who wasn't as green as he was cabbage-looking, knew a scam when he saw one. Any retraction would doubtless not be beneficial to his reputation.

Ford agreed to match the headlined donation figure.

£50,000 for a new hospital.

On one condition: an inscription, near the entrance, reading, 'I Came Amongst You, and You Took Me In'.

Double meaning very much intended.

It feels rather that I have been taken in – and then *taken in* - brought here on false pretences: that my prior purchases are now being held against me; that I am to be fiscally bled until I have nothing left to give, with no concern as to the detrimental health effects this might have on the patient.

Enough!!

As an antidote to the constant hawker barrage, I decide to spend my last full day in Srinagar away from the boat, in Gulmarg (2,650m), Kashmir's premier – well, *only* - ski resort, long abandoned, now eerily deserted, its modern, French-built POMA gondola lift providing a weird juxtaposition to the wild-looking, crazy-full-bearded local tribesmen to whom I am now being introduced. I neglect to enquire as to which tribe of Kashmiris these fine-looking fellows belong; forgive me, for I am young, and enrapt with the ease with which they handle their horses, and the wide, beaming grins they all perpetually possess.

I am here to ride.

For Horse Riding.

Not as my American friends would say, 'Horse-Back Riding', for on which *other* section of the horse's anatomy do you ever plonk your rump?

I am a true novice at this horse-riding malarkey, keen, but lacking in experience or any form of conventional schooling. True, I have sat on many a horse, these horses have proceeded to achieve a moderate cantering pace, and, despite my lack of instruction, I have always managed to remain in the saddle, somewhat tenuously at times, in a state of mild panic always, and all the while counting down the seconds until the horse decelerates to a gentle walking pace, my chances of being thrown off and maimed thence returning to near zero.

Quite why I have now decided to go Horse Riding is, therefore, a mystery. It seemed like a good idea at the time. Anything to get away from the constant hawking barrage, I guess.

Our group sets off at a brisk walking pace. I realise that the skill I am performing should probably be termed 'Horse *Sitting*'. My ability to time my posterior's rise and fall in rhythm to my horse's own rises and falls, as is the traditional manner, I believe, is not quite there. Indeed, to say it is non-existent wouldn't be too much of a stretch. The rhythm required, and that being beaten out, are, worryingly for my long-term ability to remain on top of this horse, totally out of kilter.

But at this gentle walking pace I think I will be alright. I think I can survive this moderate degree of horse motion. At this gentle pace I can calmly survey the scenery around us, the green, alpine fur trees packed tightly together either side of the piste-cleared slope we are now following.

Yes, at this pace I think all will be OK.

The ten of us, our horses formed into a tight formation with me, for some unknown reason, towards the front, break into a canter.

This canter was *not* my idea.

It seems my horse has a mind of its own.

Now, my horse wants to be at the front of this horse pack, not back in fourth place, so suddenly accelerates past its buddies to gain the lead.

Fourth becomes, third; third becomes second; second become Leader of the Pack.

Way to go, horse!

Sadly, the instant my horse's nostrils are even a whiskered millimetre ahead of the previously leading horse he (She? Didn't look) slams on its brakes just as suddenly as he/ she had initially accelerated, squashing my nethers uncomfortably into the horn of my saddle.

Thanks. Cheers for nothing there, mate.

Just whose side are you on?

The horse adjacent to mine then senses there could be a race on - What Fun! - so ups its own pace. My charge, despite my loud, 'Wow there, Buddy!'-ing, takes up the challenge, striding faster and faster as the other horse's pace accelerates, until our swift canter becomes an almost full-striding gallop. Maybe my horse only speaks Kashmiri, but the tone of my 'Wows!' should be sufficient for the message to get through its thick skull that I want it to slow down a tad, as should my constant pulling back on the reins.

But no. Now is Race Time.

To my horse, it appears - somewhat worryingly - I have become a complete irrelevance.

We are now all moving at quite a lick. The fun has, mysteriously, vanished from this endeavour. I bump and grind against my saddle, each time being thrown higher and higher into the air, with each passing stride my failure to time my rise-and-fall with the horse's rise-and-fall becoming exponentially amplified.

I am now holding on to the cantle for dear life.

I am now shouting and cussing and 'Wow!'-ing and generally proving my complete ineptitude at this particular equine pastime, something competent riders make look so simple, but at which I am currently failing in spectacular fashion.

At the sight of my being flung higher and higher into the air, my position atop my horse becoming more tenuous and precarious with each passing stride, the crazy tribesmen start to laugh.

One laughs.

They all laugh.

They laugh heartily.

They laugh with their bellies.

They laugh as fully as any man (or woman) in the history of laughing has ever laughed.

This is the funniest thing to happen here in quite a while, or so it would seem.

I am happy to be providing such entertainment, I guess.

I don't mind people laughing *with* me, but I wonder if they are maybe laughing a tad too heartily *at* me.

Whatever.

I decide to join them in laughing at the absurdity of it all; there is really nothing else you can do in such situations.

Clouds form swiftly, as is their want in the mountains. Soon, what were clear blue skies are fully covered with ominous, dark grey, rain-heavy clouds. Just like that, rain starts to fall. We all seek shelter under the eaves of an abandoned building, inside yet technically still outside. It is now bucketing it down in stair rods. The tribesmen, sporting long, ankle-length, herringbone-patterned woollen coats up into which they shuffle their bent knees, perfectly covering their feet and legs, appear totally at peace with the elements.

Lacking a suitable jumper or overcoat, wearing thin cotton trousers and top, I start to shiver.

A little, then a lottle.

My obvious discomfort, my amateurish fish-out-of-water-ness, results in the tribesmen all smiling some more.

'Stay here with us for a week,' they suggest, through my interpreter Anil. 'We will teach you to ride a horse!'

This causes them to all laugh some more. The thought of teaching such an obviously clueless novice is quite the laughing matter. I have no doubt they would be excellent instructors, and good to their word.

'Alas, I have no time,' I tell them.

They seem not to understand this word 'Time'.

Possibly, they think I should *make* Time, for to learn to ride with this region's foremost equine masters would be an honour no doubt.

I take my last supper as I had my previous evening meals, on the roof of the houseboat, with glorious panoramas over the lake as my backdrop. Supper is once again a wonderful selection of vegetarian delights, lightly curried dishes with delicately spiced exotic flavours.

I am not a vegetarian, but in India, well, why take the risk of eating tainted meat?

At home, we have the 5-Second Rule, that food is still good for consumption for up to five seconds once dropped onto the floor.

In India, the 5-Second Rule refers to the time *prior* to the food hitting the floor.

And that is probably a *wild* underestimation.

****

I am leaving the following morning, making the 48-hour bus journey across to Leh, the summer capital of the Ladakh region.

'I am losing a Brother,' or so Gupta keeps repeating, over supper.

My typical British reserve does not know what to make of these over-wrought histrionics.

'You must be helping us', he pleads, beseechingly.

I am not sure how to help, how I *can* help; I am not sure what I am expected to do. I have purchased a few thousand pounds-worth of local hand-made arts and crafts, which I trust will be delivered to me in England in a few months' time, as per the signed deal.

Just how does Gupta expect *me* to assist in bringing a political solution to this obviously troubled region?

I know not how I am supposed to act. I am but a young man.

Gupta speaks of our UK Prime Minister John Major with high regard. Major is, Gupta tells me, the only world leader currently engaged in trying to bring resolution to the Kashmir Question. I tell Gupta I am ever hopeful a solution will be agreed upon, soon.

Yet, as I sit here in the darkness on the rooftop, I hear bomb blasts from across the water in Srinagar.

I hear the distinctive sound of gunfire. Multiple shots ring out.

I look to Gupta for an indication whether this is something to be concerned about.

He has a look of resignation on his face.

'No, my friend', his face seems to say, 'this is not unusual. This is Normal.'

That a night curfew has once again been imposed is *normal*.

Is this something to worry about?

Not for us, right here, at this time. But there is indeed much for everyone to worry about.

Just two years later, six Western tourists - two Brits, two Americans, a German and a Norwegian - will be kidnapped from nearby locations by *Al-Faran*, a Kashmir-based, Islamist militant organisation. One of the Americans will manage to escape. The Norwegian will tragically be found with what the press would today euphemistically describe as 'deep neck wounds' but, in the harsh reality of the world as it actually is, with his head having been removed, the words *Al-Faran* reportedly carved into his chest. The remaining four hostages will never be found, believed sold on to other terrorist organisations and later shot when ransom or political demands will go unmet.

Elsewhere, insurgent bomb blasts will kill and maim scores of locals.

Crowds of protestors will be shot at and killed by Indian Government forces.

The Struggles will intensify. The carnage will escalate.

A suitable, peaceful resolution will become a distant dream.

Chapter 8

That's Some Numb Bum

Just after dawn.

We, Gupta and I, are standing at the bus station in Srinagar - what passes for a bus station in Srinagar - aside the rickety bus that will be transporting me on the two-day quest to Leh. We have arrived in excellent time, it would appear, having for some unknown reason risen at 5.30am for this 9am bus. There is no one here except for us two, and the driver.

Gupta seems once again close to tears.

'I am losing a Brother', he keeps repeating.

Gupta dabs constantly at his eyes with a stained, off-white handkerchief, somewhat theatrically to my own eyes. I cannot ascertain whether the tears being brushed away are genuine, or of the crocodile variety.

It is hard to know the precise nature of *anything* with Gupta.

He asks me which seat on the bus I would like.

I peer inside. The seat pitch appears poorly designed to cater for someone with my dangly leg measurement. From past experience, this is of course not wholly unexpected. I view with some covetousness the front row seats above the steps up from the door.

No hindrance to stretch out my legs here, I deduce.

'This one', I tell Gupta, pointing at the front seat on the left-hand side of the bus.

He asks for 40 *rupees*. The equivalent of £1.

'For the driver', Gupta says.

Possibly.

Or for him *and* the driver. Or maybe just for *him*.

This is the same amount as the bus ticket for this entire two-day journey.

I give Gupta 40 *rupees*.

He speaks with the driver. The front seat is now mine, Gupta tells me.

This will prove to be the best £1 I have ever invested.

Our appointed departure time approaches. The bus is now full, mostly with locals, but also a smattering of Westerners, their faces peering expectantly out from the window seats.

I step down from my own seat for a final farewell with Gupta. There really does appear to be a stream of watery issue now running down his rounded, flushed cheeks.

Yet, still I wonder. Are these honest tears, unfeigned tears, or just Part of the Show?

'I am losing a Brother'.

I shake Gupta's hand, thanking him heartily and sincerely for his hospitality.

'I am losing a Brother.'

The words remain eerily with me as the bus gently rolls out from the station.

****

A great distance and much challenging terrain awaits us before we reach Leh. It is more than 450km along a very rough, rutted road – the National Highway 1D – that runs between the two main northerly cities, over the Zoji La pass at 3,500m, and the Fotu La pass at 4,100m, before we're due to roll into Leh, still a cool 3,500m above sea level. This route can only be travelled in the summer months, during the brief window in the calendrical year when the deep winter snows that render the route unpassable for six months (or longer) have melted, and once the numerous landslides have been swept aside. Our presence on this narrow strip of road is precarious; the road's own presence in this vast mountain landscape is equally tenuous, nature continually doing its upmost to erase this scar from the terrain, to return the land to its original, unblemished condition.

Despite my luxurious leg stretching space, it is not a wholly comfortable ride. For lack of comfort, in return there is exhilarating scenery. Majestic views lurk around the road's every twist and turn, vast vistas of wild mountain ranges. There is untold beauty waiting to be discovered wheresoever you look. Staring out of the bus's grubby windows, for hours at a time is, in such wondrous circumstances, a real joy. We are wandering; my mind, too, is free to wander, free to choose its own musings and considerations on the nature of existence, on the never far from thought, *Meaning of (My) Life*. It is in these rare moments of unfocused meditation, when cognitions are given free rein to roam unchecked and undirected, that those epiphanic, momentous, *a-ha* moments might occur. Staring for hours on end out of a moving bus (or train) window, for no other reason than to let the mind wander, doing nothing, without the need for external stimulus or other interactions, is a joy to which the must-be-doing-something sections of society have not an inkling.

It is a forgotten artform; a lost source of hidden treasure.

At a rest-stop, I chat with a fellow bus rider, another British escapee, a former financier, an ex-high-powered honcho in the City of London, who quit his job six months prior, or so he tells me. Once a Venture Capitalist, this man has now ventured forth to find the Meaning of It All whilst Travelling the World.

I ask how's he getting on with that.

He smiles.

I think this means he's still working on the All of *It*.

Life as a Venture Capitalist was not, the man tells me, all it is cracked up to be.

I am not *exactly* sure what life in the world of Venture Capitalism is supposed to be cracked up to be; the limited amount I do know merely covers the knowledge that VC most likely provides a non-immodest level of income, which is surely the reason the vast majority of people enter that profession.

I ask what he felt was lacking.

'Oh, a deep sense of Personal Fulfilment from bringing Betterment to the World.'

Ah. Is that *all*?

Aren't the salaries stratospherically high precisely *because* the soul finds little sating in its midst?

There are many more like him, the man says, who become similarly trapped inside the Financial Industry's midst, having myopically rushed in, overly keen and eager to get a foothold on the ladder to the Land of Wealth and Comfort, and Beyond.

'Don't worry, it'll only be for a year, or two. Three at the most. Just until I've saved up sufficient resource to be able to quit and take up a cool Not-for-Profit, philanthropic role that will allow me to fulfil my true vocational needs', is what they all say.

Of course, the underlying fault with this plan, the ex-VC tells me, is that Outgoings increase just as rapidly as Income increases. If not more so. Before you know it, you've moved into a lavish, new-build pad in one of the fancier London postcodes, a spanking new, shiny fast car parked in the carpool, and a stonkingly hot, uber-chic boy/girlfriend whose interest in you is not necessarily unconnected with the briefcases of crispy moolah you bring in each month, and the luxuriant trappings this level of wealth thus affords.

Then comes the next big shock to the system: you discover your savings are mysteriously not in fact increasing, despite earning a cool annual six-figure sum, plus hefty six-, occasionally seven-figure bonuses (a Brucie-B swallowed up almost entirely by your equally non-insignificant credit card balance, accrued at all the fashionable night spots and bistro restaurants your paramour insisted he/she be taken to with all too frequent regularity).

In a flash, the three years pass.

Bam!

You might still be wanting to leave, but, wait, what's that?

Yes, you're trapped!

You daren't move on to that Vocationally-more-Fulfilling-yet-Fiscally-less-Rewarding role as intended, lest the lad(y) in your life dumps you for someone *better suited* – i.e. more moolah'd; in any case, you can't afford to take the hit a substantial drop in salary entails, for much of what you 'own' is merely leased on finance, and the monthly repayments are eye-wateringly staggering.

At such junctures, many simply 'forget' their promise to move on; their current rate of income attainment is actually quite appealing, now they come to think about it – maybe the partner is now the spouse, and the patter of tiny feet has added an additional burden into the mix. Despite the fact their jobs are eating away at their souls, their bellies are constantly replete (indeed, waistlines are expanding on both sides of the aisle).

So, erroneously, they kid themselves that all their spiritual needs are equally well sated.

It is a surprising, cautionary tale to be hearing so far from the luxuriant trappings of fiscal excess. The City, the Square Mile - pin-striped suits, bowler hats, shiny patent leather shoes, brown leather briefcases in one hand, FT and umbrella under one arm - that life seems more than a world away from the almost Middle Ages rudimentary existence of this stark land here. It is hard to believe that There and Here are indeed part of the same global sphere of existence.

'Isn't following one's true vocation a luxury, a dream – maybe even a pipe dream?' I ask the VC.

For dreams are surely the preserve of the foolish head-in-the-clouds Dreamer.

You can't raise a family on dreams, can you? Or *can* you?

For some – for many? – for most? - the luxury of following our dreams is simply not part of the equation.

My fellow traveller might be the Exception that Proves the Rule. He had is Epiphany, he broke free, and what's more he managed to do so with a suitably swollen bank balance - he tells me, not that I asked - a tidy amount with which to ease the pain of this Epiphany: that there might be more to life than the 9-5, *Metro-Boulot-Dodo* World of Finance, working crazy long hours but seemingly achieving nothing in the real world, of putting profit before anything else more ethically or morally nuanced, creating nothing tangible you can actually touch and say, 'I built that'.

How I wish my own Epiphany had occurred with my bank balance similarly engorged.

How much simpler it must be to navigate a Philanthropic Path with a healthy surplus squirreled away.

****

It is already late in the day when we pass through Kargil, the northern-most village in Kashmir before you reach the dotted line indicating the approximation of the borders between India, Pakistan and China on maps of this region. Little do we now know, but in 1999, Kargil will be destroyed by hostilities between Pakistan and India. Almost three months of fiercely contested skirmishes will see Pakistani forces pushed back across the LoC and India regain the village. Kargil will become virtually uninhabitable despite the victory. Few villagers will return to their devasted homes. The road to rebuilding will take decades. It will be yet another tragedy in this part of the world.

We are making painfully slow progress along the narrow, rough and rarely tarmacked road. Our average speed is not improved by the frequent army checkpoints we are required to all de-bus and pass through, passports in hand, entrance stamps and visas open for show.

Thank goodness for being *official*.

Around 1am, we finally reach our overnight stop - a tiny, unnamed hamlet that appears out of nowhere - many hours behind schedule, legs sore, bums numb, backs achy, bellies empty.

There is precious little time for us to recover; the bus will leave again at 5am, we are told.

I ask the driver whether he is joking about this departure time.

It appears that, no, he is deadly serious.

Four hours is barely enough time to sleep, to find sufficient comfort to even *contemplate* sleep.

You must take what you can.

I seek out lodgings for the night. There are few lights on at this hour. I find an old lady still pottering around outside who shows a couple of fellow weary bus passengers and I up a flight of rickety stairs to a dark, dingy, dusty room with three rickety metal-framed beds inside.

This is not in any way suitable accommodation. It will have to do, however. The charge for the night is only *Rs5*. I chain and padlock my rucksack to the bed and try as best I can to get some rest. After sixteen hours bouncing and bumping along inside the bus it is tricky to achieve a feeling of balanced equilibrium. The rocking motion seems to have followed me off the bus and onto my bed, the rusty springs beneath my dusty mattress squeaking with each minute movement my body makes.

5am arrives far too soon.

****

Day Two.

Everyone resumes their previous positions inside the bus, with exact precision, no one daring to attempt a sneaky upgrade lest someone take offence. Who knows what the response would be in any case were someone to be so underhand as to change position? Seats were not allocated in any order, purely a First-come-First-served basis; the bus conductor is a short, fresh-faced Tibetan lad whose ability to mediate a heated disagreement appears somewhat limited. This renewal is a wonder of self-selecting organisation rarely seen in other parts of the world, where this sense of 'seat ownership' would not even be a glint in the conceptual eye for people to contemplate. My luxurious leg space position has been much coveted by travellers and locals alike. I am in no mood to give it up now. Not unless Gulliver himself makes an appearance.

On the move again.

The scenery is changing. We are still in a ruggedly mountainous region but gone are the densely forested slopes of pine trees we traversed yesterday morning. The land is now almost completely barren. Green vegetation-covered slopes have been replaced by vistas of white-tipped mountain tops, flora-free, pastel-hewn slopes – layers of deep iron-ore reds, bands of soft beiges, patches of dark mocha browns – all contrasted against the verdant, cultivated valley floors, each section of mountain complementing strikingly with its neighbour, dramatically enhancing the views. We have now entered the rain shadow, annual precipitation reduced to a mere fraction of its western cousin due to the consistency of the strong westerly winds pushing weather patterns from west to east, up over the towering mountain ranges that suck all the moisture out of the air.

The result of this water deficit is other-worldly.

The stark beauty is mesmerising.

Our bus bounces along, *once again*.

Our bums are *once again* numb.

Once again, darkness falls.

We are all mighty relieved to eventually reach Leh.

Drinks Break

Zipolite, Oaxaca State, southern Mexico.

Oaxaca: pronounced – *Wa-ha-ca*.

Yes, just like the restaurant chain. The pronunciation, that is, not the spelling.

Zipolite (*Zippo-leet-ay*) is (*was*?) a cool, laid-back beach destination for backpackers, hippies and alternative life-stylers alike, first achieving notoriety back in the '70s, and still popular with those who prefer to shun the bright lights of 5-Star Resorts.

In **Zipolite**, the alternative life-styling covers most alternative lifestyles.

In **Zipolite**, you can *do* as little as you want, *for* as little as you want, *in* as little as you want, or so the saying goes.

Zipolite's 5km long white sands, bookended by two small coves at either end of the beach, are pounded constantly by large Pacific breakers, uniform, rolling waves that crash with a thunderous *Boom!* every thirty or so seconds, day in, day out.

Peaceful the Pacific most certainly is not.

'The Place has Amazing Energy', one sagacious, dreadlocked individual, who might quite possibly have been stoned, might once have proclaimed.

Like, yeh, Dude. I hear ya.

Zipolite. From the *Zapotec*, 'Beach of the Dead', a name bestowed, according to legend, due to the strong rip currents that used to drag an average of fifty people a year to an early, sodden demise. The beach has life-guards now, but, in the early '90s, your only hope, as the strong tides dragged you out to sea, or off round the headland to the neighbouring deserted bays, was to relax, to not fight against the current, and to wave your arms as wildly as you could, whilst calling out at the top of your lungs, hopeful that one of the handful of surfers near the beachfront was still sufficiently *with it* to come to rushing to your aid on his (or her) board.

It is currently Midday.

Hot. *So* hot.

Too hot to be out in the full glare of the sun.

I am taking a cool *Dos Equis* in the shade whilst chatting with a local Mexican lad from the *Cabanas*.

The pace of life here is slow. *Real* slow.

Cicadas are chirping.

The beach's scruffy looking canine inhabitants, who do their bidding in the night's cooler air, are all currently curled up under the huts, snoring to their hearts' content. A cockerel, or two, crow their 'doodle-do' crows, impervious to the inaccuracy of their time keeping. A strong, southerly wind strains the palm fronds overhead.

Barely a soul stirs.

Barely a soul, apart from the ever-present flies that flitter annoyingly around, buzzy-whizz bugs that take great pleasure in annoying the hell out of anyone they find to pester.

Then again, do flies *have* souls?

In front of us, walking with only slightly more pace than an asthmatic snail afflicted by painful bunions, but only just, is an old man - weathered, wrinkled, stooped - carrying a large bundle of firewood resting precariously atop his head, and down most of his arched back. The dude's progress is *painfully* slow.

I suggest to my *amigo* that perhaps we should, you know, offer to assist the poor man, such is the agonising sloth of his progress. The old fella looks to be in his 80s, I guess. We lads are both young strapping twenty-year olds, in the full flush of youth. Surely, it's not right for us to continue to sit there, supping our cool *caguamas*, whilst this octogenarian struggles so valiantly, but so onerously, with his ungainly load.

I am surprised to be met with a stern rebuke. I am told, in no uncertain terms, that to assist this man would in fact be the worst thing we could do for him. Whilst we would certainly be helping the man *today,* should we assist him *now*, we would not be helping this man in the *long term*, or so my friend says.

'Sure, the man is old. That is correct'.

'Sure, he is struggling with this load. That, too, is correct.'

'But he has been carrying this load all his life. He has been fetching wood, being active, strengthening his muscles, toning his body, *all his life.*'

'If we step in to help with this load, and then someone else helps with the next load, and the next, his body will soon weaken. His muscles will soon atrophy. His body will wither. The man will then end up *not being able* to carry this load.'

'In not quite the blink of an eye, the old man will no longer be able to carry this load for *any* distance.'

'So, despite your best intentions, before you know it you will have caused the old man to lose his autonomy, to become a burden to those around him, for he will thence surely age. He will surely become *aged.* You will have created the reality you had fixed in *your* mind, one of him being an *old* man, but one of which he had no inkling *himself.*'

Interesting.

So: 'You are only *truly old* when you perceive yourself *truly old.*'

'We're old,' or so we reason, 'hence we should stop performing physical tasks, on account of our advancing age.'

This is a fallacy.

We're merely *getting older.*

As such, we should *continue* performing physical tasks, because once we cease our bodies will then truly become *old.*

It is an interesting lesson for a hot, slow, cold *cerveza* kind of day.

Chapter 9

Wherever I Leh My Hat

Sun rise. Leh.

1,000km north of Delhi.

Top of India. Top of the World.

What a change from Srinagar.

What a dramatic transformation.

They are neighbours, Ladakhis and Kashmiris, but as peoples they are chalk and cheese, drawn from distinct heritages and dissimilar mindsets.

The round-faced – innocent, cherubic - Tibetan-looking Ladakhis smile and smile, and then smile some more.

It is a real smile. A wide smile. A *happy* smile.

They appear a Happy People.

Maybe the Kashmiris used to smile, too.

I can understand why they do not smile now.

In Ladakh, you are greeted with a firm handshake; a wide, beaming smile.

The Ladakhis seem genuinely happy to see you, to meet you, to welcome you to their beautiful home.

In Kashmir, the greeting ritual left you feeling as if it were your wallet, not your hand, that was being shaken.

'Hello. Pleased to meet you. And, yes, your money. Actually, mainly your money.'

Maybe I am too cynical.

Maybe, Gupta's theatrics have made me wary of accepting anything I witness as the real deal without further corroborating evidence.

I feel the need to be cleansed of this cynicism.

Ladakh seems the perfect place for such a procedure.

****

In recent times, Leh has experienced its own disputes and conflicts, sandwiched as Ladakh is between the Pakistan-Kashmir issue to the west, and China to the East. Pakistan forces almost captured Leh in 1948; in 1962-63, China was a serious threat to its position within India; in 1965 and 1974, there were wars with Pakistan. For these reasons, Leh and the Indus valley were closed to foreigners until 1974.

As a mainly Buddhist region, in contrast to its Muslim counterparts to the west, Ladakh has long sought independence of its own, to be freed from the administration of Jammu and Kashmir, desiring to instead be under the direct governance of Delhi. Tensions simmered and bubbled under the surface throughout the 1970s and '80s, reaching a peak in '89. Led by the Ladakh Buddhist Association, the usually meek and accommodating Buddhist community of Ladakh were encouraged to favour businesses run by those of their own faith, as opposed to those run by Muslims. Lately, a truce has been brokered; Ladakh will be permitted its own Hill Council within the J&K Administration. As Buddhists are by their nature a non-belligerent people, it is a good rule of thumb, I have come to think, that you must have done something considerably disagreeable to have incurred their ire. As abstinence from harming other creatures is a central precept of the Buddhist doctrine, their first consideration must be to seek a peaceful solution to this, or any other problem.

Sunshine. Blue skies.

After two days of cooped up claustrophobia, now is time to get an expansive sense of perspective over my new glorious surroundings.

Time to set forth; time to visit some of the wonders Leh has to offer. Time to shake the dust off from my Tourist Hat.

Time to go See Some Sights.

I make my way to the Spituk Gompa, 8km outside Leh, an ancient 14th century Buddhist monastery reached via hundreds of steep steps. I must have been sitting around for too long, for I have no breath left after merely a dozen. Doing anything here takes more time than you expect. The air is thin; or I might possibly need to get into better shape.

I am currently at 3,500m – just over 11,000 feet - above sea level.

Yes, it's the lack of oxygen in the air; nothing to do with my own physical deficiencies.

Slowly, slowly, catchy monkey.

The monkey here can rest easy.

I journey back into town to see the Namgyal Tsemo Gompa, also dating back to the 1400s. The region's relatively dry climate has aided the Gompa's fine state of preservation. The monastery is constructed in a simple, traditional design, although I am once again referring to my Lonely Planet for this information.

'Few flourishes; little gaiety; locally sourced building materials' is the text's general gist.

Few flourishes, except for a vast golden Buddha, a three-storey high statue.

Wow. Magnificence.

I try to take it all in: the majesty of the setting; the vastness of the statue; the deep blueness of the sky; the freshness and tranquillity of the air.

Leh sits at the confluence of two strategic routes: the main Indus river valley; and the road to the pass over to the Nubra valley (and thence almost to China). For an age, I sit, transfixed, completely absorbed by the far distant vistas - 60km, possibly further, towards the rugged peaks of the Zanskar mountain range - a land left, right and centre with scant indication to suggest the 19th century, let alone 20th, has percolated this far north.

The claustrophobia of the bus ride evaporates in an instant.

This is It. This is the Place to Be.

It is a simple land. It is a simple time.

The people are happy.

Maybe we make life too complicated for ourselves?

What if Less truly is More?

Maybe my VC companion will find the Answers to It All out here.

****

I have arrived into Leh at an auspicious moment, for the following day the annual *Trungkar* Festival is being held nearby at Choglamsar, a few kms outside Leh, what is described to me by the young lad at my accommodation as a joyous occasion to celebrate the Dalai Lama's birthday. Gupta had told me this event was not for several weeks; as my stay on the houseboat progressed Gupta had tried, quite persistently, to cajole me into extending my Kashmir stopover by several more days.

'No, no, you *definitely* won't miss the Festival' he said, many a time, with a straight face, hand on heart, Mother's Honour.

Oh, Gupta.

Why the blatant mendacity?

Why no shame?

Do the Ends justify the Means?

'Sure, sure, there will be other travellers with you on the houseboat', said the guy who travelled up to Kashmir with me.

Another case of misspeak?

Another case of being *economical* with the Truth?

Or should we call it an out and out *lie*?

Too direct? Too unforgiving of me?

I stop this train of thought, reminding myself I am here to flush this cynicism from my system.

I contend to look forwards in Time. There is no Future in the Past.

I am happy to have coincided with the Festival. I don my tourist cap once more, venturing over to join in the party. On arrival, I am not entirely sure *how* to join in the party. The Gorshay dancing is unlike anything I have seen before, guys and gals garbed in traditional Tibetan outfits all in circular formation, following one another around a large, sectioned-off performance area. The ladies' costumes appear slightly too long in the sleeve area, which cannot be very practical I fear. They are at risk of being blown away, should the wind decide to pick up. The audience claps heartily when the dancers all stop moving. It seems the choreography was very much to everyone's liking.

Elsewhere in this vast field, more large circular groups have formed, fifty people and more in each gathering. Prayers are being offered, for his Holiness, for his Eternal Good Health, or so I am told. Random individuals then walk out from the main congregation, moseying up to a centrally-plonked microphone; speeches are made, although no subtitles are provided. I am at a total loss as to what is being said.

No matter. The sun shines down on us all. Happy smiling faces in all directions. Much merriment is evidently being enjoyed.

In amongst this merriment, I spy an aged, silver-haired lady - sixty? seventy? – standing motionless whilst this throng moves hither and thither all around her position. Her long traditional robes provide her with a dignified air. Her wide, four cornered hat adds a touch of stylish flair. The septuagenarian, a rolled-up rug under one arm, mouth slightly ajar, hand on her chin, her brow furrowed and pensive, stands there in such a pose, in such a manner, as if there were something she is finding hard to mentally process, some issue currently beyond her comprehension, as if a question has entered her mind, transfixing her whilst she searches for an answer.

She is hypnotised. Engrossed. Confused. Concerned.

Oh, to now know what this lady now knows.

To be able to enquire about the life she has seen.

I wonder what is going on in her mind. It seems this lady might just need someone to put an arm around her, to tell that everything, whatever *everything* may be, is going to be OK.

Right on cue, a younger lady – her daughter? – arrives, taking hold of her arm, leading her back towards a small gathering of ladies of her own generation.

The lady's concern concerns me. I wonder what was troubling her mind.

****

I meet dozens of other intrepid travellers who have also made it to this rugged northern outpost. It appears I am in the company of a wondrous self-selection of traveller finery, the most hardened, the most inquisitive, the most open-to-new-experience, the *true traveller* wheat sifted from the *suitcase traveller* chaff. At the cafes that dot town, conversations are easy to start up. They continue for time immeasurable. It is a relief to once again be in decent company, after the days spent in isolation on the houseboat.

Most of these wanderers have come in by way of Manali, others along the same Srinagar-Leh road I have just endured. Some, instantly branded disdainfully as *Outsiders* by the tougher elements of the group, have flown in directly to Leh – lightweights with evidently deeper pockets then the rest of us. The hierarchy within the travelling community instantly rejects those who clearly didn't suffer sufficiently to reach this place; the greater the hardship, the higher your imbued ranking.

In any case, flying directly in to Leh from Delhi may only take a couple of hours, but the swift rise from sea-level to 3,500m knocks your body for six for the better part of two or three days. You'll have saved Time, only to then lose Time lying flat on your back in your hotel room, gasping for oxygen, whilst enduring the mother of all headaches and a whole series of weird body aches and digestive gurgles that for the better part of sixty hours will leave you feeling really rather peculiar.

Thought you could save Time, eh?

A Fool's Errand.

See, you, too, will be Learning.

****

A football match is arranged between the travellers and some of the young local lads. We travellers are all prime physical specimens, in the full flush of youth, or so we think. In the first half the local lads run rings around us. It is barely possible to run even a few paces with the ball before you must stop, hands resting firmly on your knees, trying desperately to catch your breath, trying desperately to suck oxygen in, as if you've just remerged from a lengthy underwater foray.

The local lads smile and grin as they dart around the pitch like over-caffeinated moths.

Each time they score, they smile some more.

Half-time comes.

We travellers all collapse in a destroyed heap of raggedly worn out bodies. There are no half-time oranges with which to perk ourselves up. No physios to massage our weary limbs. No manager to provide the much-needed motivational team talk to rekindle the fire now burning as mere embers inside our dejectedly broken spirits. Instead, one of our team lights up a large chillum, packed to the brim with strong Manali hash. The chillum is passed around, each team member taking a long tug from the base of the clay tube. I politely decline. I am not sure smoking this concoction will enhance my lung capacity, nor boost my competitive spirit. Maybe smoking the chillum will mean I will no longer care about my current physical inadequacies.

Everyone seems back in good spirits after inhaling from the pipe.

I doubt this restorative process will catch on in the sporting world at home, though.

In the second half, the teams are jumbled up, locals and travellers now comprising both sides. The score is reset to 0-0. The locals still score all the goals, but this time each goal scored equalises out their own earlier efforts.

In any case, the result is unimportant.

We have all learnt a lot. Everyone has won.

As I gather myself after the match, I encounter a trio of intrepid Aussie guys, also in their early twenties. You'll meet Aussies scattered far and wide around the globe, no matter how remote the place you have managed to reach. As a nationality, Aussies might be few in number, but they're mighty wide in scope.

Enlightened as the Aussies are, travelling is more ingrained into Australian culture than within most other nations. Travelling is considered a positive addition to their better, fuller understanding of the world. The World Trip, or Six Months in Europe Break, is considered a Fair Dinkum Must Do for those of a certain age: finish your studies; get yourself Out There to experience the wide variety of life outside their own shores; return with a hefty stack of hard-earned Aussie Dollars, maybe a decent Sheila, too; then bang out a few blonde-haired sprogs and spend the rest of your life surfing, drinking cool Stubbies from your Esky, whilst following the Rugger (or Cricket, or Aussie Rules) on the telly, which, come to think of it, might be an outcome slightly short on True Enlightenment.

These lads have been climbing a few of the local high peaks, they tell me.

Not for the incredible physical challenge, or the mind-blowingly stupendous views, mind you, but to have their minds blown in another, altogether different, manner.

The Enhanced Tokers' High.

The secret, they inform me, is to find a peak, one at around 5,000m (we are surrounded by quite the choice) and venture up to its summit, no mean feat in and of itself. Once summited, you need to skin up a joint (or maybe produce a *Blue Peter*, as in, 'Here's one I rolled earlier'). Said joint should then be enjoyed from a squatting-down-on-your-haunches position, taking several long puffs in quick succession.

Inhale – hold – count to ten – exhale.

Repeat.

Threepeat.

As the effects of the hash kick in, you must then, the Aussies say, leap up majestically from your squat in a Starburst – that X-shape body form where your arms are extended overhead. As you ascend serenely into the air, rapid blood pressure changes mean you will promptly pass out (if this hasn't already put you off attempting this malarkey yourself, for obvious reasons this whole shebang does not come with any endorsement from me – I accept no responsibility for any issues that may arise should you be crazy enough to try this out yourself, although I imagine finding a suitable, 5,000m high peak *chez vous* might be something of a challenge).

Recently rendered unconscious, this mad manoeuvre is not best suited to solo travellers, the Aussies tell me, for you ideally need at least two buddies still of sufficient alert and wherewithal to then catch your currently lifeless body before it smacks face first into the ground with a bone-crushing thud.

When, moments later – hopefully – you come round, the rush, they say, is quite the hit.

I am not sure whether to be impressed by their inventiveness, or concerned at what seem the obvious flaws in their antics. I wonder, too, if the lads might be missing out on the cultural wonders of this place.

But, each to their own, I guess.

Live and Let Live.

There may indeed be numerous sound medical reasons why the lads should not be attempting such a stunt. They're also not exactly in the best catchment area for medical evacuation should something, quite possibly, go wrong. I wonder what their insurance policy might have to say about this specific activity, whether there might be an explicit exclusion for High Altitude Drug Taking Mishaps lurking there within the small print (they're not dumb, these Insurance Adjustors).

The Libertarian in me reluctantly admits the risk is all theirs'; the lads are not harming anyone whilst they monkey around, as far as I can tell. And they're happily paying for the services of a local guide during these ascents.

Who knows, maybe with this novel experience the lads are actually mining gold. Maybe they'll go on to establish a successful business for fellow Antipodean Travellers wishing to experience similar fun-filled highs. Something a little different to the Tomatina, or the Pamplona Bull Running festivals the Aussies normally flock to in their thousands.

At least they're not being Unoriginal.

****

Night of the Full Moon.

In the World of the Traveller, this means one thing: All-Night Party.

Luckily, the Israelis are in town. The Israelis always throw the best parties. They always bring with them the best sound systems, the best music. They always dress up the party area in their own unique style, daubing sheets with multi-coloured, fluorescent paints in an array of wonderfully psychedelic designs. Sometimes, they daub fluorescent paint onto the cows, too. Cows are considered deities in India; fluorescently-daubed cows roaming randomly amongst a group of raving, off-their-tits travellers adds an air of *je ne sais quoi* to the proceedings. The Indian perspective on that particular use of their bovine gods is unclear, however.

Tonight's Party is being held on a small island in the middle of the Indus river, about 9km outside Leh. It is a magical setting. Moonlight glistens off the gently rippling streams of water flowing either side of the set up. There is a Buddhist Gompa a few kms away, resting high up on a rocky outcrop, its façade illuminated by the fullness of the moon.

The Israelis play Trance music. *Good* Trance music (no, not cheesy Euro Trance, or really any Trance produced since 1999), with added Psychedelic-Mystical elements inspired by the Goan Hippie Vibe. High Tempo Electronic Dance music is a relatively new phenomenon, having emerged in the late '80s from the German Techno scene (with nods to the Chicago House scene, too). This new style of music, of social gatherings, of dance vibes, attracts creative types from other genres of the music world, producing something new and innovative with the aid of computerised synths and beat generators, all with wondrous results.

An exciting time to be part of the Scene. Musical Revolution is in the air.

Without breaking between tracks, our DJ mixes the tunes on his twin turntables for maximum effect, like a conductor controlling an orchestra's tempo. The music ebbs and flows - faster, louder, quieter, slower - dropping the hook, bridging the breakdown, then hitting those peaks, the repetitive beats creating trance-like states for those who have sought out the Man Who Can, those who've added a little chemical augmentation to their digestive processes, who've ingested MDMA, or Ecstasy, or Speed, or Coke, or LSD, or 'Shrooms – uppers and downers, or something to twist their minds sideways, through a portal into another dimension – affording them a temporary, alternative perspective on Reality, and the stamina to keep gyrating rhythmically to the rapid 130bpm tempo for what seems like an Eternity.

These people are going to be here all night, and probably some of the following morning, too. For them, Time will stretch and bend, Reality will shift and distort, their moods will rise and rise, higher and higher, until, as their brain receptors flood with waves of dopamine and serotonin, of oxytocin and norepinephrine, a wildly uplifting *euphoric* high will be experienced.

Love will be in the Air.

Love will be All Around.

Love will be Everywhere.

Many will doubtless claim this to be the Best Night of their Lives, Man.

I walk home around 3am. I am content.

I lie awake, though, deep in thought, my mind brooding on the old lady at the *Trungkar*.

I wonder what had confused her so.

Surely, this place is too perfect for danger to be lurking in our midst.

****

The following day, rain arrives.

This is an odd occurrence, the young lad at my accommodation tells me.

'It *never* rains in Leh', he says.

It is the curse of the Brit to bring rain with him wheresoever he goes.

I visited the Sahara Desert, near Ouarzazate, Morocco. The rain started almost as soon as I arrived over the Atlas Mountains from Marrakech.

A vast dust storm, darkened skies, thunderous downpours.

The rain then continued for four, non-stop deluge days.

Bridges washed away.

Roads out of town impassable in all four directions:

Back across the Atlas Mountains?

Nope.

Parallel to the Atlas Mountains?

No, in either direction.

How about further into the desert?

Still a resounding 'No'.

'You bring us luck!' the locals extolled, despite the loss of life that had occurred, as drivers unaware of the force of the torrents crossing the roads had attempted to drive through the gullies, with disastrous and occasionally fatal consequences.

'It has not rained here for two years!' they informed me.

I had just arrived from the UK, where it had rained for the entirety of October, every sodding day.

No, Sir. I do not consider *myself*, nor this situation, *lucky* at all.

The buildings in Leh are not designed to repel rain of any quantity nor duration. They all have flat, untiled roofs with no guttering. Puddles on the roofs quickly morph into small lakes. My lodgings soon become damp and unappealing as the drip, drip, drip envelops a rapidly compounding percentage of the floor space inside my room. I continuously shift my bags and possessions into an ever-smaller pile as the remaining safe, dry spots on the floor diminish rapidly. If this rain continues much longer, I fear I am in danger of floating out of the hotel.

The temperature has dropped dramatically. There is no heating in the room.

I must wear half my clothes to stave off the chills. I appear to have significantly over-achieved in my attempt to rid myself of the Delhi heatwave.

I have insufficient funds for alternative arrangements; there are no means in Leh to acquire more cash, neither from credit card advances, nor from travellers' cheques. The hotels accepting credit cards as payment are *way* outside my meagre budget. The information filtering out over the grapevine is that all roads out of town are blocked, with torrents streaming down the mountainside in numerous locations, cutting us off completely from the outside world. Flights south to Delhi, or further afield, are booked out for a fortnight, and more.

There is no choice. I will have to wait it out.

My host is unnecessarily apologetic as the rain continues, day after day, after day, after day.

'It *never* rains in Leh', he says, again. 'I am so sorry'.

He is still smiling, though. He is happy whatever the weather.

The marooned travellers begin the ritual of congregating each morning in the smattering of small cafes in the centre of town.

Tales from the road are shared, thoughts from the road are aired, visions for the future bared.

There is something about a perforced halt and subsequent incarceration you initially push back against – the claustrophobia from not being able to move forwards, even if you don't actually *want* to move forwards, for the travellers here consider themselves autonomous beings, at the beck and call of none, free to come and go entirely as they please.

Or so they think.

In truth, we have merely managed to lengthen the rope affixing us to our individual poles of fiscal or societal responsibility to such a degree we can trick ourselves into *believing* we are truly autonomous creatures.

I mention my observations on the differences between Kashmiris and Ladakhis, how the Ladakhis seem to be purer, in a spiritual sense, and more intrinsically fulfilled – and therefore more happily content - than their counterparts to the west. I wonder aloud whether these differences are 'nature' in causality, or due to recent events on the ground over in Kashmir.

Those travellers in the Humanistic camp – those with the matted dreads, drinking the weird-smelling organic cappu-latte coffee whilst rolling their tenth ciggie of the morning - think we're All intrinsically Good People; it's our negative interactions with, and within, Society that turn us to the Dark Side. No one *chooses* to step from the Path of Righteousness; Society's negative influences *blows* us off course. Societal influence is the causal attribution should someone steal, or commit an act of unprovoked violence, or worse; external factors are the most important drivers for human behaviour. We must always seek to understand a person's deeper motives for acting before condemning the behaviour – and especially the person *behind* the behaviour - or so the Humanists contend.

The Freudians on the other side of the café - those sporting clean, well-pressed clothes, drinking the freshly squeezed fruit juices, chomping on the towering Club Sandwiches – disagree vehemently, spitting their toasted bread out in the process.

No, they say. *That's all far too Fatalistic.*

Where, they ask, *is Individual Agency in that belief?*

The Freudians think we're all intrinsically Bad People, that it is merely Society's Rules, and the Repercussions of Breaking those Rules that stop us from swiftly regressing into a barbaric, there-is-no-consequence-to-our-actions rabble, everyone out for themselves, and Lord help *you* if you choose to get in *my* way.

I am uncertain into which camp to pitch my psycho-analysis tent. Anyone with even a cursory eye towards history could easily provide ample examples showing valid support for either side of the debate; wide-ranging horror stories emanating from those desperate lands where law and order has broken down, the absolutely debased acts some humans appear capable of, atrocities the minute details of which are more than sufficient to send shivers down your spine, sending you running into the 'all people are barbaric' camp; on the other hand, the world is blessed with those who ritually perform acts of pure altruism, of kindness and selflessness, of generosity and sacrifice, acts in such stark contrast to the horrors seen elsewhere.

How could anyone then conclude that we humans are intrinsically Bad Creatures?

In any case, I have neither dreads, nor are my clothes neatly pressed.

Much to their chagrin, neatly into either camp I do not fit.

Maybe, I suggest to the two factions, they might *both* be correct; and therefore, might *both* be wrong.

Maybe, I tell them, there are only two Types of People in the world; those who Divide the World into Two Types of People, and Those That Don't.

Much sagacious nodding occurs.

The rain continues, unabated.

We ruminate on our Reasons for Travelling.

For whose benefit *exactly* do we cast ourselves out into the world?

Perpetual motion might appear to many outsiders a self-indulgent pastime, bestowed with rank and awe at odds with the far more worthy, less self-indulgent occupations undertaken by the majority of Society back home.

Some consider travelling purely about Escapism, a tactic of Conscious Avoidance, avoidance of the harsh realities of day-to-day life.

There is some truth to that belief. Travelling *is* Escapism, but to a greater or lesser degree, for if you are considering running off to a far-away land to run away from *yourself*, there will be no Escapism for you. You can *never* escape yourself, for, no matter what else changes, there you are, *you*, the one constant in your life. Those issues you might think you are running from will pack themselves into your luggage whether you like it or not. No matter how fast, or far, you run, they will catch up with you, eventually.

There is an unspoken sense of commonality amongst the long-term travelling community, a sense of being Outsiders, separate from Society – some even consider themselves *above* Society - but the reality is that not even the hardest hardcore Traveller could exist without the order the Society they criticise continuously creates, without the infrastructure and systems provided by those for whom the urge to live an unstructured, peripatetic life holds no allure nor fascination.

There'd be no Electricity; no Water; no Transportation; no Banking System.

No Police, no Law, no Courts.

No Sewerage; no Communications; no Construction; no Agriculture.

With no one to Steer the Ship, or Power the Ship, or Repair the Ship, or Feed the Ship, for how long will you be able to simply Play up on Deck, eh, Hardcore Traveller?

With no Order, what then? A return to a world-wide Subsistence Existence, with Medieval Justice replacing the Presumption of Innocence and Trial by Jury?

And this benefits *who*, exactly?

It is a quandary, a form of hypocrisy, a dilemma that appears best swept under the carpet, lest it shatter the illusory world these Travellers have created.

Outside, the rain continues to fall.

Discussions frequently commence on the reshaping of World Order into a world with different priorities, different goals, different measures of success, whilst the trusty chillum does the rounds once again.

You know, like, yeh, *Life*, man.

To some extent it is hard to disagree with the need for change. Not everything in Society is imperfect; the values many individuals possess, the means used to measure the success or otherwise of their lives is certainly a personal and individual issue – that should be respected - but too many seem to equate and measure their success by the physical trappings of their lives, lording their bling over the 'less fortunate', championing Conspicuous Consumption, feeling superior to those who simply prefer a less ostentatious path. The pursuit of Validation through Acquired Wealth appears to be spreading like a cancer, or so seems to be the point raised time and time again as the chillum continues to make the rounds.

We wonder whether wearing an expensive *Haute Couture* shirt should provide the wearer with greater status than someone in a clean, crisp non-logo shirt; or even someone in a tatty old top?

We wonder whether driving a flash car with all the latest gizmos and gadgets really should bestow its pilot more kudos than the man who decides to rock along in a badly beat-up banger, complete with sticky locks and no electronic accoutrements; or to someone with no vehicle at all?

We wonder at the multitudes weighted down by the need to be continuously comparing themselves with their peers, and with Society as a whole, continually seeking validation, perpetually concerned about their place and status within the Social Hierarchy?

We wonder whether, instead, we should – all of us - simply get on with the task of trying to be *the best version of ourselves* we can possibly achieve, whilst encouraging everybody else to commit to this same fundamental task.

For there are no short cuts to Perfection.

Constant attention. Repeated application. Target well-defined.

Believe me, it was a well-packed chillum.

And outside, the rain continues to fall.

The wealth of the True Traveller cannot be measured from external inspection – success for them is equally not to be found in the digits of their bank account - for the True Traveller will spend any spare cash or sudden windfalls on experiential wealth, on what they consider Personal Cultural Enrichment, on expanding their realm of understanding about the many varied peoples with whom we share this planet, seeking new, fresh perspectives to otherwise cliched and blinkered reasonings. The TT marvels in the beauty of Mother Earth, her rare habitats, her pristine wildernesses, her varied and unique fauna, all in constant need of preservation from the never-ending march of Progress. Of course, the True Traveller then needs to keep completely schtum about the beautiful scenery they have just marvelled in – that *amazing* new hidden spot on the coast/ in the jungle/ in the middle of nowhere - lest mass tourism march in to despoil this once pristine wilderness. Yes, the Progress the TT wishes to keep in check might itself arrive on the soil of their own boots, if they're not too careful.

An Eternal Traveller Paradox. *The* Eternal Traveller Paradox.

Then it is the practical application of this Knowledge Wealth that remains the dominant issue.

For how can you enable others to see the world through your own eyes, to see all the wonders and eye-opening visions *you* have been blessed to witness?

How can you convince others of the advantages of applying alternative perspectives to the many, enduring issues continuously affecting society Back Home?

How might sharing this Wisdom improve the lives of the world as a whole?

The Eternal Traveller Conundrum (answers on a postcard to…).

Outside, the rain pours down incessantly.

The travellers huddle ever closer together inside the chilled, stone-walled cafes, their windows profusely steamed in condensation from the non-stop, constantly brewing pans of water, for the non-stop, never-ending orders of coffees, teas and noodles, the three elements considered by travellers the fundamental nutritional requirements.

The Nature, the Essence, dam it, even the Meaning of Life – of *their* Life - is discussed, ruminated on, over and over, like a cud chewed repeatedly in an attempt to extract the last morsels of goodness.

Many seek the Solution to this one fundamental Dilemma.

Who *Am* I?

For some, this is their *raison d'etre* here on the Road.

For some, the solution – the Meaning - appears to be right there – there, on the tip of their consciousness - so tantalisingly close, lurking behind a matted clump of grey matter in their collectively hashish-addled minds.

Elusive. Transient.

There one second, gone in a puff of smoke the next.

So close. Yet tantalisingly out of reach.

So close, yet we are all in danger of over-thinking, of over-analysing, of going round and round in ever-decreasing circles, never achieving anything of any note nor permanence.

This lockdown has made us all too introspective, perhaps.

If this rain is to teach us anything, I think, it is not to think *too much*, I think.

If this imposed pause has left any lasting impression, it might be that it is not the right answers we should be seeking, but the *right questions*; for once we are asking the right questions, the answers will surely come.

I am in danger of disappearing into the Ether, into a gallimaufry of galimatias, up into that orifice where the sun, like our distant valley here, rarely shines.

I take a pause from the mind strain of these conversations. Sometimes, the best ideas, those Eureka-like moments, occur not when the mind is deep in contemplation, but when it is freed of the rigours of thought and allowed to roam, unencumbered by the necessity of being engaged in a cognition-heavy task.

Those Eureka moments occur when we least expect them to; and are more joyous as a result.

Outside, the rain falls relentlessly.

A week passes, although not quite in the blink of an eye.

As the days drag on, I endeavour continuously to seek out the positives, to maintain a bright outlook over our continued incarceration, to stave off the longueur that looms ever present. I remind myself it is far better to be stuck in the rain in a place such as this, than be stuck in the rain back at home. But in spite of my determined attempts at good cheer, there is a worry I seem unable to shake, for as each day is crossed off the calendar, I am a day closer to needing to be in Bombay – a mere 2,400 land-based kms away - for my flight to Egypt.

I have no means of contacting the airline to alter my date. I am unsure if I can alter the date on my ticket in any case, nor whether I would want to pay what is bound to be an exorbitant fee for making the change even if changes were permitted.

I need to move on, and soon.

The rains need to stop, even sooner.

I make constant trips to the bus station.

Is there a bus heading down to Manali today?

Tomorrow maybe?

The day after tomorrow?

Soon?

'Come back later,' I am told.

I come back later.

Again, and again.

It is necessary to persevere. One must endeavour to persevere.

After a week of virtually incessant heavy precipitation, the rain finally ceases. Over the grapevine, I discover there might be a minibus leaving early next morning. I rush over to the company offices to grab myself a seat.

Yes, there is a bus scheduled for the morning, but it comes with the usual caveat, the standard small print: until it is certain, nothing is *certain*.

The young lad of a driver says the road, rough at the best of times, and peaking out at over 5,300m, is in terrible condition, but he will see if we can make it all the way to Manali, some 480kms from Leh. The trip will be an assault on both engineering, and our bodies, or so the lad tells me.

Just nine days remain to reach Bombay.

Chapter 10

Bash, Smash, Crash

I head out for the bus station in the brain-damagingly early hours of morning. The hour, an ungodly 3.30am. Outside, all around, is pitch black – no streetlights, no building lights, no moon, no stars - and brutally cold, the short walk to the bus meeting point doing little to warm me up.

My mood increases somewhat when I meet my fellow travelling companions for the first time. We are a motley assortment of young Brits, Israelis, Swiss and Germans, all in our early-to-late twenties. Despite the early hour, and the blisteringly chilly temperature, everyone is in the best of spirits, glad to finally be on the move once again, despite the many formidable challenges lying ahead, sight unseen, mind unknown. Once again, youthful ignorance acts like a soft comforting rag for us all. No one queries the inherent wisdom of our imminent departure. We are all blithely optimistic of a successful conclusion.

There is a ragtag assortment of locals with us on our quest, too, carrying with them the standard paraphernalia of the Ladakhi farming peasant: an assorted collection of hefty rice bags; squished and pre-crumpled cardboard boxes, tied firmly, yet precariously, with fraying cords of string; stained hessian sacks filled with who-knows-what; plus the ubiquitous clucking of chickens, thin ropes tied firmly at their feet to ensure the chucks don't run amok inside the 25-seater bus. The chickens blink occasionally, just to let us know they are still alive. They all have the 1000-yard stare of someone who would rather be somewhere else entirely. Their chicken sense is, quite accurately, telling them today may not be their day, that it would be unwise for them to be making plans for tomorrow, either. Maybe we should ask them what their chicken senses say about how *we're* all going to get on.

The minibus is full, both inside, and rooftop. Indeed, the roof rack is piled so high I hope our equilibrium is not fatally affected. I sure hope this bus crew knows what they are doing.

This time, I don't have Gupta to snag me a seat with extra-long legroom. This time, I am cramped cheek to jowl into the back row like a sardine squished into a tiny tin. This is not a conducive space in which to sit in comfort, squashed as I am, for what will be another 48-hour journey, and that's assuming things run smoothly, which, surely, they will. Fortunately, during my stay in Leh the secret to relaxed and comfy Indian bus travel has been divulged to me, an over-the-counter remedy requiring of a prescription should one need to purchase said powders in the UK. One tiny pill should do the trick, or so I have been informed.

The advice is road tested. The desired result is achieved within twenty or so minutes of ingestion.

My knees and gluteals gain a satisfactory numbness.

I bliss out.

Soon, I fall asleep.

The bus trundles along the road, me drifting in and out of consciousness from my wondrous slumberland stupor. Occasional checkpoints along the route mean we are required, to much quiet muttering, to all de-bus in order to once again provide the soldiers with our passports, and to show our visas, an annoyance that punctuates our otherwise restful repose.

We top out over the Tanglang La Pass, at an eye-watering, brain-mashing, oxygen-lacking 5,328m.

Over 17,000 ft for those still in Imperial.

As we all stand outside the bus, trying to take in the rugged scenery, wondering what stupendous views might have been on offer had the clouds not decided to come rolling in just now, one of my fellow passengers informs me, with some pride, that this is the world's 2nd highest Navigable Pass.

My brain is in a too-far-gone state of hypoxic shock to be able to register this information, or anything else for that matter, right now.

I am not currently a Well Man.

Just what is that weird feeling?

Terrible headache; just the weirdest, dulled, head-achiness.

My temples throb and pulsate uncomfortably. My brain feels as if it wants to both explode *and* implode, simultaneously.

To add to my woes, a worrying looseness in the bowl region is then detected.

Some of my fellow passengers are sick. Nausea sick.

Many have turned a deathly pallid off-white-dull-grey, looking decidedly unwell to my non-medically trained eye. We all scatter away from the bus to our own personal space, ready for any eventuality should it decide to afflict us now.

The sound of guts being forcefully emptied echoes in the otherwise silent mountain air.

This has rapidly morphed into a scene of physical carnage.

We tell the driver we need to keep moving, to descend from this unpleasant altitude, before we all collapse into hypoxically-induced catatonia. The driver agrees without argument. As we slowly descend, the feeling of being human again gradually returns.

This is a most welcome relief. We feel we have survived the worst of things now.

We pass small clusters of guys riding their iconic Royal Enfields in the opposite direction, slowly, slowly up the mountain road.

This is a Classic Ride along a Classic Route on a Classic Motorbike. These lads are certainly travelling with more style than us. Alas, though, there are bikes dotted along the roadside at irregular intervals, bikes that have decided to quit working, their riders standing forlornly over their immobile machines, scratching their heads as to what they should do next.

The altitude's rarefied atmosphere has affected the normal operation of the carburettors.

A quite possibly terminal problem. There is no Roadside Assistance out here.

We pass on by, unable to assist. For all I know, these riders might still be there now.

****

Darkness falls once again.

We in the back of the bus have nodded off once more, now off and away in the Land of much-needed Sleep. Being in the Land of Sleep is by far the most comfortable manner in which to participate in this bus ride. At some point, however, we are all rudely brought out of our slumberland, greeted by a scene of unmitigated hullaballoo, of wild commotion taking place right here inside the bus.

Our forward motion has ceased. All the passengers are currently standing and shouting, shouting at each other, at no one, at anyone. Everyone appears to be rapidly collating their possessions and making to exit the bus, all in a state of utter panic. There is much pushing and forceful physical cajoling, the one narrow door at the front not conducive to rapid de-busing.

There is more shouting; more raised, angry words, voices seeped in frantic desperation.

Something appears to have occurred. Not a good *something* either.

Being at the back of the bus, I am one of the last to establish a more detailed nature of this specific something.

This specific something is a large boulder, a large boulder that has decided to bound down the mountainside and crash into our bus, narrowly missing our driver. Immediately thereafter, the bus has rammed nose-first into another, even larger, boulder, a second boulder that has also decided to hurl itself down the mountainside, settling in the middle of the road, waiting patiently for us, or indeed anyone, to show up.

A case of 'Bash, Smash & Crash'.

After much pushing and nudging of my own, I eventually manage to step outside to survey the scene.

The bus is indeed quite badly banged up.

The window behind the driver's position has been caved in.

The front of the bus is badly dented from its impact with the large, 3m x 3m road-based rock.

The axle is bent, too, for good measure, or so the rumour mill says.

A state of pandemonium and confusion exists amongst this now ragtag group of individuals.

'So, what now?' appears to be the question on everyone's lips.

My fuzzy head is trying to make sense of it all, without much success.

'It is not safe to stay here', the locals tell us. 'More rocks might decide to follow suit and throw themselves down the mountainside. The bus could be crushed at any time'.

None of this sounds a Good Thing.

'We must', they say, 'walk down to the next village to seek shelter for the night'.

It is *very* dark. The full moon we had enjoyed a week before is nowhere to be seen. It is also raining hard, which explains the complete lack of moonlight.

We ask how far the next village is.

'8km', they tell us.

The thought of an 8km – 5 miles in old money - walk in these circumstances does not fill me with much joy.

Did I mention it is *dark*?

And worse, it is also *raining*?

The usual maxim in situations where the best course of action is unclear is to follow the locals' lead, on the presumption that no matter how bizarre or unusual a certain situation may be it is more than likely this has happened to them before, more than once, and that they are therefore equipped with the wherewithal to decide upon the most sensible and effective response to their current predicament.

I am about to put this maxim to the test and begrudgingly gather my things for the long walk, when the Israeli lads in our party announce they are planning to stay put on the bus for the night.

This announcement is somewhat out of the blue.

I am now a rabbit caught in the headlights, unsure which way to run.

Israelis in their mid-to-late twenties have all recently completed Military Service, choosing to head off travelling once their mandatory period is up in order to regain a sense of Peace, Harmony and Tranquillity, a change of scene after running the near ever-present risk of shots being aimed their way. These tough and resourceful individuals are not the molly-coddled young men and women when compared with those produced by countries where National Service has since been scrapped. They are hardened soldiers, toughened from the days, weeks, months and years they will have spent patrolling the borders between their country and their neighbours, with whom they aren't on the best of speaking terms, to put it mildly. (I heard a rumour about one group of about a dozen Israelis, who were allegedly kidnapped in Kashmir in the '80s. Rather than do as you or I would - that is, wait for our governments to intervene and negotiate our release - they decided to take matters into their own hands, overpowering their guards, capturing their weapons, and shooting their way out of their predicament. Whether true or not, it certainly sounds plausible).

It is interesting that the Israelis want to stay, although I'm not sure their underlying motivation matches mine.

No matter.

They stay, *I* stay.

Then, the rest of the travellers announce they, too, will stay.

The locals all shake their heads.

Exhortations of, 'It's Not Safe', hang in the air as they disappear off into the blackened night, down the narrow path to the next village.

Suddenly, those of us who remain find ourselves all alone in complete darkness, in a minibus 4,000m high up in the Ladakhi mountains, miles from anywhere of any note, the statistical Risk Coefficient of our situation on this specific stretch of road a figure far higher than any of us has the experience or wisdom to evaluate.

Yes, *Staying Put* is probably a flawed decision, made for the laziest of reasons. Sloth is not usually the most effective underlying paradigm with which to fashion those all-important Life Decisions the Fates enjoy throwing our way.

Choosing the *Easier* path over a *Harder* one, not so much either.

The Innocence and Ignorance of Youth have yet again won out. For now.

Well, here we all are. As the saying goes, if you make your bed, you need to lie in it. There are no beds in sight, though. I seek out more soporific-inducing powders from my bag, take a quick sip of water to wash them down, extend my legs out from my position in the middle of the back row, tip my Fedora down over my eyes *à la Eastwood*, pull my arms inside my long woollen coat (as previously modelled by the mad, long-bearded Kashmiri horsemen: see, they taught me well), and fall swiftly into the land of Deep Unconsciousness, without break, until the dim light of morning returns ten hours later.

Travellers often talk of the *Ultimate*.

The Ultimate Juggle?

Two chainsaws and a baby.

Best to practice with someone else's progeny until you've perfected your routine, or so They say.

The Ultimate Sex?

In a hammock. With someone else.

And *without* falling out.

The Ultimate Place to Fall Asleep?

On the back of a mule.

If you can sleep there, you really can sleep *anywhere*.

It was a freezing cold night, the cruel chill made worse by the steady stream of fresh mountain air breezing in through the gaping hole in the window at the front of the bus.

Not quite the *Ultimate* place to fall asleep, but more than sufficient challenge.

The others have endured a restless night, or so their constant early-morning mutterings maintain, the paucity of adequate warmth and comfort disabling their smooth transition back into the glorious Land of Slumber.

'You didn't move all night,' a fellow bus passenger says, in amazement. 'How *do* you do it?'

Well, I *could* tell you, but then reflect my tradecraft might be best kept to myself.

The rain has thankfully stopped. Bleary-eyed, unkempt, and somewhat bedraggled, our ragtag collection of stowaways scoops up all its belongings, commencing the long walk down a narrow, windy path leading to the nearest village. On the way, we pass the bus driver and his mate, with a few other locals for support, making their way back up to the bus.

We exchange cheery and much relieved greetings.

They are pleased to see us, all still evidently very much alive.

I wonder to myself whether bets had been placed on our chances of making it through the night.

The lads say they are hoping to fix the bus in an hour or so, that we should all be under way again in the not-too-distant future.

They are a resourceful lot, these people. Fixing a bent axle is not an easy undertaking, even with the most modern, well-stocked garage workshop.

We wish them the best of luck. They will, I suspect, need all the positive vibes Karma can spare today.

****

The tiny hamlet is reached after a 2-hour slow trundle down the hill. An elderly couple, for whom this distant outpost appears 'home', provide us most kindly with a breakfast of fried eggs, dried bread and warm, milky, sickly-sweat tea. The food is most gratefully wolfed down in no time at all.

The hamlet is a ramshackle set up consisting of only one main habitable building, with three smaller outbuildings whose doors all lie dormant on the ground by the entrances they were supposed to be guarding, and whose tiny glass-paned windows are either cracked or missing.

Nearby, a garrulous gaggle of chickens squawk and crow, scurrying past us in their quest for sustenance, clawing frantically and optimistically at the muddy ground, before moving on to the next spot they feel certain will provide for them.

Then another spot, and another, and another.

'Cock-a-doodle do!' cries a rooster, grandly, from somewhere out of sight.

'Cock-a-doodle-Do' I call out in reply.

Why?

Well, I dunno. Something to do. Something to pass the time.

The other nationalities in our seated breakfast circle regard me with a look of some confusion.

The Germans tell me, 'No, you should shout, *Kikeriki*'.

I tell them that is plainly nonsense. They must listen.

The rooster crows again.

Definitely, 'Cock-a-doodle-do'.

'Not so', say they Germans.

I wonder what they are hearing.

The Israelis tell us it should be, '*KuKuRiKu*'.

I tell them they, too, are mistaken. They must listen again.

The rooster most definitely calls out with five syllables, five moments of hard emphasis.

Cock.

Ka.

Doo.

Dle.

Do.

Right on cue, the rooster crows again.

'There you go', the Israelis say, gleefully, 'definitely *KuKuRiKu*'.

I wonder what they are hearing.

The Swiss are French speakers. They tell us the rooster is *actually* crowing, '*Cocorico*'.

'This cannot be right', I say, as again this word is comprised of just *four* syllables.

The cockerel's crowing *clearly* contains *five*.

The rooster crows again, aware, it seems, he now has an audience. Each of us is rigidly convinced of our home country's onomatopoeic conversions, that this rooster has just produced our own nationalities' specific variation of the doodle-do'd crow.

There is then much animated discussion, on the feasibility of roosters crowing differently in distinct regions of the word, of roosters exhibiting vernacular variations, just as we humans might be polyglottal.

Maybe French chickens really do say, '*Cocorico*'?

Maybe German roosters really do go, '*Kikeriki*'?

Maybe British roosters, and British roosters alone, crow, 'Cock-a-doodle-do'?

Or, *maybe*, our home language's onomatopoeic offering has primed our expectations of what we hear, and we therefore hear only what we *expect* to hear?

The rooster crows, again.

Once again, we are all convinced his crowing corresponds to our own mother tongue.

We cannot *all* be correct.

It has been an interesting discussion. An unexpected development.

There is evidently much to consider about global rooster crowing I had hitherto not considered.

I am unsure how this new-found knowledge will assist me in later life, though.

****

It is early afternoon before the bus arrives back down at the hamlet. We are unable to establish to what level of repair the bus has been re-engineered, whether the patch-up has been rigorously applied, or is simply a '*Doofa*'.

You know. As in:

'Might not be the best repair ever, but it'll *Doofa* me.'

'Didn't have time to complete a proper fix; it'll have to *Doofa* now'.

'It's a *Doofa!*'.

Excitedly, and without wishing to interrogate the driver or his mate about the roadworthiness (or otherwise) of the bus, we all reembark and regimentally regain our previous positions.

That the bus is once again running is no small miracle.

Provided it gets us all to Manali, who cares whether the fix lasts a day, a month or a year.

We are on the move again. This is all that matters.

We have survived the worst the elements and the mountains can throw at us.

We are *certain* we will make it now.

Chapter 11

Having The Last Laugh?

25km further down the road, we are all once again out of the bus. This time there will be no miraculous recovery. The road ahead has been completely cut by the force of a raging torrent, a torrent now barely slowed to a *mildly thundering* torrent. The force of the flow has carved a deep, wide rut into the road to make onwards travel impossible. Detouring around this obstacle is simply not an option.

For this bus and this crew, and this group of passengers, this signifies the End of the Line.

All Change, Please.

We fortunately find ourselves adjacent to a larger, better provisioned hamlet, with a far greater choice of lodging options. This choice has, alas, been whittled to near zero by the vast numbers who are likewise stuck here in the same predicament. From where these people have all suddenly materialised is initially unclear (it transpires they were all heading up to Leh when the rains came, trapping them some time ago in this spot).

The hour is now late. After much legwork, being turned away time after time after time – So Sorry, *No* Room - I finally find lodgings for the night; being last available room in town, I am perforce required to share the solitary double bed within with a Sargant in the Israeli Defence Forces, one of our bus team who has been accompanying me on this quest for nocturnal sanctuary.

I am initially uncertain about these arrangements. Luckily, it transpires she does not snore. Indeed, she provides much needed body warmth on this bitterly cold night under a thin and still-getting-thinner blanket, the only bedding provided with the room. I am informed that sharing body warmth – Enhanced Close Physical Contact - will minimise our chances of succumbing to the crippling effects of hypothermia, a technique my bed fellow learned during her time in the Army (I imagine the IDF being quite the Communal Love-in, but receive a firm dig in the ribs for my trouble. *Not* what she meant, apparently).

I decide against teasing. Best to agree to her snuggling suggestion. Some Israeli women are not only super-attractive – long, silky, wavy brunette hair; smooth, tanned skin; and chiselled beauty - but knowing they come armed with the skills to kill you with one strategically placed blow brings an added frisson to the mating game.

Best *not* to argue; acquiescence, the wisest option.

Thankfully, I survive to tell the tale. Despite the less than salubrious surroundings, this night is not an unpleasurable experience.

Next morning, the nature of the problem with the transport links becomes clearer. The road is cut here at this hamlet, and again 15km further down the road, where sit currently most of the buses, trucks and cars that were making their way up to Leh when the rains first arrived.

If I want to continue onwards, I am informed, I must ford the not inconsiderable torrent flowing through this village, cover 15km on foot, ford the second road cut, before seeking fresh transportation back down to Manali.

My load has increased during my travels, as my gear has bulked up from the plethora of local handicraft items I have purchased *en route*: rugs, clothes, blankets, *et al.*, all bought without the expectation of having to *actually* carry the stuff more than a km, two max, between my accommodation and the next train or bus station.

Anything further, the taxi-*wallahs* would *most definitely* now be having my custom.

There are no taxis in sight.

A 15km hike at this altitude - still way over 3,000m - with two fully laden rucksacks - one front, one back - will be a tad more than a stroll of a yomp.

But Needs Must when the devil Bites your Bum, and all that.

I bid a fond *Adieu* – sadly, this is not *Au Revoir* - to my bus buddies, who have all decided to halt here for a day or two to regroup, not being so time constrained as am I. I seek out the narrowest section of torrent over which to perform my bound. There is a short stretch whose width I evaluate - in a rudimentary, Mark-I eyeball fashion - is doable with a single long-legged leap.

Thankfully, I am able to provide legs of sufficient length for such a leap (my lanky protrusions do *occasionally* have their golden moments).

The weight on my shoulders is too great to permit me a long run up (I am not keen on throwing my packs over the stream), so I rock slowly, back and forth, on my heels and toes, feeling the pressure in my thighs tightening, like a spring, tightening to the point I deem the springs sufficiently tensed for their then rapid unwind to launch me high over the stream to the far bank.

At least, that's the plan. If you've got a better idea, now's a good time to share.

No?

OK, well, here goes.

The pent-up pressure is released; up and over this body of water I commence my deft pounce.

Alas, as I become airborne, I notice the *up* is present, but the *over*, alarmingly, is almost entirely lacking. In a flash, with some considerable confusion at my evidently incorrectly evaluated Force requirements, the realisation hits me: the far bank will not be achieved without getting my feet, and other more sensitive body parts, quite wet. My inertia evidently a far greater coefficient than had been input into the hastily convened Thrust-Required-for-River-Traverse equation.

This proves an invaluable Scientific Learning Experience.

Nothing like on the job, You're Buggered if you Mess This Up-training to focus the mind.

With nothing to lose, I endeavour to convert my upwards trajectory into a forward roll, twisting my shoulders with the hope of landing on something firm and dry, rather than soft and distinctly damp. The end product is most certainly not pretty, but what the manoeuvre lacks in Style it makes up for in Execution. I am on the far bank, having landed heavily but successfully on my back, my fall softened by the clothes contained inside my backpack.

My somewhat comedic performance has not, alas, gone unnoticed.

There are ironic cheers from the smattering of others who have made or are about to make the same leap.

Ah. Being laughed at once again. I'd missed *that* experience. Not.

As I lie there brushing myself down, regaining my composure, the others all manage the leap across with way more Style *and* Execution than I have just performed.

I like to think my failure paved the way for their successes.

Enough piddling about, enough wasting time. Time to get serious.

I stand up, readjust my two rucksacks, salute my fellow travellers once more, and set off on my yomp.

****

I find myself suddenly alone in this remote mountain wilderness, alone with the perfect silence of this land. It is a wonderful feeling, to now be free of the claustrophobic space inside the bus; to now be free of industrially manufactured noise, just the echoing sounds of my own hollering, calling out to the mountains, to say 'Hello – lo – lo – lo'.

The air is cool and fresh. Thankfully, the rain stays away.

I am happy to once again be on the move.

The road undulates gently as I traverse this high-altitude plateau. Vast, snow-covered peaks tower high above, a few kms off in the distance to either side. Thankfully, no protracted, lung-busting climbs block my path, no steep mountain passes. This most-welcome paucity of anaerobically alarming rises means I am covering good ground.

5km down the road, I encounter the day's second, and somewhat unexpected, watery hindrance, cutting straight across the road. At around 30m, this confluence is far too wide for even the longest of long-legged leaps. The swiftly flowing stream appears to be at least knee-deep, if not more. A watery transit is the only available option; and I am not 100% sure this is going to be an easy undertaking. The force of the water pushing against me, even at knee-depth, whilst carrying 20kg+ on my back, another 7-8kg on my front, over an uneven, rocky stream bed, will most likely make this process just a teensy bit precarious.

I remove my boots and socks, stuffing the socks inside the boots, tying the long boot laces together, and then chucking them over my shoulder, one boot banging against my chest, the other beating against my back. A pair of hiking poles, or a long stick, to provide a back-up balance system would be a plus, but, up here in this mountain wilderness, not a solitary tree do I see.

I am about to take my first watery step when I notice an elderly, grey-haired local perched randomly on a rock high up behind me, overlooking the stream, squatting on his haunches the way Indians so love to do. Where this fella has come from – I have passed no signs of habitation since leaving the overnight hamlet – just why he is here, is not immediately apparent.

Politely, I wave 'Hello'.

The man waves back, smiling a beaming, happy smile.

So, my aquatic adventure has an audience.

This ups the ante somewhat.

No problem. Challenge accepted.

I turn back to face my task.

Time, once again, for action.

I step out into the river's swiftly running waters.

Holy cow!

Cold!

Colder than cold!

You know, as icy-fresh as icy glacial waters *usually* are.

With as much precision as I can muster, I carefully shift one foot forward, then another, and another, only fully transferring all my body weight once I am certain I have found a new, near 100%-reliable, foot placement.

Step – wobble – balance – shift; step – wobble – balance - shift.

The freezing waters are now up, over my knees, and forcing me hard to my right, continuously trying to push me off-balance. Under foot, the rocks are both sharp and slippery; I can feel my soles grazing painfully against their jagged edges. Every fresh stance I take is frustratingly unstable, potentially unreliable; every advancing footstep, a prospective toppler into these icy waters.

My balance is being thrown totally off-kilter.

I wobble, a pronounced, unsteady, precarious, near-fatal upper-torso wobble.

Uh-Oh.

There is, I realise, worryingly, an all too real danger of my ending up dunked into the drink.

Right now, I am right in it; the sanctuary of the road to all intents and purposes a million miles away

I can feel the heat of the old man's glare burning into my back.

I feel as if I am his morning's entertainment.

I sense, probably unjustifiably, that he is *willing* me to topple over.

I feel, once again, I might be on the verge of demonstrating how *not* to traverse a watery obstacle.

No, I steel myself. I am simply *not* going to give this old man the satisfaction of seeing me tumble into the stream.

I sense that seeing someone make an arse of themselves is exactly what this man has been waiting patiently all day for; exactly what he is *hoping* for, his soul reason for leaping out of bed this morning and taking up this most advantageously-vista'd view.

Most likely, I am being unkind, I know. Most likely, the man has merely popped out for a spot of fresh air and some quality Get-away-from-the-Missus-all-on-his-Lonesome Meditation Time. There can't be all that many options on the Things-to-Do-Today list out here.

But the thought of any glee whatsoever being taken from my own misfortune merely serves to harden my resolve to cross this bugger of a stream successfully; my desire to thwart his *schadenfreude* has now risen to No1 motivation for my own success.

I pull myself together.

I focus on the far shore.

I intensify my rhythm.

I raise my pace.

Soppy wet meekness = sopping wet Me.

Boldness and determination: The Order of the Day.

Twenty bold and determined paces later, not without the odd slight wibble, and the occasional minor wobble, I reach the far shore. As the waters drain down my jaundiced-white legs, I glance down at my toes and my feet, seeing with some shock their now pruney, wrinkled condition.

My poor appendages. They need drying off, pronto, and returning to the warmth and protection of socks and boots without a moment's delay. I attend to the situation immediately.

Dried and re-booted, I stand, looking back across the waters at the old man still squatting on his perch, high above this watery breach.

I offer a second salute, another friendly greeting of acknowledgement.

Still squatting, the old man waves back; his smile, still beaming and wide.

I study his face for any trace of disappointment at the lack of true comedy value from my all-too-successful crossing.

I wonder whether this smiling and waving mask a concealed annoyance, a dissatisfaction at my success in crossing all the way over, rather than *falling* all the way over.

I'd really like to ask what he makes of the situation, of this random scattering of travellers now passing in dribs and drabs through his usually tranquil and empty neighbourhood.

Sadly, there is simply no way to know. No chance I'm heading back across that river to seek enlightenment on that issue.

No chance.

Onwards. Onwards with my trek.

The next 10km pass, not quite in a flash, but without further incident.

My 15km hike has reached its conclusion.

Or so I thought.

That second watery breach they'd mentioned, oh boy, this one's a real shiner.

For between the buses heading down to Manali and my current position sits a bloody great big, 20m-wide, 10m-deep cleft in the landscape, a cleft with another raging torrent flowing at its base.

This cleft is not one for leaping; the steep sides not ones for scrambling; the stream not one for wading.

We have reached the Daddy of all obstacles.

The resourceful locals have, thankfully, somehow managed to rig up a temporary bridge, although with less emphasis on *bridge* and much more on the *temporary*. Three, 3-feet diameter logs have been resourcefully scavenged from who knows where (seriously, where on earth did they find three logs of *any* length up here) and placed across the chasm, one positioned atop the other two. Across the face of the higher log has been drawn a long, thin, rather tatty piece of rope, probably borrowed from one of the many trucks sitting idly on the far bank.

This is the system.

You walk along the side of the protruding lower log, using the upper log and the rope for guidance and a semblance of support, all the while trying to ensure you don't slip to your right, as slipping to the right will lead you off the log, down into the raging torrent, the consequences of which really don't bear considering. The walking surface of this protruding section of log is merely one foot-width wide, barely six inches. Being bark-free, the glistening, wet surface of the lower log appears slippery as ice.

This is going to be Fun.

Fun as in the, 'Oh God, I'm bricking it' sense of the word.

Once again, it is not just the terrain making the crossing a challenge; it is having to make the crossing whilst overloaded, ungainly, unbalanced, and unhinged as I am with my packs.

I wait, studying intently as several other similarly loaded travellers successfully make the crossing, taking stock of the techniques being employed. Being the font of knowledge of how *not* to ford a watery breach would, I feel, be best avoided here. With each new crossing, as each person steps foot onto the log, my heart sinks, a lump pits in the depths of my stomach, the very real fear their crossings might end in disaster adding to the realisation that soon *my* turn will come.

Did I mention I'm not the best with heights?

Oops. How forgetful of me.

A 10-metre drop may sound like no height at all, nothing to scare anyone other than the easily spooked, but I can assure you ten metres is more than ample distance to cause more than just a few small scratches and superficial light bruising should you choose (willingly or otherwise) to let gravity in on the Fun.

But the options now open to me are either forwards, or all the way back, back to where I don't actually know, but back, an alternative that doesn't bear thinking about.

No. Having come this far, this (hopefully) final obstacle will *not* be my Nemesis.

Having summoned sufficient internal fortitude to set forth, my crossing is then frustratingly held up when a long-haired German barges onto the log, rolling with him a cumbrous Royal Enfield motorbike. The bike is positioned on the lower log, numerous ropes tied through and around its frame, wheels and forks. Ropes lead out in all directions, forwards, backwards and sideways, a sight not unlike an enhanced Spaghetti Junction.

The German has, wisely, enrolled the ropework services of as many locals as he can muster, although none appears all that keen to have been employed on rope duty. Sitting and watching is, I sense, more their kind of thing. The team moves forwards at a pace only slightly faster than the glacial glide high up in the mountains above us, its advance under the precise guidance of the German, who is shouting and whistling instructions to those ahead of him on the logs, or those holding controlling ropes from either side of the chasm.

Commands to 'Slow down!', to 'Stop!', to 'Pull!' or to 'Hold!' echo over the sound of the thundering torrent.

The system does not, to this casual observer, look very Orderly, nor Organised.

Orderly and *Organised?* In India? So why am I surprised?

The team inches their way across unhurriedly, painstakingly, until, to my welcome relief - and to loud shouts and raucous cheers that echo over and through the deep chasm - the bike successfully reaches the far bank.

The log clear once again, I rise to my feet, tighten my rucksacks front and back once more, tightening my resolve, too, and take my first tentative step onto the log.

Then another. And another.

I am now shuffling forwards, one small shuffled step at a time.

'So far so good', I allow myself the luxury of thinking.

I look up.

Much to my surprise, someone appears to now be crossing the log in the opposite direction.

Guys! Come on!

This really should be a *one-way* log.

Someone should be controlling access to allow each side their ten minutes of uninterrupted flow.

Orderly.

Organised.

I know.

Having to contend with someone stepping around me is not going to add to the Fun.

I am about half-way across now. As the man reaches my position, he smiles at me.

I return the smile, a smile that announces - at least I *hope* it does – that there is *no way* I am going to move backwards.

Or sideways. Or anyways.

If the man wants to pass, my smile says, *he* will have to go around *me*.

This means the man will have to take both hands off the rope in order to pass on by.

I lean back as far into the log as I can to make the manoeuvre slightly less risky, not helped by my large rucksacks more than doubling the space I might normally inhabit.

The man removes both his hands from the rope, then nonchalantly steps over and around me, before scurrying quickly along the remainder of the log. He reaches the bank before I even get going again.

As he steps off the log, I notice the man is wearing a tatty old pair of flip-flops. I look at my sturdy Doc Marten boots, wondering whether I have selected the correct footwear for the job; the grip from the boots does not seem to be providing much traction on this shiny, smooth wood.

I place both hands firmly back around the rope. Each forward step I take is accompanied by a very precise and firm repositioning of my grip on this rope.

I dare not look down.

I shuffle forwards once more.

I take no notice – whatsoever - of the many people in front of me, landside, beckoning me to get a move on, to come faster, to hurry along, to just *finish already*.

I ignore them.

I am doing this at my own pace, thank you very much.

Finally, I reach the other side.

I smile.

They all smile.

I punch the air.

They all cheer.

We all laugh.

It is a good feeling.

Surely, *now*, the worst must be over?

****

On the far side of the chasm, I encounter a collection of empty buses and abandoned cars all parked higgledy-piggledy along both sides of the road for several hundred metres back from the gorge.

My OCD shudders at the disorganisation of it all.

I wonder if OCD is a thing in India.

I conclude it can't be, lest the sanitoriums be full to bursting point with others who, like me, find random disorder a most unsettling occurrence.

Random disorder.

India.

Random disorder.

No, it is fair to say OCD *cannot* be a thing here in India.

I make enquiries as to which of these vehicles is heading back down the road towards Manali. I am directed to an empty 50-seater bus, its previous passengers having all decamped, their current whereabouts unclear. I meet the driver, a mid-thirties moustachioed man, and his driver's mate, a younger, slimmer version of the driver, with the same pencil-thin hair covering above his upper lip that appears *de rigueur* amongst the local lads. These guys, with their wispy facial furniture (and mullet hair styles), both have the look of 1970's porn stars, come to fix the dishwasher (or was it the oven?). I decide now's probably not the best time mention this observation (or if *ever* there will *be* a 'best time').

After a brief chat, it transpires their departure for Manali is imminent. I am invited to hop aboard.

Result.

This is a much larger, more modern – although I use that word advisedly – version of the minibus I took from Leh. The seats all have spongy, unripped cushions. The leg space, more than sufficient, even for a person with my vast dimensions. That I have the whole seated section of the bus to myself is yet another beneficial boon.

The remainder of my passage to Manali will be a doddle, I think, as I stretch out contentedly in the first row of passenger seats, behind the driver. I am feeling more than a smidgeon of pride and satisfaction at having made it this far today, at having successfully overcome the not insubstantial aquatic impediments placed in my way.

We set off within a few minutes of our meeting. There are no further cuts between here and Manali, I am told. We have the road virtually to ourselves.

The driver and his mate are, I notice a few minutes into our journey, in boisterously high spirits. The reason for these high spirits then becomes clear: the two are both *high as kites* and have ingested *copious quantities of spirits*. Given their shockingly bloodshot eyes, it appears they have been imbibing for the better part of all morning. The sun's position relative to the yardarm is anyone's guess, given the sun has, right now, decided to hide from view behind yet more thick banks of ominous-looking cloud formations. Despite this complete shrouding, the lads, I surmise, have incorporated a *de facto* yardarm reading into their imbibition schedule – presumably from their wealth of experience in this region - although it appears they have then failed to also factor in a somewhat crucial requirement, their need to now be involved in gainful operation of heavy machinery within a treacherously rugged mountain setting.

Sensing they should do their utmost to confirm my worst fears about their current conditions, the mate then pulls out from his jacket pocket a small bottle of local whisky. I am offered a swig, en route to the bottle being passed to the driver. I courteously decline, unlike the driver, who takes a nice long swig, tipping his head right back momentarily whilst he glugs on down.

Oh dear.

The driver, I fear, might have earned his stripes at the Yoda School-You-At-Driving-Can-I.

Watch where you're going?

No need, for I have learnt to *sense* the road.

The mate then rolls up a hashish joint, what I presume are the primary Mate duties. Joint rolled with impressive speed and dexterity, and equally impressive artistic and structural acumen, the mate then sparks it up, taking a couple of long, deep tugs, before offering the roll-up to the driver, who accepts the offering, although, unlike you or I were this to be happening in our vehicle - not that *we'd ever* smoke a joint whilst driving - the driver then turns his head 90 degrees to pluck the joint dextrously out from his friend's fingers.

That we are in the process of rounding the apex of a tight hairpin bend is neither here nor there to the driver.

'If we're not careful, we may end up neither Here *nor* There,' I think.

Oh dear. Just *what* I have got myself into?

We round another tight hairpin bend, with a steep, vertiginous, un-barriered drop at its apex, waiting to take you to meet your Maker should you fail to successfully make the turn. The driver decides the moment of rounding the apex is the ideal time to time to turn and offer me the still smouldering remains of the joint.

I am sitting right behind him. The back of his head now faces our direction of travel.

No, no, no!!

Jeez! Louise!

I don't know about *you*, but *I* prefer to watch the road whilst driving, especially if, you know, there's a three hundred feet drop off to one side.

Please, Sir, keep your eyes on the road!

The Force may not be as strong with you as you'd like to think.

The driver's eyes are buggy and bloodshot. The man is grinning like a Cheshire Cat. Not that I wanted to perform an internal oral inspection, but I can't help noticing his dental hygiene routine would benefit from a few tweaks.

I decline the joint as politely as I can – years of ludicrously expensive, supposedly top-of-the-range Public-School Education have apparently poorly prepared me for existence out in the *real* world.

Clearly, there are significant gaps in the Curriculum – fewer Latin verb conjugations, more Indian Hashish Etiquette, perhaps?

Nec gratias agere, quod non vis ad spliff!   Said no one, ever.

I suggest that all our futures are possibly better served by the driver at least *vaguely* looking where he is going.

The driver studies me quizzingly. Puzzled, he turns to his mate, passing the joint in his direction.

The driver then starts to laugh.

His mate starts to laugh.

They are both now laughing hard.

So, *laughing* again.

Like many things in India, their laughter is infectious.

It is impossible not to laugh at their infectious laugh.

My eyes are streaming.

We are all laughing hard.

I hope this is not what is meant by having the Last Laugh.

That evening, we reach the outskirts of Manali. The driver has the constitution of an ox, for he has not stopped swigging from the whisky bottle since our departure, yet he seems virtually unaffected by intoxication.

Oh, for sure he *is* drunk. But he does not appear, even to one who knows how much he has ingested, to *be* drunk.

We park up for the night just outside town. The mate suggests I remove some of the seat cushions to fashion a bed down the length of the aisle. It turns out to be a more comfortable sleeping arrangement than I was expecting. I fall into a deep, most-grateful-to-still-be-alive slumber.

First light next morning, I walk into Manali centre to arrange my onwards transportation to Delhi. I am greeted by quite the sight. The town has been hit, and hit hard, by the recent relentless rains. Tall, narrow, three and four storey riverside buildings hang precariously, their foundations washed away by the floods. Several sizeable structures have already tumbled into the swiftly flowing, mightily swelled river, the ruined remains bubbling just beneath the swiftly flowing, churned-up swell. The main bridge spanning the river has been severely, possibly gravely, damaged; its central span displaying far too many ominous-looking cracks running along its central arches to be indicative of a future long life ahead. The flood water has eroded the soft soil around the bridge's supports, leaving the main spans resting in thin air in more places than you suspect are safe for the bridge to currently still be operational. I am glad to be walking across on merely foot. Huge, heavy trucks stacked high with grain sacks, and taxis crammed full to the brim with passengers take their chances, speeding recklessly across. From my westernised perspective, their actions look decidedly dodgy, but I guess the locals' notion of risk is somewhat different to my own.

Health & Safety Directives have yet to reach this distant outpost. Should you suffer the misfortune to experience an incident – should you, say, fall into a large hole in the pavement, or be snagged, painfully, by low-hanging wires – well, it's your own damn fault for not looking where you were going, or so the local thinking goes.

Out here, waiting for circumstance to be 'safe', for Risk to reduce to near zero, would be a never-ending wait, a lifetime's wait. Existence in this mountainous terrain is continuously no less precarious than the buildings balanced teeteringly on the heavily eroded riverbanks; everyone, everything, clinging on by the tips of their fingernails.

Out here: Namby-pamby-ism is simply not a viable option. Risk: not a word worth losing even a minute's sleep over.

I locate a bus departing for Delhi in an hour. I have enough time to get back to my overnight bus, collect my belongings, bidding 'Farewell' once more, this time to my mad driver and his mate, before Manali becomes yet another faint flicker in my rear-view mirror.

Twelve more bum numbing hours later, I finally reach my destination.

Delhi.

I'm back. I have made it. Six days remain before my flight out of Bombay. Suddenly, I feel confident of being there in time.

I take another stroll down Tourist Main Avenue, despite the lateness of the hour.

Who should I bump into completely of the blue but some familiar faces, the guys I'd met during my previous foray through Delhi, the lads who'd planned also to head up to Leh, but were taking the anti-clockwise circular route via Manali.

What serendipity! What synchronicity!

It is a joyous meeting. A happy reunion.

We are all in the best of spirits. We are all happy to meet up once again in such random and highly unlikely circumstances.

They have, I am informed, a Tale to tell.

It's quite the Doozy, they say.

My ears prick up, for who doesn't love the telling of a fine travelling Tale?

We decamp to a nearby café. Beers are ordered, for, according to the Law, travelling Tales *must* be accompanied by beer(s).

The telling duly commences.

Chapter 12

Lord of the Flies *vs* Gandhi

My buddies reached Manali as planned.

The Hot Springs at Vashisht, 5km outside town, became a daily draw, enticing them in with its therapeutic warm waters and stunning views, the sanctity of the site augmented by the bountiful, freshly-baked strudel bearing German Bakery, and not forgetting the lashes of fine Pradesh hash sold for mere pennies by the local Manali lads.

They had settled into their daily routine with possibly alarming ease.

They had quickly become comfortable. *Too* comfortable.

Yes, there really is such a thing.

Procrastination had set in.

We'll leave tomorrow, they said.

Then, the next day.

Then, the day after the day after tomorrow.

Surprisingly, despite what many might tell you, tomorrow did finally come. The lads girded themselves up for the 48-hour bus ride over to Leh. They had been fifteen or so hours into the trip when the rains commenced, the same rains that had caused me to hole up in Leh.

The roads quickly became impassable, incarcerating bus-loads of very cold, very wet and extremely miserable travellers, plus a smattering of bus and lorry drivers, and not forgetting scores of locals, in one of those tiny one-house/ two-goat hamlets in which our own bus-load had waited, whilst the rooster Cock-a-Doodle-Doo'd.

The lads were stuck.

Stuck for three long days.

Stuck without sufficient space for even a tiny fraction of them to bed down properly overnight.

The scant food provisions in the hamlet ran out at the end of Day One. The scene swiftly descended into a *Lord of the Flies* meets *Gandhi* mash-up, with people sticking tightly to their own small groups to protect whatever meagre provisions they might still have on their persons.

Night-time was cold, damp, and uncomfortable.

And dangerous.

Just when things looked as if they were indeed descending straight to hell, a Government-sent helicopter arrived to ferry the sick and needy back to safety.

Hoorah!

Help was on hand.

Or so these guys thought.

Sadly, the definition of 'Sick & Needy' being employed was not the same you or I might think of when hearing those words. The situation quickly descended into farce, with those who could push hardest, or bribe heaviest, being allocated one of the eight places in the helicopter, which, as quickly as it had arrived, would rise, slowly and unsurely, disappearing back over the mountain ranges en route down to Manali.

The guys took stock of the situation. They worked through the numbers needing to be rescued, dividing this by the helicopter capacity, and multiplying this figure by the duration of each helicopter return trip from and to Manali.

The resulting figure = a number that did not bode well for their chances of rescue anytime soon.

Their conclusion?

Rescue be damned.

They would walk out of here.

And so, they did just that, climbing high, up and over the vast, 5,000m+ mountain passes blocking their path. After a little more than two days of tough slog over slippery terrain, with poor hiking gear and heavy packs, with only the occasional dank cave for shelter and precious little to eat, they finally made it back to Manali.

Weathered. Weary. Wasted.

Wondering just whose idea it had been to leave the sanctuary and comfort of Manali in the first place.

Finger pointing be damned, however, for the haven of the Hot Springs, and the bountiful fruits of the German Bakery had never been so welcoming.

After a week of over-indulgence in Vashisht, no scrimping half-measures, no Not-Sure-if-I-Really-Should-Have-Yet-Another-Slice-of-Strudel, they had felt sufficiently rejuvenated to once again face the rigours of forward movement.

The hardships of their Tale put my own endeavours to shame.

I feel embarrassed to compare my own ordeal with theirs.

We toast each other's Health and Resilience with a cold Kingfisher.

Or two.

Or I forget exactly how many.

Chapter 13

What a Wimpy

There is no Time to rest on my laurels.

Time waits for no Man.

Time waits for no Woman, either; some claim Time's Tick-Tocks tick and tock more rapidly for the fairer sex.

Is Time, therefore, sexist?

That might need Time (some male, *non-sexist* Time) to ponder. Sometime.

Before I depart Delhi this second time, I have urgent need to avail myself of a smidgeon of westernised luxury. I say 'luxury', but this luxury comes in the shape of the Delhi branch of Wimpy, an American hamburger chain, with just a smattering of outlets in the UK.

So, can I really mean *luxury* at all?

I am not one for fast food, for processed gunk-type establishments. But the Wimpy, nestling in N-Block of Connaught Place, is far more than simply a fast food outlet; to many, its shiny red vinyl seats represent a small Oasis of Home, of the Once-Again Familiar, of Cognitive Sanctity, in this vast ocean of Turmoil and Madness that is India. A place to mentally relax, to escape and recharge the batteries away from the incessant throng - with AirCon! - before setting forth into the mêlée once again, all whilst munching on Lamb Burgers for a mere *Rs*8 a pop.

Unlike most of the Far East - or even Nepal – India of the early '90s possesses barely any brands familiar from back home. No Coca Cola; no McDonalds; no Marks & Spencer; no Gap; no, none of *that*.

Many contend this to be a Good Thing. These brands' absence is no loss; their absence is, in fact, a draw, a positive, a boon. A world without the heavily processed crap served at McDonalds might indeed be a better world for us all (other fast food chains are also available for avoiding their equally crap, overly-processed-gunk).

In place of the familiar, you are presented with products the names of which, at first, mean nothing to you: archetypal Indian brands, such as Limca (a refreshing lemon drink); Gold Spot (an orange-flavoured fizzy drink); or Thumbs Up (a wannabe Coke substitute, but taste-wise nothing like the Real Thing) are the only alternatives to water, or tea, or beer (in those non-teetotal States where alcohol can be legally purchased).

Suddenly, any brand, no matter how tacky, or 'Not-Representative-of-You', becomes a Haven of Familiarity, a Refuge of Calm in the Wilderness of Indian Madness. These snippets of home therefore exert a serious gravitational pull on your person.

As such, The Delhi Wimpy is a place you're pretty much guaranteed to meet other travellers, the majority similarly predisposed.

'Never normally be seen *dead* in a place like this...' is how all conversations start, to wizened, affirmatory nods all round.

I munch on soggy fries, and a burger, or two, washed down with a Wannabe Coke (NO ice). The food tastes rather pleasant, it pains me to say.

As I dip a fry into a red maybe-tomato sauce, an elephant passes in front of me, walking nonchalantly down the street, from *where*, to *where* I know not.

You don't get that kind of scenery in Oxford Street, no matter which day you choose to do your shopping.

Chapter 14

Bhanged by the Lassie

That evening, bound for Udaipur.

Remembering my previous Indian Railways journey up to Jammu, and considering my recent ordeals, I decide I deserve a soupçon of *real* luxury in my life. I procure a 1st-Class, Air-Conditioned ticket, for the princely sum of £10 for this 17-hour journey, from the International Booking Hall above Delhi Main Railway Station, a queue-free - and therefore pain-free - endeavour. That I did not know of this facility on my first trip through Delhi is a source of great consternation right now.

I remember the trials and tribulations I'd endured the last time I'd passed through this place. How long ago that experience seems right now.

It is a different, more assured version of me that now boldly embarks on this next leg of my journey, that's for sure.

1st Class AirCon: oh, how the other half live.

The compartment is spacious and clean; the seats, springy and soft, just the one, two-person seat on either side of the compartment, separated from the rest of the carriage by a sliding door, a door which leads to a corridor running down the length of the carriage, a corridor not currently over-run with swarms of random people as were the 3rd class accommodations. The upper bunks are currently folded away, encased in their daytime wall enclosures, giving the compartment a bright and airy feel to it. Fresh, clean bedding has been very thoughtfully provided. If anything, the air-conditioning is perhaps a tad *too* efficient.

My compartment compatriots are a Punjabi couple in their mid-sixties, of obvious good-standing. Time flies as we while away the hours and minutes to Udaipur discussing the current state of Indian and British politics, and the finer points of Cricket.

For those unfamiliar with the sport of Cricket, there is much about the game's finer points to discuss: its tactics; the ideal composition of a team; the all-rounder *vs* single-skilled players;

and the multi-faceted formats, of 1-Day Games and of 5-day Test matches. First introduced by the British to India in the 1700s, after a slow uptake the sport was seen as a means to create better social contact between the British and the Indian elite; later, the Indians played competitively as a means with which to embarrass their colonial masters. Nowadays, cricket in India has morphed into a religion, the passion and fervour of the average supporter far exceeding that of the typical English afficionado. To be a successful Indian batsman is to be revered almost as a God in this vast land, a modern-day Prince in the Land of the Ancient Maharajas. Young lads the country over all dream of being the next Sunil Gavaskar, the next Sachin Tendulkar, the next Raul Dravid, or the next *VVS* Laxman, as they play in the dirt of their remote villages with just the most rudimentary equipment, for the bat, for the ball and for the stumps (such evocative names, those Indian legends: in England, our team comprises Foakes, Stokes, and Woakes, and a bunch of other Blokes).

At mealtime, our personal chef brings us a freshly prepared meat thali, a series of small cylindrical metal pots stacked one atop the other, dishes described to me by my new companions – *Tarkar Dal*; *Saag Aloo*; a lamb-based *Laal Maas*; a vegetarian *Panchmel Ki Sabzi*, spicy and sweet, accompanied by soft, thin poppadums and rotis with which to mop up the sauces; all finished off with a tooth decaying dessert of *Balushahi* (deep-fried balls made from sugar, ghee and flour). Each serving is different to its precursor; each is delightfully delicious.

The toilets at the end of each carriage are blessedly clean and are even the modern sit-down versions, although they still deposit your waste straight down onto the tracks once you press the lever (with tissued fingers) post-episode. Large signs remind users that these Facilities are *Not* to Be Deployed whilst the train is In Station, that so doing is *Strictly Prohibited*. Experience suggests these signs are, alas, ignored with impunity. The tracks running through all stations in India are festooned with human faeces in a sliding scale of decay.

In England, mathematically, you are never more than 70 miles from the coast; in urban centres, according to legend, you are never more than 6 feet from a rat.

In India, from bitter experience, it seems you are never more than 2 feet away from shit of one description or another.

Stepping on it; smelling it; being *in* it.

You might be in 1st Class AirCon.

But you're only ever so slightly raised *above* the shit.

Oh no. You can't escape Indian shit *that* easily.

****

The *Maître d'* of the Lake Palace Hotel in Udaipur looks down his exceptionally long aquiline nose at me.

I have tried. I really have.

I am wearing clean, freshly pressed trousers; a clean, freshly ironed shirt. The shoe-shine boys have done some of their finest work with my brown leather Doc Marten boots. I feel sure I meet the sartorial requirements to now be permitted to boat over to the Lake Palace Hotel to enjoy its much-fêted Evening Meal service.

The *Maître d'* looks down his rather long nose at me once again.

'No', his contemptuous hand gestures and jittery body posturing are saying.

'*Non!*'.

Apparently, my attire will *not* do.

I do not Pass Muster.

I am summarily dismissed, shoed away with disdain as one might shoe away a fly.

'I must be deluded to think I am suitably sartorially attired for this Up-Market, High-Class Establishment', his demeanour appears to say.

Bummer.

I hail a rickshaw, heading over to another restaurant to enjoy an entirely different meal experience. The Bond film Octopussy was partly filmed in Udaipur (back in 1983), at the self-same Lake Palace Hotel to which I have just been denied access. I have heard of a restaurant in town that has been showing the film every night since it premiered - for the better part of a decade - on what must now be a very worn, over-stretched VHS video cassette. The constant repetition must be driving (*have driven*?) the waiters there stark raving mad.

I settle in for this evening's viewing.

This seems a Suitably Social Spot.

Whilst we await the start of the movie the diners all quickly become engaged in conversation.

It is the usual Traveller fare.

Where we are from (I prefer, 'Where is *home* for you?', for where you are born is unlikely to be a personal choice.)

For how long are we are away?

Places and countries visited so far?

Places and countries for future visitation?

The state of our bowels? (*seriously*, this is India).

The Never-Ending Eccentricities of this Crazy Country.

The chatter lasts well into the night. It is a most convivial evening.

****

The following day, I visit a local handicraft shop.

I play chess with its owner. The owner wins every game. I am not letting him win.

I have my eye on a beautiful, 3m x 2m, traditional Rajasthani wall-hanging currently gracing one side of his shop. The wall-hanging comprises a multitude of fabric pieces of varying ethnically hewn styles and designs, all stitched together into a wondrous patchwork tableau. The creation will have taken many hours to complete. The artistic handiwork calls out to me, that it wishes to be my latest acquisition.

Each game I lose, the price reduces a few *rupees* more.

I wonder if maybe we should play all day, until the price drops to zero.

That lunchtime - after our eighth chess game, having still failed to register a win - my haggling secures the day's first victory.

I consider the agreed fee a fair price. I am sure I have still paid over the odds.

The shopkeeper asks if I would like to accompany him to a local village, far off the tourist trail, to an ancient temple with which he is familiar. Pillion, I ride his decrepit scooter, along holed and heavily rutted un-tarmacked tracks out to the distant village. As we put-put into sight, the villagers all rush out of their homes, all eager to come see who has suddenly materialised outside the ramshackle dwellings they call home.

To a child, the kids are all unkempt – wild, never-brushed, banshee-styled hair, clothes torn and muddied, neither the kids nor their clothes appearing to have seen soapy water for many months (if ever at all). As if a compulsory fashion accessory, the kids all sport delightful balls of snot, hanging precariously out of at least one nostril, clumps that seem on the verge of performing their earth-bound terminal tumbles, but never quite tumbling free, reconciled to dangling a never-ending final dangle.

This bogey-hewn look is not one I think will catch on back home. A box of Kleenex - or a hundred - would work wonders out here. This would seem a prime business opportunity for a Tissue Selling entrepreneur. I am surprised no local has cottoned on to this.

India lacks many things; but it does not lack Entrepreneurs.

I wish I had known about the snot issue whilst in town, plentiful as tissues are back there. Stacks of tissues would be far more useful gifts than the sweets the kids all heckle me for – unsuccessfully - as we pass through their midst.

The kids scurry around, playing amongst the detritus and the human dirt and the animal muck, their only toys sticks, or small balls fashioned from waste.

No matter. They all have wide, beaming smiles. They have no awareness of their situation being anything less than ideal, that they lack even the most rudimentary conveniences British children possess as a matter of course.

The children here are happy, despite their less-than-perfect lot.

For they know no better.

For them, this is the only existence they have lived. This is simply how life *is* Lived.

Life, their life, *any* life, is a wonder, a joy.

Life is Great!

Their current state of Blissful Happiness might also have something to do with the absence of Advertising being pummelled continuously into their heads. Out here, there are none of those subtle, subconscious sales pitches, pitches for a plethora of useless toys and trinkets with which advertisers at home like to bombard our own kids.

The Marketing is relentless. The Bombardment, persistent.

'Your child's life cannot be considered complete without Gizmo A'.

'Not purchasing Gadget B for your kid is akin to child neglect, you *Terrible* Parent', or so the Promotional Slogans extol.

All Balderdash and Piffle.

The curse of a consumption-lead economy.

The kids here in this village might show few signs of *external* washing; but they've thankfully escaped washing (of the brainwashing variety) *inside*, too. No tellies for the kids to waste hours entranced in front of, spewing forth their mesmeric marketing.

My Time away from home has, imperceptibly at first, cleansed my own mind of this perpetual bombardment, to continually desire *This* Useless Item, to perpetually aspire to own *That* High-Falutin Object.

Gone is my own excessive time spent glued to the telly. Gone, too, are the large, on-street advertising billboards, at least billboards in a language that can be understand. Sure, the signs might still be there; but what they *say* is anyone's guess. Freedom from the glare of marketing has been a welcome - and totally unexpected - boon these past months since departing Australia.

'Oh, Advertising doesn't work on me,' some are want to boast.

Really?

You think?

You think advertisers fork out on expensive commercials because they have no effect on anyone?

Perhaps, you're exactly the person they *do* work on; indeed, the person they work on *most* effectively.

At the temple, I take many photos of an ancient, hand-painted mural inside, its colour faded, yet still with sufficient detail to show off the artist's considerable talent. The wall shows the traditional tableau of a typical farmers' village, the villagers standing and working alongside their ripening crops, with their herds of goats, plus the odd chicken or two scratching around for scraps in the foreground. The scene the painting depicts is from a hundred+ years ago, yet from an era when daily life appears remarkably similar to that experienced by the farmers today. It is a simple painting, but wonderful to witness.

Alas, the temple is in a state of disrepair, of imminent collapse, or so the shopkeeper says. No money is available for the temple's upkeep, for its renovation, for its hoped-for restoration. The shopkeeper wants me to take some photos of the mural, to preserve the images on film. He intends for the images to be employed in restoring or repainting the tableau, at a later stage, should the funds ever be found.

I oblige unquestioningly.

****

That evening, prior to supper, a novel idea enters my mind. For the purposes of fulfilling this idea, I am required to hail an autorickshaw. I request the driver take me to the nearest establishment for me to sample the finest *Bhang Lassie* Udaipur has to offer. My departure from India is only days away - *assuming all goes to plan* – and I have yet to partake of one of these much-fabled delights.

My autorickshaw driver duly obliges. I am delivered to a random roadside stall on the edge of town. My driver acts as intermediary to the transaction.

'One or two?' the driver enquires.

'One or two' *whats* I know not.

Two sounds better than *one*, I guess – more plural, less singular.

A *Bhang Lassie*, for the uninitiated, is a yoghurt drink, with hashish blended into the mix.

Mine tastes delicious. Most refreshing.

In a flash, it's all gone, down the hatch, ingested, slowing oozing its way into my stomach, waiting for my digestive juices to commence working their magic.

I have, however, unbeknownst, just made a rookie mistake, a mistake with potentially drastic repercussions: for I should have enquired further into the system of measurement to which the *BL* maker just referred.

Specifically, the one or two *whats*?

For the *what* here is a *tola*.

Also written *tolah*.

An ancient system of measurement dating back to the 1500s. Introduced to Indian by the British in the 1800s. Based on the weight of 100 ruttee seeds. Still employed today as a unit of measurement in the gold bullion markets in India and the Middle East.

One *tola* = approx. 10 grams.

Two *tola* = twenty grams.

0.7 of an ounce.

This is the quantity of hash now wending its way, silently, stealthily, into my digestive tracts.

It is, I later learn, a non-insubstantial quantity to be hosting for the Forthcoming.

I request the rickshaw driver return me to town, to the Octopussy restaurant. I am hoping for another socially convivial evening.

It is still relatively early. The restaurant, still sparsely populated. I am directed to an empty table for four, taking my seat facing the small screen a few feet away.

I order. My food swiftly arrives. The restaurant is rapidly filling up.

'Do I mind sharing?', the waiter asks, as I munch down my supper.

It is evidently a rhetorical question, as my new guests have already taken their seats before I can answer. I have been joined by a party of three. Americans, alas, and not, as it transpires, the best kind.

The conversation is somewhat stilted, the topics of conversation a machine-gun scatter of irrelevances. I pray the film starts soon to shut them all up.

I am sorry to be so critical. I have nothing *whatsoever* against Americans as a whole. But if you're not on the same frequency as the *someone* who's currently nattering away in your close milieu, there's really nothing that can be done to improve the situation if they won't take a hint.

You know what I mean.

Over share. Too much information. Tedious small talk.

Three against one makes getting a word in edgeways tricky in any case.

Well over an hour has passed since the *bhang lassie* first entered my system. I am a little surprised nothing discernible has yet ensued.

If I am being honest, I have no idea *what* to expect; I also have no idea *when* to expect that which I do know not *what* to expect.

With perfect timing, and right on cue, I detect a slight wobble in my reality sphere.

The Giggles are welling up inside.

Suddenly, for no apparent reason, my current situation seems incredibly hilarious.

Something appears to be happening. *Something* a little out of the ordinary.

Whatever that *something* may be, I think it best to not be seated here with my new American buddies - and I use that word most loosely - when it does. In a flash, my arm shoots up, beckoning the nearest waiter please bring me my bill. I pay, and head out into the crazy nocturnal circus that is Udaipur.

Thousands of people are roaming the streets, even at this late hour. This late hour is more like rush hour, such are the swarms of people hustling and bustling along the streets, people making the most out of the cool night air.

Out Here is a busy, noisy ruckus.

I roam hither and thither.

I find a bazaar. I swear that looks like a Tsar.

A Tsar in a Bazaar? How Bizarre!

OK, where's your head at?

I test for residuals. All appears to be in order, although which particular order I could not possibly say.

The rest of the evening passes in a hazy daze, as if in a Dream.

It is impossible to distinguish between Reality and the Dream.

To say *exactly* where I went, and with whom I interacted, is like asking someone to affirm whether a dream is really *real* (no, but also, *yes*).

In my Dream, I encounter a coven of cows.

In my Dream, I speak to them.

In my Dream, they *moo* right back.

In my Dream, I reply to their *moos*.

In my Dream, they *moo* once again.

In my Dream, this process repeats several times.

In my Dream, we are engaged in conversation.

In my Dream, the cows might actually be making sense.

In my Dream, I understand their *moo*'d musings.

In my Dream, the cows tell me what they have learned, information passed down through generations of cows, dating back hundreds, if not thousands, of years.

In my Dream, I feel they have imparted radical, earth shattering News.

In my Dream, I am in awe of their Knowledge.

It is here, frustratingly, the Dream ends. What Knowledge the cows imparted - sagacious ruminations on the otherwise Unfathomable Nature of the Cosmos - is lost, only temporarily misplaced I hope, somewhere deep inside my dreamtime memory banks.

If only this information could be recovered, I would have the Keys to the World.

No wonder the Cow is so revered in India.

These Indians might not be as daft as I have come to think.

****

Bright and early, I awake in my bed.

Something, I quickly sense, is Not Quite Right.

Something is Out of Place.

I glance down my supine torso.

Oh dear. Oh my. No, that's definitely *not* normal.

Something *Down There* is in a state of unusual enlargement.

No, not *that*!

Strewth! Seriously, People?

For it is my *stomach* currently displaying a state of worrying distention. If I didn't know better, I might think I was suddenly 'with child'.

I lie there pondering just what is up, and what I might need to be do about this recent development.

The first flatulent apparition tells me all I need to know.

Giardia. *Giardiasis*.

Joy of all Joys.

If you're currently eating, may I suggest you stop what you are doing, and push your food to one side, for there is no delicate way to phrase any of this.

Giardiasis is the unwelcome outcome of ingesting food or water contaminated with the microscopic parasite Giardia. The incubation period for this disease is around seven days. This outcome is not the result of last night's *lassie*.

My recent escape from Ladakh has had longer lasting consequences than I could have known.

PART TWO

Chapter 15

Just Shout 'Jim!' Really Loudly

Long ago, before the internet and mobile phones revolutionised interpersonal connectivity, establishing a mate's exact geographical whereabouts at any given moment was an irksome test of wits and resourcefulness. This challenge would be particularly taxing if the person you were seeking was wandering overseas and not providing their **Home Base Coordination Team** (aka Parents) with regular updates of their constantly changing location. If you, too, were participating on your own peripatetic perambulations, synchronising the collective whereabouts of two Blown-Hither-by-the-Breeze free spirits was a hit and miss affair, with way more emphasis on the miss.

Notice boards, in popular bars, outside book exchanges, in well-used hostels, in the most traveller-frequented restaurants, would be festooned with hastily scribbled scraps of paper, hundreds of souls engaged in largely in vain searches for their misplaced buddies, recaps of itineraries, suggestions for meeting places, hoping to reunite in the not-too-distant future.

It was a fraught and frustrating process. You never knew how close, or how far, you were from a successful *rendezvous*. Your friend might be thousands of kilometres away in a completely different country, or merely metres from you on the other side of the bar. You simply had no way of knowing where anyone was until you bumped, quite literally, into them.

As an alternative to the randomised notice board game of chance, you could instead use your **HBCT** as a reference point for those who might be looking for you; you could use your friends' **HBCTs** for information on *their* last known location. Handing out your parents' home phone number to other travellers was as regular and normal as giving out your email address or mobile number is these days.

Triangulating someone's geographical coordinates came in three simple steps.

I say 'Simple'.

Simple, presuming you didn't happen to be a flaky, 20-something year old traveller, with borderline organisational skills, and an impressive knack for putting things off, and off, and off.

First up: the wherewithal to prise yourself away from the myriad activities utilising your normally limited, now travel-addled, cognitive functioning, remembering to remember your one vitally important task today is to interact with communicative technology in a positive manner before the day achieves its darkened denouement.

Of course, once the day achieved its inevitable post-breakfast, focus-absorbing momentum, the need for that communicative technological interaction would be parked behind other, more current, more immediate, super-important, cognitive-heavy decisions: to reapply another coat of sunscreen, or not; to hit the bar for another cool Stubby, or not; to chat up the super-cute girl on the adjacent sun lounger, or not; or whose turn it was at the German Bakery, your shout on the Sticky Toffee buns it most definitely is not. Despite setting off with the best of intentions, a day could fly by without your mind ever returning to that one vital thing you promised yourself would be achieved today.

Tomorrow then arrives, as it has a habit of doing. So far, in any case.

'Today will be the day', you tell yourself – today will *Definitely* be *the* Day – searing the message 'Phone Home' into your consciousness, or so you thought, only for the day's events to then unfold exactly as they had previously.

This painful process usually continues *ad infinitum*.

Should a miracle occur, should you manage to overcome your absent-minded forgetfulness, prising yourself away from your Sticky Toffee buns, your cool beer, or the super-cute girl on the adjacent sun lounger, the timing of this prising then needed to coincide with your target's **HBCT** operational hours, for the risk of the **HBCT** being unmanned and your call ringing through to voicemail was the stuff of nightmares, the thought of which left you trembling in a cold sweat.

Answerphones.

Beep!

'Please leave your message after the tone...'

Sure, you knew there was a chance no one would be home, that leaving a message might be a requirement, but the *Beep!* always caught you totally unaware, your brain then racing to keep up with your panicked and out of control mouth, words gushing forth in no discernible order, nor recognisable language, the resulting message being an overly self-conscious, incoherent, jabbering, indecipherable mess, a mess with no option to erase or do-over. You'd hang up, slap your forehead in despair, cringing at the gibberish you'd just left for someone else to attempt to decipher, thence returning to your cold beer and the super-cute girl on the adjacent sun lounger, your confidence ever so slightly deflated.

No, you tell yourself, this Calling Home business is fraught with untold dangers; for all the hassles and potential pitfalls, Calling Home is really best avoided altogether.

But sometimes, once in a blue moon, when the Stars, and the Planets, and the *Chakras* all aligned, you'd manage to overcome these two usually insurmountable hurdles.

You'd extricate yourself from your cool beer, and the super-cute girl on the adjacent sun lounger.

Your call answered by the intended human target.

Hallelujah!!

You were not, however, out of the woods, for the information gleaned still needed to be current and correct.

Could you bet your house on your mate being in X on the Yth of the month, as promised?

Could you trust your buddy not to suddenly change his/ her plans, diverting randomly to some amazing, off-the-beaten-track, Must-See spot he/ she had just heard about on the Traveller Grapevine, on the promise of some Super Unique Unmissable Experience - or simply on a Promise - blaming their unreliability on their free spirited nature over which they clearly have no control?

The answer?

'Not on your nelly', more often than not.

With all the tools at the traveller's disposal nowadays, relating to the hardships created by this inability to establish anyone's location might be tricky. But, save for sub-cutaneous GPS tracker implants, or nosebleed expensive satellite phones, your options were indeed limited to hit-and-miss notes pinned to random notice boards, or this randomised Phone-a-Friend's-Parents crap shoot.

Imagine that (or, at least, *try* to imagine that).

In reality, phoning your **HBCT** to let them know you were still in the land of the living, and they could therefore stop their perpetual parental stressing for an hour, or two, should not have been an overly onerous task, what with the ubiquity of call centres offering cheap rate international calls in all the main, and all the *less* main, traveller hotspots. What made the task more taxing for the young and formative mind - in addition to prising yourself away from your cool beer and the super-cute girl on the adjacent sun lounger – was the need to perform cranially challenging calculations, adding or subtracting the hours ahead or behind GMT you were currently inhabiting (Oh God, had the clocks just gone *forwards*, or *backwards*?), thereby evaluating the optimal call time to coincide with your **HBCT's** Not-at-Work-but-not-Having-Supper-Down-yet-Still-Awake time. Should this optimal hour impinge on your own strictly regimented Acronical Activities, given that watching yet another glorious sunset, in the company of the super-cute girl on the adjacent sun lounger, with cool beer in hand, is mandatory in the Land of the Traveller, then, well, there was only ever going to be the one winner.

As a result, Calling Home was often too much like hard work for the weary traveller's undertaxed yet overburdened mind.

Were degrees offered in the Art of Procrastination, most young travellers would pass with 1st Class Honours (a 'Geoff Hurst'), the course requirements hinging on you putting off attending Finals indefinitely, pressed as you should claim to be with other (not necessarily) far more urgent matters requiring of your immediate (well, *relatively* immediate) attention.

In a similar vein, the BA in the Art of Delegation is passed simply by sending someone else to take Finals on your behalf. Attending yourself, in person, is an Automatic Fail.

With all these randomised variables in play, meeting up again with a mate you'd previously encountered hundreds, if not thousands, of miles away from your current location was always unexpected; and always therefore a truly joyous occasion, worthy of detouring to the nearest bar without a moment's delay, for the first order of business when randomly meeting up again with an old buddy is to settle down somewhere comfortable, specifically somewhere with a large stock of cold beers, and catching up on all the crazy Tales from their World of Travel.

Such chance meetings were rarer than hens' teeth, and super precious as a result.

The only alternative method of communication, and of catching up with the news from home, was the written word, hard-copy episcopal offerings received via the ubiquitous global Poste Restante system. All the sender needed to do was address their missive to you at whichever post office they expected you to be passing, having given sufficient forethought to the timescales required for the letter to arrive *prior* to you having already breezed through town.

E.g., Ed Barnes, Post Restante, Kuala Lumpur, Malaysia.

Big or small, capital city or edge of nowhere, post offices worldwide all possessed boxes into which mail addressed thus would be placed, although not necessarily with meticulous care, or any discernible sense of order. To receive your mail, your task was simply to request the Post Office's stash of Post Restante, then spend an age sorting through the hundreds of uncatalogued letters and small parcels, all on the off-chance there might be a delivery for you, awaiting your arrival with hopeful expectation.

Flick too fast whilst sorting through the tightly-packed letters and parcels, miss the needle in this well-packed haystack – or, worse, change your itinerary and miss that PR altogether - and someone's hard work will languish, uncollected and unloved, for all Eternity.

Or twelve months, whichever comes sooner.

****

May 1993.

My travelling companion, Rich, and I are hot off a Thai Airways flight from Bangkok, fast approaching passport control, in hopeful expectation of soon entering Nepal via the Immigration System at Kathmandu airport.

Immediately, we hit a possibly terminal snag.

The entrance fee to Nepal has, unbeknownst to us, recently been upped to $20pp, not the $10 we had budgeted and planned for. There is no ATM at the airport; indeed, there are no ATMs in the whole of Nepal, the first not introduced until 1995. The only cash we have on our persons, other than the presumed to be sufficient $20, comes in the shape of lovely, crisp Thai *baht* notes, freshly gleaned from Bangkok.

There is no Bureau de Change at the airport, which is also unexpected.

No problem. Surely, it is simple enough for us to pay the equivalent of $10 each out of the lovely crisp Thai *baht* notes we have in our possession?

At this suggestion, the Immigration Official rapidly achieves a state of superior agitation, as if we have caused some serious, yet unknown, offence to his person.

'Thai *baht*?'

'No!'

'No?'

'No!'

'No?'

'No!'

I'm sensing that's a, 'No!', then.

After more than an hour of bungled wrangling and frustrated non-communications, the impasse is finally resolved by the head of Immigration Services taking hold of our passports. This rather stern, overly serious man suggests we obtain the necessary dollars within the next 24 hours, thence return to the airport Immigration Services office, where, on payment of the additional $20, we will be able to retrieve our freshly stamped *Entrance Approved* passports.

Return without the dollars, you'll be on the first flight out; fail to return at all, you'll be on your own *in country* without passports.

Good luck with that, Sirs!

In anyone's book, such close-run, near-miss, almost-failed-entrance stress on arrival means one thing, and one thing only.

Beer (as if we *really needed* an excuse).

Rich and I head straight to our hotel, dump our bags, locate a Money Changer offering Nepalese *rupee* on Visa, and head straight out to sample the finest ales that Kathmandu has to offer, having left our lovely crisp Thai *baht* most trustingly with a rather shady local taxi man, who has assured us he will be able to exchange them for a decent quantity of fine US greenbacks by the morning.

We hit the town running. And hard.

Many ales are consumed in celebration at our arrival – well, *almost* arrival - into this new country. Consuming many ales on our first night in a new country is a tradition initiated way back in Australia, some five countries ago now. It is a tradition running concurrently with several other traditions also requiring the consumption of ales, such similarly noteworthy events as: 'Days containing the letter 'A''; '6pm'; 'Sunshine'; '8pm'; 'Night time'; and 'Rain' (in truth, there are numerous other noteworthy, Must-be-Celebrated-with-Beer events. Space limitations prohibit them all from being listed here).

Rich and I are so single-mindedly focused on our ale consumption task we fail to notice it has suddenly turned quite dark. It has also somehow managed to get rather late in the day. Indeed, it is now so late in the day it has already become quite *early* in the day. We have somehow ended up in an odd part of town, although to be sure all this new town looks odd (although, oddly, some of this new town also looks quite *familiar*). Sensing it is now time to depart the ale house, we decide to eschew taxi assistance, and commence the wending of our homeward way on foot. We progress - maybe a little unsteadily, if truth be told - down narrow, dark, hush-quiet streets, absorbing the sights and smells of our new location with much fascination and wide-eyed wonder. The urge to sing, as can occur in such times of merriment and excitement at the new and wondrous opportunities that Nepal has to offer – as well as the multitude of opportunities this marvellous innovation *Life* permits - lurks just beneath the surface of our ever-so-slightly impaired cognitive functioning.

Fresh in our minds is information gleaned from a letter received at the Bangkok PR, a letter from a mutual friend, Big Al, news that another mutual friend, Jim, has recently headed off to India, most likely in a Heroic Quest for Mystical Enlightenment and a Deeper Comprehension of the Mind's Inner Workings.

'Don't know *exactly* where Jim's gone,' Big Al wrote, 'but the best way to find him', the letter explained, 'is surely just to shout out his name, loudly, as you journey around India. Simple. *Certain* to do the trick'.

Certain to do the trick?

Big Al's otherwise brilliant, fool-proof plan contains just the one, tiny yet potentially fatal flaw.

A tiny yet potentially fatal flaw: that India is a *vast* country, a mere 1.25m square miles, a mere 2,000 miles from North to South, and pretty much the same again East to West.

It is also a country of a mere 1 Billion+ inhabitants.

If we want to find our friend, all we'll need to do is call out his name whilst we wander around.

Sure. Why *wouldn't* that work?

Rich and I come to a tight bend in this narrow, dark, hush-quiet Kathmandu street. Suddenly, Rich – I will resist the urge to provide you more background on the fella, he is a quiet, shy, introvert who simply *hates* the spotlight of attention – announces he has an idea.

He is, he says, a Man with a Plan.

Or rather, he is a Man with Big Al's Plan.

'Yes', Rich says, 'now is the time to try out Big Al's Theory'.

Here, in Kathmandu, after midnight, in a random, narrow, dark, hush-quiet street, here is the ideal spot to see whether That Man Jim is somewhere close by.

That we're in a completely different country - Nepal, not India - doesn't seem to have registered with Rich.

Geography. Not his strongest suit.

'Yes', Rich suggests confidently, 'we shall call out Jim's name, loudly, and see what thence occurs'.

Before Rich has had time to put the Plan into action, someone appears.

Who could it be at this time of night?

Who could be stalking us down this narrow, dark, hush-quiet Kathmandu street?

Who might be seeking our acquaintance at this most wee of hours?

That someone is the Voice of Reason.

You may already be familiar with the Voice of Reason.

The VoR is a visitor who shows up from time to time; a usually *most welcome* visitor.

The VoR is a hushed voice whispering into your ear from the deep recesses of your consciousness.

The VoR speaks sense when there is danger of sense being worryingly overlooked, with potentially disastrous consequences.

Here, now, in this dark, narrow, hush-quiet street, the VoR has taken human form.

Mine.

Boring old me.

After all the fuss we experienced being permitted entrance into this fine country, the VoR suggests it might be, you know, *less than ideal*, somewhat *ironic* even, for us to be hauled in by the Police for causing a major disturbance of the peace; Police who, on entering our details into their records, would recognise us as the two gormless nincompoops who'd not been in possession of the correct sum to fully pay for the entry stamp, so didn't currently possess the necessary authority to be actually in the country, and who would duly - and with doubtless much glee - thence kick us out of Nepal without so much as a by your leave.

'How was Nepal?' people would ask, in years to come.

'No idea,' we'd have to reply, 'we only spent five hours there before they kicked us out.'

I know.

Live a little.

What a Tale to tell.

I hear you.

Surprisingly, given his general disregard for authority, and the volume of ale currently sloshing around inside his guts, Rich doesn't flick the VoR the bird; he doesn't say, 'Bugger That for a Game of Soldiers'; he doesn't veto the VoR's 'Keeping Quiet so as to Not Get Arrested' suggestion.

Rich, for once, is a picture of meek compliance.

This event on its own is something of a singular novelty.

The pair of us continue our silent - and if we're being honest, far too sensible - homeward-bound stagger.

No singing.

No raised voices.

A pair of model, if slightly less than sober, citizens.

Next morning, the shady taxi driver presents us with a paltry amount of dollars from what had been quite a large sum of Thai *baht*. We immediately query the exchange rate utilised in this transaction. The taxi driver greets us with his finest, 'Best that I could do, and I strived arduously to achieve that' look, a look clearly honed over many years of similarly dodgy dealing.

Such an acting masterclass really deserves a long, non-sarcastic round of applause.

We give him a sardonic look instead.

Really, mate?

You can't Kid a Kidder.

But what can you do?

Done like a Kipper. Lesson learnt.

Nevertheless, we are now in possession of the dollars required for our entrance stamps. We hail a different taxi, and head straight to the airport to complete our arrival formalities.

Success.

We are now *official* Nepal visitors.

Let the singing commence!

But no. The singing must wait. It is still several hours until beer o'clock.

Yes, even *we* have standards.

On a whim, we decide to head over to the central Post Office, on the off-chance mail might be sitting in its PR, waiting for us in hopeful expectation. As the only means of keeping up with life developments back home was contained in the many letters friends kindly posted along our itinerary, receiving mail felt akin to winning the lottery. As a result, the urge to take a look 'just in case' was always strong should a Post Office be close by.

You Have Mail (?)

Literally.

Possibly.

I scour the vast box of Post Restante mail, flicking through the hundreds of grubby and creased white and brown envelopes packed tightly into the case. The large, 1m x 1m box is quite the sight to behold.

I stop to ponder a moment.

A thought suddenly hits me: that this pile of papers is not simply a pile of papers, but a physical manifestation, an accumulation of hundreds if not thousands of hours of creative input; of news (happy and sad); of love and regret; of gossip and tattle tale; of pain and sorrow, all intended to be shared with the name scribbled on the envelope's front façade. I am, in fact, casually flicking through a sea of emotional turmoil sitting here, currently unclaimed, currently unopened, waiting to be fulfilled, potentially unrequited, the love and sadness on these pages possibly never reaching its intended target, the creativity never to be appreciated.

Significant life outcomes might hinge on the news contained inside these flimsily formed missives.

Romance could blossom, or fade, should the recipient receive, or not receive, their rose-scented correspondence.

Vital information might linger, un-promulgated, should the beneficiary not access their critically, crucial correspondence.

The random Nature of Life, of Fate and Destiny, sits here, awaiting the outcome of the Crap Shoot of Chance.

These thoughts suddenly cease when my eye catches a very particular - and *wondrously* unique - style of handwriting, the way a familiar face in a packed crowd stands out from the other, anonymous, mugshots you look at, but don't *really see*.

It is scrawl belonging to our friend Jim.

Yes, most definitely Jim's scrawl.

This scrawl could belong to no other than That Man Jim.

I extricate this letter from the stack.

Yes, this really is Jim's scrawl, for his scrawl is written on the exterior of an envelope addressed to none other than *me*.

'Staying at Hotel *SüchundSüch*,' Jim writes, 'leaving on **This Date**, heading thence to Pokhara. Maybe see you soon?'

I check today's date.

Today is **This Date**.

Shit. Shit shittety shit.

Jim has given no indication as to his departure time today, so we need to get our sorry arses over to the Hotel *SüchundSüch* pretty damn pronto.

Or, faster than pretty damn pronto.

Shit. Shit shittety shit.

From being in a state of serene calm and chill, we've suddenly achieved Full Blind Panic mode. Rich and I rush out of the Post Office, into the lung-busting fumes of the busy Kathmandu streets, and frantically hail a taxi, demanding the driver speed us over to Hotel *SüchundSüch* as fast as, if not faster, than the law permits.

'Don't spare the horses', we cry, excitedly.

The driver points out with some confusion that he doesn't have any horses – *obviously* doesn't have any horses - so what the hell are we talking about.

Such is the use of idiom with non-native speakers.

With more than a little luck at not colliding with a plethora of other road users – the driver would doubtless attribute this successful carriage to his own not-inconsiderable skill, and insanely quick reflexes – we reach our destination in less time than was probably scientifically possible. We alight, paying the good man for his excellent services, simultaneously scouring our new location for the entrance to Hotel *SüchundSüch*. As my eyes flit over this neighbourhood scene, I am overcome with a weird feeling.

A weird feeling; a weird, vague feeling of familiarity with this locale.

Hmm. There is, however, no time to spare for this *déjà vu*.

Rich spots the entrance to Hotel *SüchundSüch*. We rush inside, and enquire of the receptionist the whereabouts of Jim, describing our good friend in as much detail we can. The young lad remembers Jim distinctly – something about Jim's distinguishing (*distinguished*?) bald spot, or so the lad said.

The lad is most apologetic, for he must inform us that Jim and his companions have departed the Hotel but a couple of hours earlier, taking the early morning bus down to Pokhara.

It is as feared. We have *literally* just missed him.

Shit. Shit shittety shit.

Even worse than having *literally* just missed him, is the fact that there is no way to let Jim know we have *literally* just missed him. Our close encounter will not register with him in any way, unless our close proximity to his person has sent a ripple through Jim's auric consciousness.

So, no, this close shave will not register with Jim in the slightest.

Oh, Universe, where is your technological progress now?

As we stand outside in the street in front of Hotel *SüchundSüch*, musing, mulling and cussing our misfortune, I ask Rich whether he thinks this locale has a familiar feel.

Rich surveys the scene.

'Hmm', he agrees, 'yes. A little'.

When you've been travelling for the better part of eight months, from country to country to country, from city to city to city, there is a tendency for many places to exude a slightly familiar feel. One tightly packed, narrow street lined with shops and restaurants merges into the next, your world dissolving into something of a blur, evoking fallacious feelings that you've been somewhere before when you really have not. After a while, you simply dismiss the flashes of *déjà vu* for the mind tricks they are, heeding them no second thought.

But this place. Hmm.

Why this place looks so familiar comes to me in a flash, riding roughshod from the deep recesses of last night's hazy, ale-afflicted recollections.

This spot is the *exact* same spot - the narrow street, the distinctive sharp bend to the left – where, not a dozen hours earlier, Rich suggested we shout out Jim's name, an evidently lousy idea over which the VoR had poured icy cold water.

I digest the ramifications of this for a second.

I consider the incredible outcome the VoR has probably thwarted.

Imagine this.

Imagine the VoR hadn't been such a killjoy.

Imagine we'd followed through with the idea.

Imagine we'd shouted out 'Jim', as loudly as we could into the hush quiet night air.

And imagine, whilst we'd been laughing at the absurdity of shouting out Jim's name - in Nepal, not India mind you - knowing that no matter how loudly we'd been shouting we wouldn't have had a rat's chance in hell of success, imagine a figure appearing, a figure summoned by our loud hollering, a figure then standing at the door to Hotel *SüchundSüch*.

A figure taking the exact same form of that Daft Bugger Jim.

A figure that then said, 'Greetings, my Good Fellows. How the devil are you?'

Instant heart attack territory.

Two minds blown instantaneously by the sheer holy-cowness of what had just transpired.

A One-in-a-Trillion outcome for sure.

An outcome that would have gone down in the Annals of Legend for all eternity: 'The Moment the Universe Played Silly Buggers".

Just imagine.

We imagine.

We shake our heads.

We laugh.

Oh.

So.

Near.

Alas. The Universe, courtesy of the darn VoR, has decreed *The Moment* was not to be.

Understandably, we are more than a little deflated and dejected at missing Jim by the merest of whiskers - at having missed out on the Moment the Universe Played Silly Buggers - so we retire to our lodgings, setting our minds back to arranging all the necessaries - the victuals, porterage, permits and guide – for us to be able to head off trekking in the next couple of days, as had originally been the plan before the Jim situation had thrust its bald - sorry, *double-crowned* - head into the spokes of our well-oiled organisational machine.

The following evening, after much wrangled negotiations with a local fixer, all the minutiae for us to head off into the Nepalese Himalaya for a magical fortnight of high-altitude trekking have been finalised. We are super stoked at the adventure awaiting us; this is a long-held dream about to come true.

But the Universe has, it seems, yet another surprise up its sleeve.

For nothing in life ever runs as smoothly as it should, as you expected it would, as you hoped it could.

That evening, the night before our hiking departure, Rich places his daily call to Australia, where the young Scouse lass he'd been courting during our three months in Sydney is awaiting his ritualistic evening contact.

Tonight's call will, alas, be different from the many dozens that have gone before, for young love is fiery and self-absorbed, irrational and possessive. Despite planning to meet up again in Egypt in only a few weeks' time, leaving me to travel India on my lonesome, Rich's girlfriend Chloe decides now is the optimal time to descend into an irrational, lovelorn, full-blown meltdown.

Women, eh?

Like Real People, only *Different*.

Rich returns from the call ashen faced. It doesn't take Hercules Poirot to deduce something is up.

He explains the current state of play *vis à vis* his Liverpudlian love.

'If you *really* loved me, you'd never have left me', is the general gist of what she'd said.

Oh dear.

Oh dear, oh dear, oh dear.

It is, for sure, a quandary.

Much as I am looking forward to our trekking adventure, I tell Rich if he feels he must go and sort out this mess, then he should go.

'Seriously, don't worry about me,' I say.

Rich then has absolutely no worries about not worrying about me.

Two mornings later, Rich is on a plane to Cairns, by way of Singapore. At Cairns, he takes the airport bus into the town centre. As he steps down from the bus, the first person he bumps into is an English girl, Sally, one of a group of four, lovely young ladies he and I had travelled with during our month in Malaysia, seven weeks prior. Rich and Sally had hit it off like the proverbial house on fire, but Rich was adamant he was now most definitely ready to play the hitherto un-played role of Monogamous Man, so nothing untoward had transpired.

But oh, how the undercurrents of Deepest Desires and Potent Procreational Pinings had run fast and run deep.

Even though Sally and her friends were known to have been travelling southwards from Malacca when we had parted ways, what were the chances of Rich, on his romantic rescue mission to Chloe, now coming face to face with Sally, straight off the bus from the airport?

And what *exactly* did this chance encounter mean?

Was it a Sign?

Was it an Omen, an Augury?

Did the Universe have some Important Deed in store for Rich and Sally?

Was this a Portent of a future Life?

Were the Fates shouting, with as much force as they could muster, 'Forget Chloe!! Sally is the one for you!!'?

Could be (tune in Next Time for more details).

Chapter 16

Don't Chicken Out Now

Back in Nepal, for want of a plan I decide to continue forwards in the general direction of Jim, so the same day as Rich is jetting back to Oz, I board a bus, destination Pokhara, Nepal's second city, nestled on the shores of Phewa Lake, a bumpy 5-hour bus ride away from the capital.

It feels rather odd to now be travelling alone. It was never the plan to set out solo: both from the 'having someone with whom to share day-to-day life' aspect, but also from a security point of view. Two naïve pairs of eyes are always better than one naïve pair of Bunny-in-the-Headlights, scared and startled eyes. But events have transpired such that on my lonesome is now how it is.

The main issue confronting a naïve, fresh-faced traveller is: 'Who to Trust'?

Trusting no one seems the safest course of action, but not trusting, or opening up to, anyone is a lonely way to live, let alone travel; that way might create an impermeable screen between the rest of the world and me, shielding me from the benefits of interactional experience.

So then, how – *exactly* - to establish whether someone is Trustworthy, or not?

Ah. Therein lies the rub.

Societal norms back at home are founded on largely trust-based suppositions; we presume, unless evidence to the contrary shouts otherwise, what we are told to be True and Reliable.

We presume those we interact with don't possess malevolent or nefarious attitudes towards us.

The general default setting: 'The people we meet are not motivated to deceive nor trick us.'

We consider ourselves *Nice, Kind* and *Trustworthy*; we presume everyone else similarly *Nice, Kind* and *Trustworthy*.

Oh, that this were always so.

Alas, experience teaches this to be a Rose-Tinted Specs view of the world, and not the most effective paradigm on which to base your interpersonal interactions. Sure, not *everyone* is out to trick you, amazingly kind, helpful and altruistic people *do* exist, but it is far safer, when asking random strangers for information - for directions, for assistance - for everything imparted to be taken not only with a pinch, but a heaped bucket-worth of salt.

A healthy dose of Scepticism can, quite literally, be a life saver.

Oftentimes, the information imparted is not *entirely* inaccurate - cultural face-saving requirements mean you might receive a sort-of answer, even were the person you've asked to have no idea *whatsoever* of the details you request - or is more or less true, but only if considered from a certain, very specific, perspective; or the information's veracity is such that its truth just happens to be of benefit to the imparter – That bus you're searching for? No, sadly it doesn't run any more, but *this* one does (no mention that it is slower, more expensive, and run by a company paying your informer commission); no, no, the Tourist Booking Office you are seeking has sadly shut down, but the office *over there* is still operating (not actually the *Official* Tourist Office, but a rather shady establishment, also paying your informer commission); and so on, with too great a frequency to be random chance you're simply being accidentally misinformed.

Those guys continuously shouting, 'Hey there, Buddy!'

Guess what? Not the best choice for Who to Trust, either.

Sadly, our inherent decency, our inherent need to be *Nice*, to not Make a Fuss, or Create a Scene, will often, quite deliberately, be used against us.

Our desire to instinctively trust people might just be our Kryptonite.

Deduction?

Don't take *anything* at face value.

Don't take *anything* simply on Trust.

Much better, to be wary; much safer, to be sceptical; much more effective, to ask multiple people before committing to any course of action, and certainly before handing over any money.

In short, don't be a Mug.

Don't be *that* Mug.

And *never* trust anyone who says, 'Trust Me'.

Trust Me.

Right now, a solitary figure far from home, all I can do is make the most of whatever is thrown my way.

And grow an extra pair of eyes in the back of my head.

On arrival in Pokhara, I get the feeling I am chasing shadows. Jim and his gang are nowhere to be seen. I am only a couple of days behind, but it is more than likely they have already passed through town. I search high and low, at dozens of hostels and trekking outfits, for news of a sizeable group of travellers recently arrived but hear nothing concrete from anyone with whom I speak.

Darn.

Jim and his buddies are, most likely, already trekking high up in the majestic mountains; the majority of people coming through Pokhara are destined for the Annapurna Circuit, or Annapurna Base Camp, rather than simply spending days pottering around in boring old town.

Unperturbed, and not fancying a full, week-long trekking experience - Base Camp is a 7-day round trip - I seek out the services of a local guide, to take me up to a mountain village for a few days.

Spot of hiking.

Capture some cool vistas.

Be immersed in Nepali village life.

A simple, authentic experience.

My guide, Harry – he is Krishna, he tells me, so it seems an appropriate moniker - proves quite the character. Our scenic day's hike up to the village ends not at our final destination, but at the local pub – really, a single-storey mud hut on the village outskirts - a decision made not just because it serves what he informs me is the finest millet brew for miles around, but because the pub happens to be run by Harry's girlfriend. Whilst I probably should have made more detailed enquiries into the nature of the accommodation being provided over the next four days, it turns out I am to lodge at Harry's house, with his wife and five kids, only he no longer lives *at home* on account of him having been kicked out by said wife for his all-too-frequent philandering, extra-marital dalliances in the shape of this very pretty bar lady.

I am still trying to get my head around the ramifications of this set-up as the millet brew kicks swiftly in, a discombobulating effect magnified by the raw strength of the brew, and the lofty altitude, around 2,800m, we have now reached.

This millet brew has the effect, if drunk in copious quantities, of being hit over the head by an elephant, or so the saying goes. I fear I may have been struck by the whole herd. I am suddenly struggling to remember which way is up. A long lie down seems the most sensible option.

My head goes into something of a spin.

As I seek equilibrium, Harry enquires what I'd like for supper.

'Er?' I reply, unsure what options are on the table.

'You know, what meat?'

'Er, chicken?', I reply, the first thing that comes into my head.

Chicken: usually a safe, reliable, Go-To bet.

Just like that, Harry is up and gone. In what seems like no time at all he returns, a live chicken held firmly under one arm. The poor chuck appears not best pleased at her hitherto peaceful, run-of-the-mill day having been so rudely interrupted; her startled crowing and clucking suggest she has a fairly good idea what is about to transpire, and that this development is not necessarily going to be making her currently shitty day any better, any time soon.

Poor thing.

I presume we are now about to set off down to his dwelling. But no.

'One more mug', suggests Harry.

One more mug turns into yet one *more* mug.

One for the Road.

Another for the Trail.

And again, this time for Luck.

We consume more of this millet brew concoction than we probably should have, although I really don't think this over-indulgence can be laid squarely at my feet. My pace of consumption has not, thankfully, matched my guide's. Harry has drunk maybe six or seven medium-sized tumblers to my humble three.

He asserts - categorically, emphatically, swear on his Mother's life, and on the good Lord Krishna's - that he doesn't *usually* drink. He is making an exception just for my benefit, for my own Cultural Enrichment.

He does, however, appear a tad reluctant to move on; maybe because he doesn't want to say 'Goodbye' to his girlfriend.

Or maybe, he is a tad reluctant to see his ex-wife again?

Who knows?

It is, thankfully, only a short, bandy-legged stumble down a rough path to my guide's (former) house. His (former) wife emerges from the house, followed by his (their) five kids in single file, in ascending height order, not quite the Von Trapps, but close.

Harry's ex is a homely figure of a woman, late forties, I guess, but almost certainly much younger, with the fuller physique of a shot putter, someone built for comfort, not for speed, someone you sense could pull a plough whilst also carrying a half-ton oxen across her shoulders, whilst simultaneously breast-feeding at both teats, whilst *also* corralling vast herds of goats and flocks of chucks into their pens.

She is for sure a stout and sturdy woman. A hurricane would not blow *her* over.

The welcome line-up greets me warmly, thankfully *sans* singing, beaming smiles all round. Whether these smiles are a result of my presence, or the guide's, is hard to tell. The kids may not have seen their father in quite some time, for all I know.

If my description of Harry's ex-wife seems a trifle unkind, it should be known that those characteristics are, in fact, the *most* sought after from a female spouse in this part of the world (and in many others, too). Describing her thus is therefore to pay her a sincere compliment. Skinny, petite, or effete women are of next to no use in the wife stakes, or so the general understanding here goes - except maybe for providing eye candy in the bedroom, or down at the pub - when you've got five acres of tough ground to plough, large paddies of rice and fields of potatoes to plant, sugar cane to harvest, half a dozen children to look after, and a stubborn ox currently having one of its notoriously foul moods to coax into action.

Sturdy, resilient, tough: that's what gets a man's juices flowing in this part of the world.

If you want eye candy, you'll need to head to the nearest bar and flirt with the woman who runs it. You will then have to pray you don't get caught in your extra-marital rovings.

Or be prepared to pay the price if/ when you do.

Harry's ex-wife glances at her ex-husband.

Then at me.

Then back to him.

In an instant, she clocks that both Harry and I are more than a little worse for wear; that we are both, indeed, somewhat severely soused. In a micro-second, her face morphs from joy and happiness, into a look of resignation, of disgust, of outrage, and, worst of all, of pity.

It is a face seething with undercurrents of deep, thunderous rage.

Yes, I sense an ever-increasing rage is currently bubbling just beneath the surface of her already angry demeanour.

I stand there in silence, suddenly feeling rather awkward and out of place. I am unsure what to say, or how to act. It feels as if I am intruding on a domestic dispute. I wonder whether there is anything I can interject into this scene that might smooth over this Could-Go-Either-Way scenario. I feel sure this is a good time for a joke – there is pretty much no tense moment that cannot be smoothed over by a snippet of quick wit and ribald repartee - but for the life of me nothing suitable pops into my mind.

'Did you hear the one about the mountain guide and his client who turned up as his ex's pissed as newts?'

No, me neither.

Thankfully, Harry, who evidently is no stranger to being cast out into the doghouse, knows exactly how to smooth over the ripples of his misbehaviours. From his jacket pocket, he suddenly pulls out a large wad of cash, the money I have paid for his services. He hands this large wad over to his wife, rather too dramatically and flamboyantly if you asked me, but I'm guessing no one did.

In a flash, the wife's smile returns.

Problem solved.

All is forgiven.

Whether all is forgotten, who knows.

All is suddenly well again with the world (*well*, that is, until Harry's next transgression).

I can breathe again.

And relax.

I am shown to my extremely basic, no mod cons room. No expense spent. It is a small coop around the back of the single-story house, the bed being simply a thin bamboo matt atop a bamboo platform, a foot or so off the ground. Thankfully, several rough, straw matted woollen blankets have been provided for the inevitable bitterly cold nights I am about to endure, although from a distance of several feet I can already sense they've not seen the inside of a washing machine for the better part of ever. The blankets are probably used as bedding or insulation for the lesser livestock I can hear bleating and grunting merrily nearby behind the house.

Ah, you can't beat true agricultural aromas for creating a more realistic rustic setting.

With no time to catch my breath - or suggest checking into the nearest 3-Star Resort - Harry beckons me over to where he is standing, chicken in one hand, machete now in the other.

'Supper', he announces.

Time to dispatch the poor chicken.

Harry hands me the machete.

I look at the blade.

Then at the chicken.

Then back at the blade.

Then back at the chicken.

It appears I have no idea where to start with the poor creature's journey, from Alive-and-Clucking, to No-Longer-Alive-On-the-Table-Ready-to-Eat.

It seems whichever way I try to cut it, I am a hand short.

As far as I can work out, you need one hand to hold the body, another to hold the neck out in an elongated position, and a third to apply the cutting blow.

This is evidently a job for an octopus.

Or, more likely, two people.

Harry senses my quandary. He sits down on the ground beside me, takes the machete back from my loose grasp, placing it between his feet - just so, blade facing upwards - demonstrating the actions of what must next be done.

I sit down next to him. He hands me the blade, which I place between my feet as shown. The less-agitated-than-a-second-ago chicken is then handed over to me, such that I am now holding its head still, and its neck out straight.

'If I am going to do this', I think, 'for the chicken's sake, it had better be quick and painless'.

Thankfully, the machete blade is extremely sharp. The force required to sever the neck is not a great as I had anticipated. Rather startled that I suddenly have a severed chicken's head in one hand, I loosen my grip on the rest of the chicken.

The dead carcass falls to the ground.

No matter. It is a lifeless entity.

Or so I think.

Not so. It runs away.

The corpse of the chicken bloody well ups and runs away.

My mouth drops open.

Harry laughs the drunken laugh of someone who's seen this a thousand times before.

The chuck doesn't get far. There is no escaping the pot.

An hour or so later, the chicken is served. I don't want to criticise the chef, who is obviously working under the most primitive and challenging of conditions inside the thatched hut, but the meat - despite being as Organic, Free Range and Fair Trade as it is possible to get - is, most disappointingly, extremely tough to eat.

Not tough as in, 'I am awash with guilt, Oh, what have I done?' but tough as in, 'chewy', 'rubbery', 'hard to swallow'.

I persevere in any case, to give the poor bird its due consideration, and given I am also ravenously hungry, and there is no supper Plan B.

Chapter 17

Free at Last?

June sees the start of the rainy season in Nepal.

Fortunately, it doesn't rain all day, every day. The mornings are clear and bright, but with each passing hour after sunrise, as the heat of the day rises, in roll the clouds, large banks of menacing cumulonimbus, completely obstructing the views of the majestic mountain ranges that are this region's main draw. This regular, dependable, early-morning-clear-skies-soon-clouding-over routine means, if you want to catch the scenery at its best, you have to venture out into the landscape with the clucking of the cockerels, before dawn's imminent rising.

0-5 Hundred.

What does the 'O' stand for?

Oh, my God, it's early.

As per my instructions, the following morning, in the chill mountain air before the sun has graced the horizon with its presence, Harry rocks up, banging loudly at my door. I am a somewhat reluctant riser. Harry has almost to drag me out from the warmth of my crib, bleary-eyed and swearing like a trooper, for the pre-breakfast stroll I had requested during our pre-hike negotiations.

'You *did* ask me to wake you this early', he points out, rather unsure as to why not I'm leaping about madly with the joys of this pre-dawn perambulation.

I must confess: the teenager in me is not yet fully expunged.

I might have resisted this pre-dawn reveille, but as the horizon gains a white tinge the silhouetted mountain ranges come into full relief. My mood improves dramatically.

Machapuchare (6993m).

The Fish Tail mountain, with its distinctive triangular upper section.

White turns to dark orange, dark orange to butter yellow. The pain of rising at such an ungodly hour dissipates with dawn's early light show. It is moments like these that fuel the soul, that dissolve the hardships and rigours of existence, that are etched eternally into consciousness, deep reserves on which to draw sustenance whenever circumstances, in years to come, might dictate.

I am glad it is just the two of us here to witness this morning's majesty. Harry and I sit there, in silence, no words needed to add to this glorious scene: no narration, no play-by-play account, nothing. There have, alas, been far too many occasions when a glorious sunrise vista has been ruined by fellow early risers chatting incessantly – usually noxious nothings – people constantly moving around in your peripheral vision, or worse still, pointing out - unsolicited – that, pleasing as today's sunrise vista is, 'You *really* should have been here yesterday. Yesterday's sunrise was *so much better*'.

Really?

Why on earth the need to share this information?

For right up until the moment, 'Yesterday's was *better*', was uttered, you had been more than happy with the glorious offering our wondrous Universe had been supplying.

Mention of 'Yesterday's being *better*', suddenly, you're not so sure.

Suddenly, you're feeling rather let down at the spectacle you'd been enjoying just a minute earlier.

Now, you're cursing your bad luck. Why weren't *you* here yesterday, too?

Sometimes, knowledge gained is of no benefit to the newly wizened. Sometimes, knowledge gained instead makes us poorer.

So, why does the imparter feel this overwhelming urge to impart?

Have they come to *gloat*?

Have they come to Lord it over the rest of us poor Here-for-Today's-Sunrise-only unfortunates?

What is *wrong* with some people? Why can't they just keep their thoughts on the merits, or failings, of today's sunrise to themselves?

Indeed, why can't they and the rest of the chattering masses just shut the blazes up, and enjoy the free show without all the natter?

And I swear, if you don't put that stupid selfie stick down, right now, it'll end up where the sun don't shine.

Trust me: the Beauty is in the Nature. The Beauty is not enhanced, *in any way,* by adding your ugly mugshot into the frame.

Ah, Bolshie Teenager, I suddenly sense, pupating perfectly into Grumpy Old Man.

****

Over the next three days, whenever I am not out trampling the mountains marvelling at and photographing the many superb scenic delights the local area has to offer, the local area comes to me: the local area in the shape of the local school teacher, who spends a couple of hours each evening chatting with me, practicing his English; the many neighbours who pop by with the obviously lame excuse that they have dropped in to see my hostess, and look, *what have we here*, some Strange Alien from Another Planet (*me*, by the way)?; and the many neighbourhood kids, who want to inspect the new Circus attraction now in town, for a limited period only (*me*, too, by the way).

I mind not one bit. These interactions are very much part of the all-inclusive Village-Life Experience, although it turns out communicating non-verbally with the kids is significantly more straightforward than attempting proper conversation with someone who tries hard, who means well, but has only a meagre grasp of the English language – but is improving fast - happy as the kids are to simply play, to chase or be chased by this giant ogre of a man, to kick or catch a ball with this giant ogre of a man, or simply to sit and stare at this giant ogre of a man, who towers above even their fully-grown parents like a character from a Roald Dahl novel.

I ask Harry for details about the villagers' lives. He explains that they have only recently been connected to the electricity grid. The addition of light after sunset has enabled a seismic shift in their daily routines. No longer are the villagers rigid slaves to the perpetual cycle of the sun's celestial meanderings. Work can now be conducted long after darkness prevails, continuing inside their basic, poorly illuminated, thatched houses, homes which would otherwise be pokey, and ill-suited to intricate handicraft and other such creative endeavours. Daylight is strictly reserved for external activities, for work in the fields, attending to the sustenance they all need for survival. Now the villagers can attend to their artistic aptitudes, too.

As welcome as the advent of electricity has been - it has certainly eradicated a massive hurdle to the villagers' economic advancement – one consequence thus created arrives in the shape of the dreaded monthly Electricity Bill. Suddenly, from not having to contend with regular monetary outgoings, the farmers must now, each month, barter and trade successfully to earn sufficient funds to meet the Electricity Company's billing requirements. The costs are minute compared our Western World monthly bills, but the concept of Earning and Budgeting is novel, a skill for which not every villager has the mathematical nouse, nor organisational dexterity, to cope. Some villagers complain that with these monthly payments their sovereignty – indeed, their *autonomy* – has, in fact, been surrendered.

There will be quite a few tricky, sticky issues whilst the new system beds in, Harry predicts.

Harry tells me there is also talk of a system of water pipes being installed before long, too. As the farmers must make a tricky – and daily – trudge, down several hundred metres of mountainside to the river, and back up again, in order to collect their water rations, sometimes multiple times each day, this new addition will, one might presume, also improve their situation greatly. Again, not all the villagers are convinced this new service will be a boon; there will then be *another* Monthly Bill payable for this second utility. The issue has divided the community, with some quite vocally opposed to this added development.

Harry is unsure how future developments will transpire. He is certain, however, that the water pipes are coming, whether the villagers want them or not.

Progress, he says - if *progress* is what this can truly be called - cannot be resisted.

Harry says this is a lesson in 'Freedom'; what price true 'Freedom'?

What price Freedom from the yoke of another, in whatever form the loss of this Freedom might take?

Freedom from owing money for a service, no matter how that service might improve the quality of your life or livelihood.

Sure, you are being provided with a Service - tangible or otherwise - part of Transactional Contract, but in return something else, something intangible, but very real - and not just monetary - is taken from you as part of this Transaction.

Only the *truly* free, Harry says, would notice the subtle situational change even the imposition of one monthly bill imposes, for there are real and negative consequences to not maintaining the terms of the Contract.

I ask Harry more on the true nature of *Freedom*.

For whom amongst us, he suggests, is as Free as we might *think* we are?

If we *are* Free, Harry says, we are no Freer than a goat tied to a pole is *Free*.

The goat thinks he is Free; inside his wide arc of movement, the goat can indeed perceive himself Free.

The goat is indeed Free to move hither at will.

But the length of rope decides just how *Free* the goat truly is.

I think I see. I think I understand; that there is an invisible pole to which we all are tied; that we are held subtly, yet inexorably, in our place by an invisible rope.

How long is *our* rope?

Is it of sufficient length to mask the limits of our own Freedom?

Harry appears to have had access to a more than decent standard of education; he appears well-informed, to be a rational thinker, and smart. He speaks English to a more than decent standard. He is well presented (or else I would have been reluctant to procure his services – the booze issue might be a bit of a letdown, though). He is smart enough to have solved the power issue in his own home by rigging up a system of pipes and valves so the methane produced by the anaerobic decomposition of his household's daily latrine visits can be harvested, and utilised to their advantage. The important factor, he tells me, is not to add any paper to the waste, instead sprinkling a thin layer of wood chippings on top of the daily deposits. The methane is piped back into the house, in what I presume is a fail-safe system that could never suffer leaks or blow backs, providing power to light the many small lamps switched on each evening as darkness falls. This is an impressive, Low-Tech-High-Output set up. This setup also means that his (ex) wife does not have the worry of the monthly electricity bill afflicting her neighbours.

I wonder where Harry learnt the details of rigging up such a system. I wonder, aloud, whether he could teach his neighbours to do the same, but he says that as he is *persona non grata* up here in the village, except when *en passant* with a client, he is unable to help any of them out. I get the feeling they are all – both Harry and the villagers - losers because of that.

All of Harry's good works over the course of the first two days, at making amends for our less than perfect entrance, count for nothing when, on Day Three, he shows up for supper pie-eyed once again. So much for *not usually* drinking (Krishnas are supposed to be not only vegetarian, but also teetotal. Sex is only permitted for the purposes of procreation within a marriage. I feel Harry might need to swot up on these rules again, or possibly choose a different religion to follow).

Harry has been on the millet brew again, with his girlfriend.

Many, many glasses. He might have fallen face first into the vat this time.

His legs appear to have turned to rubber. Or the earth's gravitational pull is suffering wild fluctuations inside the sphere of his close physical proximity (and the sphere of his close physical proximity, alone).

There is then, between Harry and his ex, an almighty row. Almighty rows between two once amorous and caring people appear, from the physical mannerisms and forceful tones of speech employed, to be identical the world over.

Sforzando voices.

Increasing levels of indignation.

Doors being slammed. Indeed, the same door being slammed, over, and over, and over.

I wonder whether removing all doors from all houses would reduce divorce levels, or instead make things worse.

Poor doors – poor, innocent, minding their own business doors – having to endure the world's anger being taken out on them.

Harry is sent packing, off to the doghouse to lick his wounds, or possibly back to the pub, where one presumes his girlfriend will do the licking for him.

Chapter 18

That Man Jim

All too soon, the time arrives to head back down the mountain to Pokhara. During our descent along narrow, windy paths, with the occasional precipitous, vertiginous drop off to one side, we pass through many-acre fields of 12-foot high marijuana plants, swaying rhythmically in the light breeze. For those who prefer to indulge in such herbal medicines, this sight might invoke a truly spiritual moment, an 'I've-died-and-Gone-to-Heaven' experience.

To them, this might quite possibly be the physical manifestation of Nirvana on earth.

I make a throw away comment to Harry as to how much these fields of prime bud would fetch on the open market in London. I tell him how much people in the UK pay for a single ounce of the stuff. I fail to spot his eyes bulge at the news, for when we are back in town at our final destination, saying our goodbyes, it comes as a total bolt from the blue when he stops my chatting, and enquires about implementing the importation of this particular herbal crop.

I laugh.

No, Harry, it seems, is deadly serious.

I point out to him that the importation of even the tiniest amount of marijuana across UK borders is ever so slightly illegal.

Football fields' worth of the stuff, *very much so* illegal, I'm guessing.

Setting up in business doesn't even bear thinking about, not even for the briefest of moments.

To analyse the situation, to run the numbers, to evaluate the potential profit, that way lies way too much temptation for some people to ignore.

So, 'No dice here, *amigo.*'

Whilst in the full throws of this discussion, another Nepali man passes close by. He enters into conversation with Harry. The conversation appears to get rather heated. The man then leaves, waving his arms at my guide in a display of frustration, or annoyance, or who knows what, it's hard to tell.

I ask Harry what they were discussing so animatedly. He says the other man had enquired how much Harry had charged to guide me. The figure Harry stated was met with some horror.

According to this Nepali, Harry's had significantly undercharged me. Harry should, according to the Nepali man, have over-hyped the risk posed by the few Maoist rebels still operating somewhere up in the mountains, and whose antics have resulted in the loss of hundreds of innocent people's lives.

More risk = greater price.

Harry had dismissed this man's suggestion. Harry says that such lies and deceit are not the ingredients of successful, long-term tourism. I am relieved to learn that he is a highly moral and ethical man in this regard. I am pleased, and I must say more than a little surprised, that this is a consideration of his. In future years, I will encounter far too many shady tricksters more than happy to screw you and every other tourist over for a few pounds – or dollars or *whatevers* - with absolutely zero compunction to how this might then affect events even a day ahead. The Future be well and truly damned (there are some countries where stability is such an elusive trait that even if the tourists are here today, it's a very good chance they won't be in a month or two's time. The underlying motto? Milk the Tourists Now, for Tomorrow is Another, not Necessarily Profitable, Day).

Despite Harry's sound moral compass in this regard, it seems he has no qualms about disregarding the UK Rule of Law or overlooking the moral and ethical considerations of running a large-scale, drug importation business.

Drugs are drugs, I guess; one man's Legal High is another's Illicit Vice.

The history of drug laws around the world shows how views can change drastically over time, in either direction. Christmas hampers, purchased from well-known Central London Victualling Merchants, sent by loved ones to soldiers on the front line in the 1914-1918 War, often included gelatine lamels prepared with concoctions of both cocaine and morphine, to aid with hunger suppression, and prolonging endurance during difficult and stressful times. Whilst the general population had no qualms about the use of opiates in the course of their daily lives, those in charge of military efficacy became concerned about the effects this drug use might have on their troops. So began a campaign to clampdown on the widespread 'excesses' of these soldiers.

Attitudes to marijuana use in the US in the early 1900s shifted primarily due to the advent of technology for the manufacture of wood pulp into paper, rather than using hemp as the main ingredient, as had been the case for many decades up to this point. Hemp paper is of a much higher quality than the wood pulp version, lasting much longer than the quickly yellowing pages created from wood pulp. Certain high-profile US industrialists, concerned that this hemp product – a different, THC-free strain than is used as a narcotic – was not only affecting their wood pulp business, but was also competing too successfully against their petrochemical businesses, hemp oil being considered in many instances a better product than oil derived from these fossil fuels. Hemp was also a major contributing ingredient in the manufacture of sails, of rope, and of twine. Hemp was therefore the evil competitor these Industrialists considered must be expunged.

Enter these Industrialists, and their Cunning-Yet-Evil Plan. Petrochemical companies were a good source of newspaper advertising revenue, so the editors of these papers decided to jazz up some tales about this evil *marihuana* being responsible for a number of evil crimes being committed by evil minority immigrants (Mexicans were known to be keen partakers of this evil herbal smoke). Public opinion was swayed to endorse legislation against this evil *marihuana*, even though most of the population had no idea that *marihuana* and hemp were one in the same. 'Ban *marihuana*'; most had no idea this also meant 'ban hemp', the important crop that had been grown in the US for over 50 years. Secrecy and lies followed within the legislative process, leading to the total banning of all hemp products in 1937, a ban that favoured a number of US Industrialists greatly in the forthcoming years, hemp products no longer being in direct competition with their inferior products.

On such small details can public opinion and sentiment be swayed.

How easily the population can be influenced on matters of societally approved norms.

Any of this sound familiar?

I ignore Harry's repeated attempts to reopen the Export/ Import discussions.

He is, however, most persistent.

I finally tell him a firm, 'Goodbye' – it is a bizarre note on which to part - and start to make my way along the lake shorefront back to my lodgings, where I deposited the bulk of my gear prior to heading up the hill.

I've only walked a short distance when I espy up ahead of me a distinctly familiar form, more facially hirsute than usual, and distinctly more dishevelled than his normally well-dappered state of attire.

It is the unmistakeable form of That Man Jim.

I approach from his blind spot, tapping him on the shoulder.

'Think you need a shave, young man', I suggest.

Jim turns in total shock, a look of abject terror etched on to his face. Whilst I obviously have a notion he is roaming somewhere hereabouts, Jim will have had zero inkling I am anywhere even remotely nearby.

The shock for him is, therefore, very real.

To those who have lived entirely in an Internet Connected World, you can only guess as how incredibly unlikely this sort of chance encounter is (*was*).

This meeting with Jim is, to put it bluntly, a Mind Fuck.

At this juncture, I've been away from home for approaching nine months. *Nine months* in your twenties operates on the same schedule as dog or cat months - the equivalent of a decade to those past 50.

Nine months is an eternity for an era where our social group would gather multiple times each week, without fail.

Suddenly, here we both are.

Here, in a Far-Away Land.

At a total loss what to do next, we stand there shaking and mumbling like a pair of jabbering idiots.

We need to pull ourselves together, and fast.

When doubt strikes, the Go-To answer is *Beer*.

The Finest Ales Known to Humanity.

Or, failing that, bucket-loads of watery Nepalese Tuborg lager.

But they do the trick.

****

A few days later, we – Jim, myself and a baker's dozen of stragglers from the group of hikers he'd met on the Annapurna Base Camp trek - have all relocated to the Hotel at the End of the Universe, a rustic affair perched high on a vantage point in Nagarkot, an hour or so outside Kathmandu. The ride up from Pokhara passed by in a flash, buoyed on by fine conversations, and booming dance music from the boys at the back of the bus.

Here, at the End of the Universe, we are afforded one of the most stupendously majestic Himalayan views, right there in front, just there, everywhere, to the left and to the right, as far as your eyes can see in either direction. The vast mountain ranges are seemingly close enough to reach out and touch. For sure, it is a view that transfixes, drawing you in, further and further in, until hypnotised, losing all sense of time and situational awareness.

Currently, I am reading a book. I am also wondering how my ankle has become so bloodied, for I have just noticed a not insignificant trace of claret dripping down from my heel. The trail of blood continues several feet along the floor behind me.

What the heck?

I follow the trail, noticing a leach crawling slowly away from the scene of the crime. It is a guilty crawl, I surmise. The leech looks bloated - although I must admit I am no Leech expert - as if it has recently suckled from an unsuspecting victim, *aka* me.

I am about to take some sort of retributional action on the bugger when the guy who has been my room-mate for the past couple of nights comes rushing onto the decking area at quite a lick, out of breath, asking for - no, *demanding* - the room key.

'Why the rush?' I ask, but my room-mate glances at me without responding, grabbing the key from my hand without so much as a 'Thanks', disappearing off in the direction of the room at breakneck speed.

Those on the decking who also witnessed this give each other the 'Look', nodding sagely.

One of those '1000-Yard Dash' moments, all are sure.

Poor lad.

On those occasions where I have been perforce required to share a room, I think I offer that person quite the optimal roommate experience.

Oh, I might take a little too long in the bathroom.

I can be a tad messy.

I am certainly not perfect in that or several other regards.

But what I do offer potential roommates as compensation for these deficiencies is a very particular set of skills.

Skills that are not of my own making, but skills you, as my roommate, will appreciate, nevertheless.

For I am a prime, high grade, almost-100%-guaranteed-to-be-the-only-one-bitten, Mosquito Magnet. If there is a mosquito within a 100-yard radius, or *anywhere* inside the room, it will leave you, my lucky roommate, totally alone. The mosquito will, instead, make a beeline (mosquito-line?) for tasty old me. I will awake with one hundred bites before you get even the one.

Over the years, my curiosity in ascertaining just how potent my mosquito attracting skills are has lead me to consider proposing a Mosquito Bite World Cup, a paired-up, knock-out contest to see who really does possess the World's most potent Mosquito Attracting Skills.

I am a semi-finalist, for sure.

About an hour after handing the key over in such a hurry, I make my way back to the room to check in with my roommate/ drop off some stuff/ dab my still bleeding heal with some antiseptic cream. I come around the corner of the accommodation block, and there, directly outside our room, stands my roommate.

The man has bucket of soapy water by his side. He has a mop firmly placed in both hands, a mop he is currently swishing over the ground outside our shared room, from side, to side, to side. The man is sporting a completely different clothing ensemble to the one he was wearing just an hour or so earlier. There is quite the smell of disinfectant in the air. A sizeable patch of ground in front of our room door appears to have been given the more-than-once-over mop treatment.

I am, once again, about to speak, about to utter the immortal, 'So, what happened here, then?' line, when my roommate's gaze catches mine.

His look stops me dead in my mental tracks.

Immediately, I decide to park that question.

No, now is not the time for *that question*.

Indeed, *never*, his looks suggests, will there *ever* be a right time for the 'So, *what* happened here?' question.

His is a bathetic look that speaks volumes. It is a hollow-eyed look of utter, thorough dejection; a look that says, 'Seriously, mate, do not even for one iota of a millisecond consider raising the question of what has previously occurred here in this spot, specifically events within the last 1-hour time window.'

'Not now. Not later. Not ever.'

'Of this thing, we will never talk, nor refer to, nor allude to, even in the feintest of ways.'

'Capiche?'

I leave the poor lad to his doleful mopping, backtracking to the restaurant to resume my reading.

Of course, I *capiched*.

'Back so soon?' one of the decking gang remarks.

I re-take my spot on the cushion on which I had previously been resting, staring once more deeply into the pages of my novel.

Not a word of those terrible occurrences is spoken.

The unfortunate lad's nemesis?

Giardia. Giardiasis.

Poor chap.

That no one was there to witness his ignominy at that most unspeakable of moments is at least one tiny, comforting mercy.

PART THREE

Chapter 19

The Shitty Shits

The Second Law of Thermodynamics states, at its core, that Disorder is the End State for any closed system. Our own finite Universe, therefore, prefers Chaos over Order: Maximised Chaos, even, to amplify its potential towards Disruption.

It is a fallacy that buttered bread when dropped will *always* land buttered side down. This fails to consider this need for Maximised Chaos: if your floor is Yellow, and your butter also Yellow, the dropped bread will almost certainly land buttered side up.

A topping of Yellow, against a backdrop of Yellow, does not add significantly to the Chaos.

The vitally important element to be factored into the Probability Equation is the contrast between the colour of the spread and the colour of your flooring (the Price of the Flooring *psm*, and its Relative Absorbency Value, are also variables inside the PE).

Inexpensive Red Flooring + Sticky Red Jam: the bread will, again, more than likely land spread side up, for there is little to no Chaos from Red on Red action (nor from ruining a low-grade flooring option).

Expensive White Carpet + Sticky Red Jam: an almost 100% chance of the bread now landing jam side down.

Red/ White contrast + Prized Carpet Forever Stained = Chaos.

Maximised Chaos were the carpet to have been *freshly laid*.

So, according to this Law of Chaos, were I ever to catch a debilitating illness such as *Giardiasis,* then I was going to do so at such a time when this setback would have the potential for causing Maximum Disruption, for maximum potential blowback from the effects of the affliction.

I once again apologise for the forthcoming, but, well, I have no pictures to illustrate, nor diagrams to draw. I have but words at my disposal. My artist's palate is coated merely with words, words that need to evoke in you as true a picture of this sad, sorry, terribly awful event as my amateur scribbling skills permit. It would be remiss of me to gloss over this tragic episode and, much as I wish it hadn't, pretend these sullied events never transpired.

Those of a scatologically intolerant nature might probably wish to skip ahead a page, or two.

Don't say you weren't warned.

There are many symptoms to *Giardiasis*.

The two I am currently experiencing are Severe Bloating.

Severe Bloating, accompanied by Excess Gas.

Excessive, continuously building gas that perforce must be expelled; out of which orifice this expulsion occurs is of zero importance to this Excess Gas.

So, yes, the two current symptoms are Severe Bloating, and Excess Gas. And a distinct Looseness in the Bowel Arena.

The *three* current symptoms are: Severe Bloating, Excess Gas, and a distinct Looseness in the Bowel Arena. And a general sense of Lethargy.

The *four* current symptoms are...

With some relief from the pain this stomach distention is creating, wind passes from my Bowel Arena Gateway.

The waft hits my nasal passages. Instantly, I am transported atop a gently smouldering volcano. I am returned to the rim of the crater, for what has emerged from my BAG is the foulest, eggiest, most sulphurous smelling nether eructation I have ever had the misfortune to emit. Were I still the spotty prepubescent youth of my teenage years, surrounded by my similarly greasy-haired, spotty peers, this fart would surely have won me access into the Pantheon of Legend, such is its lethal potency. My schoolboy buddies would doubtless have been in absolute awe at my unparalleled aptitude for producing noxious effluent of such a hideous nature (the things that impress young boys, eh?).

A second nether eructation emerges, unbidden.

Holy cow. These follow-up wafts are even more ungodly.

Giardiasis be damned; something has crawled inside my guts and passed away, many weeks ago, its sad, sorry corpse now entering a highly developed state of decomposition.

As I mull over the potential significance of this sudden development, without warning, without any guttural advance notice, an oral eructation suddenly emerges into the outside world.

Urrrrrrrrrrrrrrppppppppppppppppp!!

A peculiar taste residue now resides inside my mouth.

I do that thing we all do when trying to establish the nature of a particular taste. I pucker my mouth and tongue a few times.

Oh, how I wish I had not.

For the residue confirms my worst fears, fears of having just performed the foulest, eggiest, most sulphurous tasting oral eructation, ever. It is a new high (*low*?) score in the land of foul-smelling burps.

I am now more than somewhat concerned at this new turn of events.

None of this can be a Good Thing.

None of these symptoms are indicative, even to a non-medically trained person such as me, of being someone currently in the rudest of health.

No, actually, I *am* in rude health. Just health that is *rude* to those around me.

An urgent race into the bathroom suddenly appears on my To Do list. The smells and sounds created are both disconcertedly wondrous, and deeply concerning. The effluent appearing has the consistency and colour of, well, picture a radiator being emptied for the first time in more than 50 years, into a vat of festering, rancid rice pudding.

Sorry. You *were* warned.

The timing of this affliction is indeed unsurprising, for I am booked this evening onto a bus, destination Bombay.

It is a 24-hour journey.

See.

Chaos. Maximised Chaos.

I currently cannot begin to imagine how I am going to endure a 24-hour bus trip, riddled as I am with microscopic parasites, and stools looser than a 16th Century Coaching inn. My schedule has no laxity with which to work in a delay until there has been noticeable improvement in my condition, whenever that, in any case, might be.

I seek out the services of the nearest Medical Practitioner, who happens to be a Homeopathic doctor. I describe in full technicolour detail all my symptoms, although I am by now in no doubt whatsoever as to the name and nature of my ailment. The lady practitioner prescribes me a course of Homeopathic pills, pills which as we all (should) know have not been shown to have any rigorous, scientifically evaluated efficacy, so will almost certainly have no positive effect on me whatsoever. I was really hoping to be proscribed something to block me up good and tight.

Tighter, if possible, than a Yorkshireman's wallet.

Cement, maybe. Or failing that a large corked bung.

Back in my lodgings, I am joyed to discover several Imodium tablets lurking loosely at the bottom of my washbag.

I take as many as I can find. Three, four, what the hell, chuck'em all down.

More than the recommended dose. I do not care for their recommended doses.

Imodium is, as I found out earlier this trip, a potent bowel blocker for those in need of such services. On the eastern flank of Java, prior to a pre-dawn amble up Mt Bromo for the stupendous sunrise enjoyed from its crater summit, I pre-emptively took just the one tiny, red-and-green tablet, having detected a few worrying rumblings, you know, Down There. Better to be blocked up than to experience a bowel-related emergency whilst crossing a rugged, jagged lava plain at 4am in the pitch black, or so my thinking went. Eight whole days later, having traversed the entirety of Java, and thence up to Singapore, I was still blocked tighter than a nun's gee, and deeply concerned I had pooped my very last poop (the relief at the First Movement of my New Underground Symphony was tantamount).

This might all be over-share – please, no, I sure hope I am not turning into *that type* of American - but, well, you've come this far with me; I'm hoping you and I have reached a suitable level of familiarity.

There are no boundaries between friends, are there not?

I take all the Imodium tablets I can find. I am not certain this dose will be nearly enough - the tablets are up against quite the adversary after all - but, thankfully, the desired effect soon occurs.

At least, my To Do list no longer contains continuous urges to race to the loo every thirty seconds.

Trepidatiously, I take my seat on the night bus. As we set off on our 24-hour quest for the coast, I am extremely nervous. If things go wrong, they can go wrong fast, and in the most embarrassing of manners. The gaseous build up in my guts continues, most painfully so, whilst the bus bumps and grinds its way to Bombay. The poor Indian lad sitting beside me experiences the worst of the aromas. I am afforded frequent, sideways glances, with a look of uncertain puzzlement, and utter disdain. The man seems continuously on the verge of saying something, his mouth opening to speak, but never quite finding the right words with which to initiate the conversation. Inwardly, I am sorry for the distress I may be causing to others, but in some way this is payback, payback for the six previous weeks spent sitting in close proximity to a plethora of malodorous and excessively agriculturally pungent people and their paraphernalia.

I try to drift off. I try to retreat inside my head, to remove myself from this discomfort, from the knowledge I have many more hours of this uncertainty to endure before we reach the far-away ocean.

No. I am not at all a Well Man.

Chapter 20

Enough, Already!

It is 800km, along a poorly maintained A-road, to Bombay. Single carriageway in each direction; no central barrier. Near constant traffic of all sizes and speeds heading in both directions; ox drawn carts sharing the road with heavy freight traffic and buses. A recipe for disaster if ever there was one.

Daylight has returned. It would appear I have survived the night.

We are currently overtaking an oil tanker, its length almost identical to that of our bus. We inch past the tanker, slowly, our relative speeds giving us a maybe 5kph advantage. We are by necessity on the incorrect side of the road, although, in India, the custom to drive on the left, as instilled by the British over 200+ years of Empire, is treated by many merely as a *suggestion*, rather than the Legally Mandated obligation it actually is.

Indians, or so I have learnt, are want to treat pretty much all Rules and Regulations with disdain, believing them a cudgel the Higher Classes employ to beat them down, to fix them firmly in their places; Rules are a hindrance to these people's manifest latent creative talents, and to the enterprising entrepreneurial spirit that provide their means of rising out from the dirt and squalor, and to thence realising their full potentials.

To comply with the Rules is to always remain poor, to never Get Ahead; to do things by the Book, to languish in your torrid position of lowly status, in Perpetuity.

You'll never rise (*up/ out*), you'll never find your *niche* – nor your *edge* - if you pay heed to those pesky things called *Rules*.

We are still inching, ever so slowly inching, along the length of the oil tanker, half-way to being able to move back onto the correct side of the carriageway.

Now, we are no longer inching along the length of the oil tanker, our relative speeds all of a sudden corresponding.

Now, the oil tanker is, in fact, inching forwards.

Now, the oil tanker is, in fact, level with the front of our bus.

Now, the bus is speeding up.

Now, the oil tanker is *also* speeding up.

Now, the bus is accelerating some more.

Now, the oil tanker is *also* accelerating some more.

Now, it would appear, we are having a crazy race with an oil tanker, whilst on the incorrect side of the road.

Now, there is much shouting and arm waving coming from the driver and his co-pilot conductor.

Now, they are banging on the windows and door of the bus on the tanker's passing side.

Now, we are all travelling at a reckless, suicidally breakneck speed, horns blaring constantly.

HONK, HONK, HONK!!

BEEP, BEEP, BEEP!!

I stare out the window. I am wondering whether these two maniacs, with their puerile racing, are going to get us all killed. Colliding with an oil tanker is rarely an event that ends with a positive outcome. Unless the bystanders happen to be planning a barbecue.

Whilst this side-by-side race has been unfolding, the other road users have, thankfully, so far managed to duck their vehicles out of the way; they have all avoided becoming entangled in this childish dispute.

If they want to successfully navigate from A to B, Indians drivers have learnt to expect the very unexpected.

The ones still alive, that is.

By now, our forward momentum has been somehow sufficient for us have gained a full bus-length over the tanker. Our driver turns in hard to the left, back onto the correct carriageway, dead ahead of the tanker. Rather than deciding to continue onwards, brushing this incident off as a silly episode of imbecilic tomfoolery, our driver then suddenly slams on the brakes.

What the f...?

The oil tanker, thankfully, brakes too, the rig coming to a halt but a few metres shy of the side of the bus.

This is obviously a *Very* Good Thing.

Our driver gets down from his seat, and rushes around the front of the bus.

The oil tanker driver gets down from his cab, too.

I stare out of the window at this farcical scene.

The two men square up to each other. Heated words are exchanged. Much shouting and arm waving ensues.

Other bus passengers alight, presumably to see what all the fuss is about, or maybe to place bets on the outcome of the scrap that is sure to follow.

The shouting is now very loud. A fist fight is an imminent possibility.

The bus driver cocks his arm as if to administer the first blow. As he makes to drive his fist forwards two of the passengers dive in, holding the driver back. Now the conductor is saying something to him, right up in his face, a seemingly frantic exchange but with I hope the intent of calming the driver back down to a more even, passenger-friendly, keel.

Yes, we would all prefer a calm driver in charge of our bus, rather than one, you know, intent on homicidal retributional rage.

Please, please, please, everyone, calm the fuck down so we can all reach out destination in one still-alive piece.

The tanker driver skulks back to his cab.

The bus driver, the conductor and the passengers all file back inside the bus, as if nothing untoward has just occurred. The doors close behind the last of them. Everyone settles back down.

Is this the end of the show?

I am awaiting to see which of us will set off first, for, if it is the tanker, I fear we won't have seen the end of this daft, petty dispute.

Our driver turns to face us all. He utters something in Hindi, something I obviously do not understand. He has a smile on his face, though, which is, at least, reassuring.

We set off, first. Blessedly, we do not encounter the tanker again.

The bus reaches Bombay. It is raining, and raining hard. The streets are awash, flooded extensively. Cars continue to drive slowly through, more concerned with avoiding the unseen potholes than the wake they might be creating. Cyclists pedal furiously, but not always with the best of outcomes, the tops of their wheels only barely peaking above the water level. To be still rolling forwards when you're almost virtually underwater requires some skill, I imagine.

Monsoon has arrived.

Hallelujah!!

Despite the hardships and mayhem these rains create, this is a happy time in this region, and in the country as a whole, for not only do the rains bring much-prayed-for respite from the last few months' absurd incessant heat, but they are also considered the Bringer of Life. With these deluges, the annual Cleansing and Renewal process has completed yet another circuit in its (hopefully) never-ending Cycle of Life.

Indian cinema is less prurient than its Hollywood counterpart. It shuns nudity; there are no sex scenes. Instead, the happy couple - whose romance is secured when the Hero, after multiple near terminal setbacks, finally overcomes his Nemesis - will be shown walking together, hand-in-hand, whilst the two become soaked under a deluge of rain. This deluge is the Indian equivalent of a sex-scene. The rains symbolise fertility. The rains symbolise the creation of new life. The two actors, their clothes now soaked to the skin, become one as their love is consummated through the potent power of these rains.

It is always tricky to view a (typically) washed-out Bank Holiday weekend in the Lake District in a similar vein, as a romantically fertile and fecund occasion. There is rarely anything fertile, nor romantic, about couples bickering furiously over whose clearly terrible decision it was to come camping in England over a Bank Holiday weekend.

I retrieve my rucksack from the storage compartment at the back of the bus. As I peer inside, I notice a not-inconsiderable volume of water has permeated into the baggage hold. My large rucksack has, it seems, been lying in a several centimetres-deep puddle of water, for who knows how long, soaking the filthy monsoon waters up well and good.

Ideal this, most certainly, is not. The bottom portion of my clothes are quite moist, much moister than is customarily optimal, I later find out. That the rain waters now soaking my clothes contain all manner of unknowable pathogens merely adds to the sense of utter yuckiness. I discover, too, that the photographic films taken at the temple in Udaipur are completely ruined. All that remains is a soggy mess of unusable tape.

These rains won't be bringing any life to the soon-to-be lost forever mural in far away Udaipur.

I do not know what I will tell the shopkeeper when he asks. I fear I have rather let the side down. There is nothing that can be done to make amends for *this* disaster.

Despite these setbacks, and keen to focus on the positives, I have now arrived at Bombay.

I have managed to survive yet another uniquely Indian adventure.

Surely, *finally*, everything will be plain sailing from here on in.

Chapter 21

The Last Hoorah

Bombay, as was in '93, since renamed Mumbai, is a large, metropolitan city of (then) 13million citizens, nestled on the Arabian sea. My arrival is fewer than six months since the city was rocked by a series of violent bomb blasts in its Financial Centre, blasts that killed 257 and wounded 1,400. Powerful underworld figures, previously revered as romantic, idealised characters, were later found to be behind this atrocity, the city's first brush with Terrorism. Tragically, this attack would not be the city's last.

The Rains do not put a dampener on my own spirits. In spite of the combined efforts of an angry and unforgiving Nature, drunken and homicidal bus drivers, runaway mountain boulders, and a gutful of microscopic parasites trying to thwart my every move, I have successfully reached my final Indian destination within the allotted time frame, to now catch my flight to Cairo the following evening (well, 2am the day after tomorrow, to be precise). I feel a gentle pat on back to acknowledge this fine achievement might be in order. All that remains is one whole day to peruse the city sights - and say my final Farewells to this vast land - before my next – Egyptian - adventure begins.

Thankfully, the following morning, my guts have regained a more reliable sense of equilibrium (*caveat*: for India). I am free to roam without the need to remain within thirty seconds of the nearest toilet facility. Refreshed, to a degree, I leave my accommodation for a stroll through town towards a special lunch destination I have in mind. I am once again wearing my cleanest and smartest; my Sunday Best. Hopefully, this time my plan will meet with some success.

I step out from the calm oasis of my hostel into the throbbing streets of Bombay. The cacophony of city life immediately hits me like a clunking fist to the head. Pollution in Bombay is not quite on the same lung-destroying level as that of Delhi, but pollution can take many forms, not just the toxic fumes that spew forth from the tens of thousands of rickety old vehicles clogging the city's streets. The persistent clamour of car horns, and motorbike horns, and bus horns, and lorry horns all being sounded incessantly pierces your frontal lobes like a sharp knife through soft margarine. There can be a thousand and one things wrong with a car in India, yet the vehicle will remain obdurately on the road. But the second the horn breaks your vehicle is no longer considered road-worthy; you must head straight to the nearest mechanic for urgent, vital repair.

The horn is not used simply as an expression of anger, or as a severe warning to other road users they are about to transgress or cause a collision.

The horn is sounded every few seconds to advise other road users, 'I am Here. Be Aware of My Presence'.

Over, and over, and over.

'I am next to you!'

Hoot! Hoot! Hoot!

'I am behind you!'

Toot! Toot! Toot!

'I am overtaking you!'

Hoot! Hoot! Hoot!

Not that the traffic flows freely in Bombay much of the time in any case, given the overwhelming volume of traffic. But rather than stationary drivers resting their fingers from their horn pressing activity, as the cars nudge forward, slowly, so slowly, the blare of the horn now takes on a different cry.

Toot! Toot! Toot!

'Move forward more quickly', they seem to be saying, despite their protestations having exactly zero effect on the pace of their progress.

Toot! Toot! Toot!

'Turn green more quickly you annoyingly red traffic light!'

Drivers foolishly believe the traffic lights can hear and understand their frustration, their annoyance, and will turn green more rapidly the louder they all hoot.

Hoot! Hoot! Hoot!

Like an addiction, an obsession, the drivers cannot restrain themselves.

As hardwired as breathing.

Toot! Toot! Toot!

The only place it will drive you is nuts.

The pavement outside my hostel is heaving, lined with street vendors and the dangerous traffic on one side, and tightly packed shops, workshops and warehouses on the other, an endless stream of pedestrians endeavouring to squeeze past one another on the narrow strip of sanctuary between these two hazards, like thousands of ants all on their way to who knows where. No one affords anyone any consideration. No one stands back to allow others to pass more easily, to allow the flow of pedestrian traffic any sense of smooth progress. It is Dog Eat Dog in the land of the foot traveller. Only the boldest and the bravest will survive this mêlée.

I focus my gaze straight ahead of me, preparing to run the gauntlet.

'Hey, you! You want girls?' a male voice off to my left enquires. 'Pretty girls. Young girls. Cheap cheap'.

Gee, thanks for asking, but that'll be a resounding *No* from me.

The temptation I am endeavouring to resist is not the services on offer – obviously - but the urge to interact with the voice, or at the very least to locate the man offering such vile services, to see whence this offer originates. But to make eye contact with the seedy salesman is a mistake, for your curiosity in putting a face to the voice would be misconstrued as possessing an interest in the services he has on offer. You would then, most likely, be followed down the road, pestered incessantly, harangued, over and over, the man sticking to you like a piece of sticky tape that won't easily be detached.

'Girls, girls, girls!'

The cry haunts me.

I walk on.

'Guns! Guns! Guns!', another male voice proclaims. 'Good guns. Many guns. Kalashnikovs. Cheap! Cheap!'

Thanks again for offering, old chap, but not really looking for a gun right now, or anytime. Thanks anyway.

Again, I resist the temptation to put face to voice.

'Passports. Passports. Hey you, you want a passport?' comes the next cry.

Instinctively, I pat the pocket containing my passport, relieved to feel its imprint.

Nope, don't need another passport, either, thanks.

'Hash! Hash!' comes the cries from the next salesman. 'Good hashish'.

Nope. Don't need any of *that*.

Things to do. Places to go. Stuff to see.

I am striding onwards, full of purpose, successfully dodging the onslaught of sales pitches being thrown my way. I have almost reached the end of the street when I detect in my peripheral vision an object being thrust towards my head. Instinctively, my left arm rises to parry this projectile, deflecting the trajectory of what on closer inspection turns out to be a 1m-long metal pole, with a somewhat rudimentary version of cotton wool affixed over its nub end. It seems the owner of the pole has the intention of cleaning the wax out of my ear, for an undisclosed and clearly unagreed sum of money, despite the diameter of the pole, even before the cotton wool bud was included, being somewhat wider than the orifice it is intended to enter.

'Dear God man, for Fuck's sake, what on *earth* are you thinking?' I cry out in frustration, as I continue onwards, not allowing my pace to be slowed by this leftfield attack.

Really, people here make a living cleaning the wax out of random strangers' ears? Urgh!!

This street appears to be a veritable One-Stop Shop. For the right person, this might be the best shopping arcade in the whole damn world. None of the boring, homogenous parades of national chains, coffee shops, old-school barbers and charity shops you find in almost every high street across the length and breadth of the UK.

This is where it is All At.

This is *the* Place.

But I am on my way to lunch. I hurry forth.

****

The Taj Mahal Intercontinental Hotel sits on the waterfront overlooking Bombay harbour, right across from the iconic Gateway of India, a triple arched monument symbolising both the harmony between Hindus and Muslims in India, and the final spot from which the British left the continent at the end of Empire (sadly, also a target for terrorist bomb blasts in 2003). The Taj Mahal is a palatial hotel, five stars - six, possibly - as much an iconic part of Bombay as the Gateway of India just across the road. The beauty and opulence of its décor, along with the meticulousness and quality of its service, makes the Taj Mahal one of the must-see destinations of the city. Sadly, in 2008 there will be others who will decide that the Taj Mahal should be a prime fixture of their own city-wide tour, but, alas, with nefarious, non-sightseeing motives, the hotel becoming the backdrop for a deadly siege lasting several days, resulting in the deaths of scores of people, both Indians and foreigners.

This atrocity is fifteen years from coming to pass as I stride confidently, but trepidatiously, up to the hotel's front entrance. I am hoping to be permitted entry to the hotel's hallowed turf, that

I have de-scruffed sufficiently to pass muster amongst its hallowed corridors and high-quality eateries.

I am greeted by a smartly dressed, turbaned brute of a door man, the very epitome of the powerful Sikh warrior, who looks down at me from his great height as I reach the doorway he governs. This feeling of sizing up short next to someone is rare; yet this man towers over me in every way.

I enquire about the Hotel's restaurants, and whether they accept American Express cards as a form of payment. I am hoping the mention of this card will boost my credentials, bestowing me with sufficient kudos to be granted entrance, making up for my lack of Armani suit and Italian patent leather brogues that seem to be uniform for all the other (male) guests.

The doorman could crush me with a single one-handed swat such are his over-sized dimensions.

I brace for disappointment.

Suddenly, I am transported back to the Lake Palace Hotel in Udaipur, and the withering rejection I had received there.

Instead, the doorman smiles, holding open the glass door, beckoning me follow him inside.

I am taken to the *Maître d'*, who then shows me into the restaurant, a vast room with high ceilings adorned with an extensive array of lighting, providing brightness to what outside is an otherwise rather dull, grey day. This is the daytime restaurant / tearoom, packed with diners, and those who have merely popped in for a cup of their favourite brew and a natter. The *Maître d'* escorts me to a table in one of the room's less well-lit corners. It is not nearly as bright here as in the rest of the room. I scour the tables, further inside, spotting a vacancy right in the centre of the room.

'Is that table free?' I enquire, pointing to the middle of the room.

The *Maître d'* nods in the affirmative, his mask of calmness and serenity and impeccable unflappability slipping just a fraction, appearing ever so slightly annoyed he hasn't managed to hide this less than-perfectly-attired customer in a more out of the way section of the restaurant.

I am seated at the new table. This spot is perfect. The room's hubbub percolates all around, and all through, me. I feel that the room's atmosphere is fusing perfectly within me; I could just sit here for an hour and leave, contented, without even needing to eat. I am however, after my recent stomach issues, ravenously hungry. I peruse the menu, but in truth the decision as to the nature of the food to grace my plate was made many days ago, without the need to be shown the culinary delights this gastronomic oasis has on offer.

After six weeks of self-imposed vegetarianism, I now need meat.

I apologise to the vegans and vegetarians amongst you, but for us carnivores, there are times when a lack of meat is quite the ordeal.

Yes, I need meat. Juicy, red, succulent meat.

A steak.

And not just any run-of-the-mill steak, but a decent, fresh, *well-prepared* chunk of protein.

And where else in Bombay are you going to find a top-quality, bloodied, juicy, tender steak than the Taj Mahal Intercontinental?

We are still in India, though, despite the cleanliness of the surroundings being so out of character with the rest of the country; it will therefore not be *beef* steak that is served.

Water buffalo steak is an acceptable substitute, not nearly as tasty as beef, mind you, but decent enough in any case if cooked to perfection, and by 'perfection' I mean red and juicy.

Sagnant, as our French *amis* would say.

Sure enough, when my plate arrives, the food is cooked perfectly. Topped with a delicious sauce of fresh *cepes*. Sides of fresh squashes.

All this washed down with a large glass of fine French claret.

OK, *two* large glasses of fine French claret.

The bill?

The princely sum of £5.

This is indeed to perfect way to end my trip, a celebratory meal after the rigours and hardships of the preceding days and weeks.

I feel as if I have earned this the Hard Way. The Hardest of Ways.

I raise a glass to my success.

To the end of my incredible Indian adventure.

Scholl. Prost. Santé. Cheers.

All that remains is the trip to the airport, for my flight to Cairo.

I can sense the Pyramids calling even from here.

Chapter 22

Suffering, so Much Suffering

Just before midnight.

A taxi has driven me the long ride out to Bombay airport, through the densest and poorest slums the city has to offer, not by way of a Sightseeing Tour, but because this just happens to be the way out to the airport. In the UK, we might regularly reflect on the disparity between Rich and Poor, but nowhere is the contrast between the *Haves* and the *Have Nots* starker than in India. In a country of more than a billion people, the rich can become staggeringly rich indeed, whilst the poorest of the poor are barely able to scrape together sufficient scraps with which to feed themselves each day, every day.

The Welfare State, as you or I might know it, does not exist in India. The relatively tiny sums allocated to assist the Poor and the Needy are slowly whittled away as they move down the line, from National, to State, to Regional, to Local levels, at each juncture a fraction of the pot being creamed off by corrupt officials who see the taking of a share of this cake as their given Right, given that they will have had to pay a not inconsiderable bribe to ensure their appointments to these lofty positions in the first place. Corruption in India sadly permeates all levels of society, inside the whole gamut of National Bureaucratic Institutions, including its Law-Making and Law Enforcing bodies.

Need a Passport?

A Driver's License?

Planning Permit for your (illegal) Construction?

Baksheesh please.

Need to dodge a Traffic Fine, an Arrest Warrant, a Crime for which you have been Charged (regardless of whether you actually did it or not)?

Another – *larger* - *baksheesh*, there's a Good Citizen.

India's Ever-Churning Bureaucratic Cogs, greased by dirty, ill-gotten gains.

So common place, so ingrained; as instinctive as breathing.

In such conditions, the gap between the *Haves* and *Have Nots* remains obdurately wide. Principled Politicians might announce new, bold initiatives to clamp down on Corruption, but their stay in office is rarely prolonged; often time, these poor, unfortunate, idealised folks end up face down in the nearest river. The System works hard to look after itself, first and foremost. We could debate the merits (or otherwise) of the Caste System, of Indian Social Hierarchy, seek solutions to end Endemic Corruption, ask why barely a 10th of the population provides a tax return each year. We could valiantly seek to uncover rationales, to offer solutions to these fundamental, overriding problems, but a decade (a century?) later we might still be throwing ideas around with no clear solutions in sight.

Maybe Mother India will find the cure herself? Maybe, when the Time is right.

To witness the hordes of beggars who throng around the city's main tourist and transit hubs – in all cities - hands held pleadingly out, desperately hoping for whatever scraps or change you might have to spare, is truly heart-breaking.

But in India, as I am sure you are learning, nothing is ever truly as it seems.

The child beggars are often time sent out by their parents – were they to be orphans, they are most likely controlled by shadier, more nefarious characters - to bring home money for the whole family, or for their handlers, which the children can achieve with such success, given their ability to tug so effectively at your heart strings, their parents never consider returning them back to school – education offering these poor unfortunates the only sure path out of their current predicament - thereby perpetuating the Poverty Trap.

During my time here, I decided against giving money to the street children, instead preferring to bring them to the nearest food vendor (usually just a few feet away), offering to buy them lunch (or breakfast, or supper, or whichever meal they felt they needed). This offer was often met with puzzled, quizzical looks, the children turning their heads to one side or other in an effort to seek guidance or reassurance from a parent - or more likely a controller - who had taken position a little way back for their own, and was ensuring the kids were doing *exactly* as they had been instructed.

Food is good, but it's not money.

It's not *cash* money the handlers can spend (on) themselves.

In India, the handicapped and maimed are everywhere, too: ankles fused at grotesque 90-degree angles; legs of patently unequal lengths; backs hunched to ungainly degrees; amputees at the knees, or the hips, or the wrists, all these cripples pulling or pushing themselves along on an intriguing array of Heath Robinson-inspired devices resourcefully cobbled together from the detritus found lying around, in order to ensure some degree of mobility.

This physical deformity is naturally extremely distressing to witness. It is even more distressing when you learn that the majority of these disabilities are self-inflicted, part of an inflationary war amongst the beggars to see who can achieve the worst disability- the most obvious, the most shocking - thereby attracting the highest levels of donations as a result. One beggar I saw had succeeded in flexing his knees fully, strapping the upper and lower sections of his legs together by the ankle over the thighs, thereby causing the muscles in his lower legs to atrophy such that they had virtually wasted away. The pitiable man moved about on his kneecaps, whilst steadying himself with his fists, around both of which he had woven large pieces of now extremely dirty cloth bound with leather, to protect the underlying skin.

Your compassion and empathy demand you provide some – any - assistance to these poor souls; you imagine yourself scooping them all up and whisking them off to some place better, to some place safer, to somewhere they can *live* their lives, rather than simply enduring an *existence* up to the end of their days.

But with so many to help, just where to start?

And where would your work finish?

The correct course of action is unclear. Your heart perpetually breaks. Your mind perpetually in anguish, for to be dismissive is to consider yourself cruel; to see the elimination of poverty and deformity as your own personal crusade, to run the risk of being too 'White Saviour'.

Is this *my* problem to solve in any case?

Helping just one person in this Sea of Neediness just seems so pathetic, so drop in the ocean, so needle in a haystack.

I discuss this issue with many normally abled Indians. Indians are largely a compassionate and caring people; the performance of philanthropic acts woven deep into the Fabric of Society, their religious beliefs shaping their compassionate views on the less fortunate amongst them.

Yet, despite these underlying beliefs, the consensus I hear could be condensed thus: to offer money to these poor cripples – those who have performed acts unthinkable-to-you-and-I on themselves – is to condone and encourage the proliferation of this form of self-mutilation.

Rewarding one self-mutilating beggar will only spawn other copycats, will only lead to yet more suffering, will only create yet more needless pain.

Their view on this most disturbing of issues is that employing a macro, rather than micro, perspective is the only viable, long-term solution to the needs of such unfortunates.

'What about Compassion?' I ask.

'Where is the Compassion in perpetuating senseless harm, in reinforcing mutilation, in rewarding such barbarism?' they all answer.

I have no option but to bow to the residents' greater knowledge – these are *their* people, *their* brethren, *their* brothers and sisters after all - no matter how all my senses are shouting at me that these souls need help in so many ways.

Just when I think I am coming to terms with India, there is another dilemma to knock me off-balance.

A sense of Equilibrium is sure hard to find here.

Chapter 23

Cairo or Bust

Bombay Airport. Main departure lounge.

I am now checked-in, and have passed, without issue, through Security. I am incredibly tired (two large glasses of red wine for lunch tends to do that), but thankful that very soon I will be on the plane, Cairo-bound, and able to shut my eyes for some much-needed *Z*.

The Egypt Air flight is scheduled to depart just after 2am. This early hour is not unusual for flights heading westwards out of Bombay. The airport throngs with hundreds of other passengers, who scurry past hither and thither en route to their *Now Boarding* calls.

I want to tell those rushing by to *slow down*.

There's no hurry, I want to say.

Nothing in India is ever *on schedule*.

They all have *plenty of Time*.

Our Departure Gate is announced over the crackly Tannoy. Slowly, I make my way down the concourse, taking a seat with the rest of the passengers at the Gate, expecting to be called to board in just a few minutes' time.

So.

This, pretty much, is It.

This is, pretty much, the End.

Time is now Up.

Time, now, has Run Out.

Time, now, to Move On.

India. Farewell. So long.

It's been Emotional.

The *Time* approaches 1am.

I sit. I wait.

So, a little more sitting, a bit more waiting.

I am so glad this is the last of the sitting and waiting.

The last of the sitting and waiting *patiently*.

I have now attained Nirvana-Black-Belt in sitting and waiting *patiently*.

The *Time* reaches 1.45am.

Nothing appears to be happening.

Surely, the boarding call will be made ever so soon.

I wonder how the flight crew plans to get everyone on board in time to depart on schedule, just after 2am.

I am a tad Dubious.

Sitting. Waiting.

This *really* has to be the last of the sitting and waiting.

The *Time* reaches 2am.

Nothing has happened, yet.

Surely, the boarding call will be made really ever so soon.

I wonder how the flight crew plans to get the everyone on board in time to depart even before 2.30am.

I am a tad More Dubious.

More sitting. More waiting.

Seriously, this is the *very last* of the sitting and waiting.

The *Time* reaches 2.45am.

Still nothing has happened, yet.

Surely, surely, surely, the boarding call will be made in the very near future.

I wonder how the flight crew plans to get everyone on board in time to depart even before 3.15am.

I am now more than a soupçon of a tad Dubious.

Still, I sit. Still, I wait.

Really. Sitting, waiting: I've almost had it up to here with the damn sitting and waiting.

The *Time* reaches 3.30am.

Still, still nothing has happened, yet.

Finally, a Representative from the airline arrives down at the Gate. I overhear her telling those who have managed to push their way to the front of her Desk that our flight is subject to slight delay.

Minor Technical Issue with the aircraft, or so the Representative is saying.

Peak Dubious has now been achieved.

Even more sitting. Even more waiting.

Really, sitting and waiting, I never wish to see your sorry arse ever again. I'm done with the sitting and waiting.

The *Time* reaches 4am.

Absolutely bugger all has happened, yet.

The Airline Representative has stopped interacting with the passengers as a) it appears she has nothing else to say apart from the fact that the plane has developed a minor technical issue, and our departure will be slightly delayed; and b) the passengers three deep in front of her Desk have turned into a rabid mob who aren't taking 'I don't know' any more for an answer.

There is much arm waving, much fist banging, much foot stamping; many deep sighs of frustration.

I have moved on from Dubious. Dubious is now a tiny flicker in my rear-view mirror.

I am Completely Resigned.

Yet more waiting. *Still* more sitting.

Sitting and waiting. Don't even go there.

The *Time* reaches 4.30am.

Guess what?

Still absolutely bugger all has happened, yet.

I push my way through the throng in front of the Airline Representative, approaching with my best fake smile and a calm demeanour that hides a seething frustration bubbling just under the surface. I tell the AR it is obvious to anyone with even a modicum of intelligence that our departure can in no way be described as *imminent*, not for *today,* nor in all probability for *anytime soon*. The airline, I gently point out, needs now to be seriously applying itself to making the necessary arrangements to accommodate all of us passengers for the foreseeable future.

The lady nods.

I point at the previously angry mob, who appear to have all been given a sedative.

'That lot are unlikely to remain docile for very much longer', I suggest.

The lady picks up the phone. She is Egyptian (I presume. She *looks* Egyptian. She certainly doesn't *look* Indian). I cannot understand what she is saying, but from her facial expressions it appears she is relaxed about what she is hearing.

She tells me in her best English that an announcement will be made soon.

I am now *utterly* Completely Resigned.

The *Time* reaches 5am.

Oh God.

More waiting. More sitting.

If you hadn't already guessed, maybe not waiting and sitting quite so *patiently* now.

Gold Medallist I might potentially be, in the Waiting *Patiently* Olympics; I resign myself to being out of the medals at today's warm-up Event.

No, not today. Today, my previous training counts for nothing. My Discipline is faltering.

Today, I couldn't give a flying fig.

I feel the last vestige of patience leave my weary body.

Sod This, I think. For a **Game**. Of **Soldiers**.

The *Time* reaches 5.30am. How on earth has it come to this?

Something, finally – Hallelujah - is about to happen.

A more Senior Representative from the airline has just arrived down at the Gate. He is briefing his colleague on what, I presume, he is about to tell all of us. The man then bangs loudly, several times, on the Rep's desk.

As one, the sedated throng opens their eyes. We are all on tenterhooks.

'There is a minor problem with the aircraft,' the SR tells us. 'This issue will take a short while to fix.'

You don't say?

So far, so bleeding obvious.

'Whilst we wait for the repairs to be carried out, we have arranged for you all to stay at a nearby 5-Star Hotel, each with a $10/ day food allowance.'

Hmm.

A *per day* allowance?

This sounds ominous.

'As the spare part needs to be flown in from our workshops in Cairo, your flight will now be departing in three days' time'.

I swear the SR ducked the moment he uttered the words, *in three days' time*.

Naturally, the rabble explodes.

Pandemonium!

'Three days?'

THREE DAYS!!

'No! No! No!'

To protect myself from the crush, I dive away from the desk as the rabble descends *en masse*.

'This is **totally unacceptable!**' appears to be the main issue being shouted out.

'**We all have jobs to get back to!**', the main source of the rabble's impatience at what it transpires is going to be a 66-hour delay.

Oh India.

Oh, *lovely* India.

Oh, *blessed* India.

Do You not wish to release Your grip on me?

Mother India, am I to deduce You are desirous for me to stay?

Is there more from You You think I still need to learn?

Or do you Love me such that You cannot bear to part with me?

If it is indeed Love, Mother India, You sometimes choose to show It in the most Mysterious of Ways.

The dawn mist of Birgunj seems a Lifetime ago.

Oh India, You have taught me much these past six long weeks.

You have shown me a Window into this Other World.

You have taught me to *Go with the Flow*; You have shown me how to *Roll with the Punches*, how to *Get Up* each time *You Knock Me to the Floor*.

I have learnt to understand the Nature of Fatalism, for Fatalism is the one and only True and Trusted route to maintaining one's sanity within the Tessellated Chaos that is India.

I check myself to see how I feel about this New Development. Good news. It would appear I am surprisingly sanguine about this turn of events and the changes it enforces to my plans, which other than landing in Cairo are, in any case, currently a work still very much *in progress*.

If three nights in a 5-Star Hotel in Bombay, with Food Vouchers, *is how it is*, then three nights in a 5-Star Hotel in Bombay, with Food Vouchers, *it is going to be*.

Suck it up, Fuzzball.

I have learnt to select which battles I fight.

See India, you have taught me much.

Around 6am, the buses arrive to ferry us all to our accommodation. Everyone appears utterly shattered. Shell-shocked, 1,000-yard stares all around.

After a 45-minute journey, back through the hubbub of the already much re-awakened city, we reach our destination, a non-descript, 5-Star Hotel, on the beachfront facing west. Everyone waits patiently in line to be checked-in, not necessarily out of politeness, more out of sheer exhaustion.

Finally, my room card is provided; on autopilot, I wander the hotel's labyrinthine corridors.

Eventually, after many a wrong turn, I locate my billet. Whilst walking the corridors, I detect a distinctly dank aroma, an odour that does not diminish on entering my room.

I touch the bed.

The bed feels damp.

The mattress feels damp.

The duvet feels damp.

The pillows feel damp.

The whole room has a musty, mouldy base note to the air inside.

It is another grey, decidedly overcast day, virtually windless. The oppressive humidity from outside has, evidently, permeated all areas inside. My room is basic but clean, the mattress, dampness aside, firm, but not too hard (**SCR**: 68).

I look around, smelling the air, sniffing the surfaces; I dare not open a window, lest the outside venture inside, exacerbating the problem, rather than freshening the place up. I ask myself whether I should be surprised, whether I genuinely believed we would be housed in a *real* 5-Star Hotel. From the outside, and on paper, this place sounded so promising; it offered so much to look forward to, at time we all so desperately needed *something* to look forward to.

The disappointment hits me like a punch to the guts; we've not been housed in a *real* 5-Star Hotel, merely one showing 5-stars adjacent to its name, stars Management evidently picked up down at the local market on special offer.

I ponder a moment, torn between letting gravity force me down onto the mattress, and venturing down to Main Desk, to complain in no uncertain terms to said Management about this distinct *excess* of moisture.

A wry, ironic chuckle passes my dry, chapped lips.

Now, there is being *too much water*.

Ha ha. India. Nice One.

No, I should probably stay put. I do not want the Receptionists asking whence I hail.

I do not want this dampness to be because *I am from England.*

Yes, this dampness I am bringing with me *all the way from England.*

I am way too tired to be making a fuss, about the damp, or indeed about anything.

I collapse onto the bed.

My head hits the pillow.

I am asleep faster than you can say 'boo'.

Chapter 24

Play Your Cards Right

Midday.

I awake, feeling only slightly less shattered than I was a few hours earlier. I decide a tour around this so-called 5-Star Hotel should be top of today's Order of Play. Maybe, I have been a tad swift to rush to judgment; a trifle unkind with my initial harsh appraisal.

An idea smacks headfirst into my weary consciousness.

A swim in the Hotel's much-feted pool, to freshen up?

I am directed to the Outdoor Pool area.

The scene greeting me provides yet another sucker punch to the guts.

On paper, Swimming might *seem* like an Option – the Hotel advertises its Pool somewhat proudly, after all - but Swimming is oh so not a *viable* Option.

Not unless you can doggy paddle in the six inches of dark green, algaed muck sitting at the bottom of the virtually empty pool. Maybe only Breaststroke would be feasible in that depth, in any case.

My heart sinks. It is yet another Major Disappointment.

I retire to the dining room and take breakfast, which merely suffices in quality.

Outside, the day is still overcast; dark, dank and stickily humid, and stiflingly hot. I decide a walk along the long beach directly across the road from the hotel should be next up on the Order of Play. It is not, sadly, a beach most people would typically picture in their minds when imagining *Seaside*. The sand is dull and grey, what sand you can see that is, the beach largely hidden under a blanket covering of rubbish stretching the length of the waterfront. All manner of flotsam and jetsam is strewn before me, left and right, as far as my eyes can see, both landside and in the watery shallows: algae-stained plastic bottles; rusty old cans;

shattered tree branches; mulched up leaves; thousands of coconut husks; scores of car tyres; the odd canine carcass or three, all manner of detritus congealed into a stinking mass, now shimmying slowly forwards and backwards with the ebb and flow of the sea's gentle swell, adding to the already 2-foot-deep pile accumulated up the majority of the beachfront.

With its 100% cloud cover, today is not, sadly, a Prime Tanning Day, nor any sort of tanning day.

Today is also not a Prime Swimming Day, nor any sort of entering the water day.

The wind suddenly picks up, carrying any dark, still-exposed sand up the beach, and across the road towards the Hotel. In the near distance, I notice a small group of men standing around a table. They have set up shop just in front of a disused Funfair, its Wave Swinger ride standing motionless, exuding a somewhat forlorn air, whilst what remains of its once ornate paintwork is sand blasted from all sides.

It seems a long time since the Funfair saw any action, any attention, any love. Any Fun.

I wander over to the group. They are playing cards, or so it seems at first glance. One man must find the Queen from three cards placed face down on the table, after the man holding the cards has done a series of moves rotating the cards' locations, two, by two, by two.

It is hard to keep track of the motions the Card-Holding Man is making.

I think that is the main purpose of the exercise.

The Guessing-Man points to the centre card – **Position Two**.

This is an **Incorrect Choice**, it becomes apparent, as the Card-Holding Man turns the chosen card over to reveal an Eight of Clubs.

A large denomination *rupee* note is removed by the Card-Holding Man from a small stack on one side of the table.

The Guessing-Man removes another large denomination note from his pocket, placing it on the side of the table.

Words are exchanged. It seems the Guessing-Man wants to go again.

The Card-Holding Man shows the Guessing-Man - and the rest of us standing round the table - the position of the Queen, then turns that card over, does the weird rotating thing again, two, by two, by two, by two, moving the cards from position one to three, three to one; two to one, one to two; three to two, two to three; faster and faster - *swivel, swivel, swivel* - until really it is anyone's guess where the Queen is currently.

If, indeed, it is anywhere at all.

Position Two, guesses our desperate gambler once again.

Once again, an **Incorrect Choice**.

I decide to have a go. It is, of course, a scam, but, what the heck, I have nothing better to do today. In a way, I want to see if I can work out how the Card-Holding Man achieves his sleight of hand. I remove a small denomination note from my pocket, placing it on the table, signalling my desire to Play.

The men all smile and laugh.

Success!

Another Sucker reeled in, they are almost certainly all thinking.

The Card-Holding Man shows me, and everyone else, the position of the Queen, then turns the card back face down, beginning the rotation sequence as before, faster, and faster, and faster, his hands and the cards now just a blur.

I am certain the Queen is in **Position One**, unless of course it has somehow made its way off the table, into the scammer's hand.

Position One is turned over.

Well, darn me.

A **Correct Choice**.

We Have a **Winner**!

Do I want to go again?

You betcha!

I proceed to lose the next three turns.

There is one born every minute. Today that *one* is me.

I smile, waving my friends goodbye.

They smile, and wave back. It appears they are all happy in their work.

Back in the Hotel foyer.

The area is a wide, high-ceilinged atrium. I notice a large grand piano sitting, alone, in the centre of the otherwise empty space, its top resting open to allow its dulcet tunes when played to travel further around the foyer, and with greater resonance. I plonk my posterior on the accompanying stool, looking forward to spending some quality time now caressing the ivories. Doing something artistic, and creative. I have missed having a piano to play during my travels. You simply cannot pack a piano of any size into a rucksack. I should have learnt to play the guitar, or the harmonica. Harmonica and guitar players rule the campfire, although I would respectfully suggest to the Harmonica/ Guitar Players' Union that the global Harmonica/ Guitar-Playing Fraternity become better acquainted with a few more songwriters than the ubiquitous Cat Stevens and Bob Marley. If I hear one more strain of 'Wide World' I swear I'll...

I check the stool's height against the level of the keys.

Set.

I am correctly centred.

I am now ready to perform.

I present my fingers to the keys.

I press my fingers into the keys.

Nothing.

No downwards movement from the keys.

Definitely no sound emanating from hammer-on-string action.

I press again, a little more firmly.

Still no movement. Still, definitely, no sounds.

I press harder - and harder, and harder - up and down the octaves - black keys, white keys - until the only conclusion I can draw is that the mechanism is well and truly stuck.

I mosey around the side of the piano to peek at the mechanism under the lid.

What, I wonder, is causing this wee problem?

I am dumbfounded.

Sure, all the strings are still there.

Everything is, from first inspection, *exactly* where it should be.

Except. Yes, this is somewhat unexpected. You don't see *this* every day.

A bird's nest – a bloody bird's nest - is resting on top of, and intertwined with, the piano's strings.

No birds at home. Just their long-flown nest.

This scene epitomises India in a nutshell.

India is a wondrous, ornate country. India is blessed with a great many wondrous possessions and ornate artefacts, all of which stunningly beautiful on the outside. But scratch even a centimetre beneath the surface, or peek behind the curtain, you find the backdrop is, by and large, mere Frontage – the beauty just thin veneer - that nothing functions as it was originally intended.

The finery, largely Just For Show.

But somehow - any*how*, who knows *how*, it *doesn't matter how* - the Show Will Go On.

Welcome to India!

Inter-Course

Amuse Bouche

Atacama, Peru.

I am experiencing the 1,200km journey, from Cusco to the Peruvian capital, Lima, a voyage of more than 24 hours' duration. (In traveller-speak, an *Experience* is an event we hated with a passion whilst it was unfolding, but have since managed, over many subsequent decades, to reshape and reframe in our memory banks into a now relatively positive entity).

Our transportation is an old, rickety, cramped, former US School Bus; we are travelling along old, rickety, rutted roads. The parlous state of both bus and road have combined to transform the journey into an Instrument of Torture, akin to being forced to sit on top of a washing machine during its spin cycle whilst being punched repeatedly in the guts, for hour, upon hour, upon hour, with no end in sight, such is the incessant bouncing, juddering and shaking thus far endured.

Time passes with all the swiftness of an apathetic, asthmatic snail afflicted with a 20-a-day cigarette habit, and a profound sense of *ennui*.

Reading a book is simply not a viable option, given the absolute impossibility of focusing on the page as we bounce merrily along. Staring out of the windows offers nothing in the way of ocular appeasement, scant rewards to take one's mind off the crushing sense of boredom our leisurely progress is instilling, for we have left the beauty of the high mountains far behind us, now crossing the vast, sparsely vegetated northern fringes of the Atacama Desert. Plastic Bag bushes, low-level gorse that ensnares the mounds of man-made detritus blown unimpeded across this flat land by the frequent, strong, dry, north-easterly winds, are all the window view has on offer.

In an attempt to dislodge myself from the tedium, I try to mentally zone out.

It is going to be a long, long day. The night might be even longer still, I fear.

Out here, right in the deepest middle of absolutely bloody nowhere, our bus suddenly comes to a halt. I look around for a reason for this unscheduled pause. I really hope there isn't a serious problem with the bus.

The long, long day, and even longer night, might suddenly have taken a turn for the worse.

The front passenger door opens. A diminutive, well-matured man, grey, wrinkled and weathered, climbs aboard. The man carries no luggage - no bags, no livestock, nothing - except for an empty pint-sized glass in his right hand. Rather than passing down inside the bus to take a seat, the man simply stands there centred at the top of the aisle, his back to the direction of travel.

The bus starts up again; the incessant bumping and grinding along the road recommences.

As we bounce and bump along, the man stands there, motionless within the confines of the bus, for many minutes. I am wondering what his situation is, what this man is doing here; it seems to me he is waiting for something.

If he's waiting for something, he could, given where we currently are, be here for a *very* long time.

Now the man is saying something, something in Spanish, something I do not understand.

The man is now raising his empty pint-sized glass up for all the passengers to see.

I do not know what significance this glass has with reference to what he is saying.

I don't know if he is offering to sell us all a drink.

I am really not sure a full bladder combined with this incessant bumping and grinding is going to be the best of combinations.

The man then laughs.

I am only back in the third row, so when the man then laughs, I catch his edentulous grin in all its glory. Great gums; but no teeth whatsoever with which to trouble the dentist.

The man positions the empty glass just beneath his chin.

He is now performing a strange stomach, shoulder and chest movement, like a wave rolling up his body, from belly button all the way up to his Adam's apple.

As if by magic - or possibly peristalsis - a marble suddenly emerges out from between his toothless gums.

The marble drops, with a loud clunk, into the glass.

Ta-da!

There is a light ripple of applause from towards the back.

Unperturbed by the lukewarm reception this first marble has generated, the man contorts and ripples his body once again, and – Hey Presto! - out pops another tiny glass orb.

Clunk!

Then another.

Clunk!

And then another.

Clunk! Clunk! Clunk!

Over, and over, and over, until, wouldn't you know it, the glass is now full to its brim.

The man holds the glass up for everyone to see. He is still smiling his toothless grin. He is evidently quite proud of his recent achievement. There is now much applause coming from this captive audience, front, back and centre.

We are, it would appear, all duly impressed.

The man passes down the aisle, receiving a few *pesos* here and there for his unusual performance. I offer whatever small change

246

I have readily accessible. The last ten minutes seem to have flown by, well worth the small price paid.

Back again at the top of the aisle, the old man now raises his glass full of marbles in salute to this fine, appreciative crowd, opens his mouth wide, and then proceeds to swallow the whole glassful of marbles, down in one.

He grins his wide, edentulous grin once more.

I wonder what he does for an encore.

I wonder what might happen were the man to suddenly sneeze. Or break wind, for that matter.

Despite the minutes just passed, we are still in the deepest middle of absolutely bloody nowhere.

Suddenly, the bus halts again.

The old man alights.

The doors close, leaving the old man to await the next ride north, or south, or wherever, his unusual party trick to once again amuse or bemuse the poor bored Peruvian souls who might happen to pass by this way.

I am left wondering, wondering about that certain morning he awoke, the special morning this man had experienced his triumphant 'Eureka!' moment, a moment that must surely have caused him to leap out from his bed like a startled gazelle.

'Ethel! Ethel! I have it! I've *found* it! The solution to our financial inadequacies!'

'Yes, dear', Ethel might have replied. 'And just *what* are you proposing?'

'Marbles!'

With that, I am sure Ethel - poor, patient, put-upon Ethel - would have considered her husband to have finally lost his (although, in actual fact, his marbles weren't lost, they were, as you and I both know, safely resting inside his belly).

PART FOUR

Chapter 25

In the Beginning

July 1988.

19 years have elapsed since my (then) tiny toes first touched down on this planet.

I find myself in residence on the tiny Greek island of Patmos, a remote Dodecanesian outpost, nestled in the SE corner of the Aegean. My travelling companions are the extended family, plus a ragtag assortment of waifs and strays. We, all ten of us, are taking our traditional summer sojourn (our *last* summer sojourn *en famille,* as it transpires), days, then weeks wiled away in all manner of sloth-like beachside inactivities: reading countless novels; playing countless games of backgammon; snorkelling amongst countless fish; pedalling countless Pedalos; drinking countless Oranginas, the only respite being the countless sessions of American football played in the bay's shallow waters with the other young lads and ladesses with whom we have become acquainted over the many years we have been returning to this exact same spot. Sloth has never been so indulged, nor so *expected.* Stricken as I am with perpetually pushy parents, this departure from the prescribed routine is a much-welcomed reversal.

Throughout the '70s and '80s, my stepfather would each year spend several months working in Greece, leading Consultation Projects for Financiers and Entrepreneurs considering building *this* factory, or starting up *that* business, and who needed someone to evaluate the merits - or otherwise - of their enterprising endeavours. Strict capital controls in this era stipulate that any money earned in Greece must remain in Greece; for more than a decade, we are, therefore, forced to return each summer – kicking and screaming, of course - to help these funds find suitable benefactors: first to the island of Skiathos, then Syros, before finally we settled on Patmos.

Thanks to its airport, Skiathos, the western-most in the Northern Sporades, was, by the mid-'70s, already a tourist hotspot, despite its diminutive airstrip ending with an abrupt, watery runoff, ready to ensnare the unwittingly imperfect landing. Island airports are a mixed blessing: the option to arrive by air makes for easy access; then again, the islands are easy for *everyone* to access. Which Grecian isle best suits your needs is a common dilemma: many years' island hopping experience suggests a good Rule of Thumb, should peace and quiet be your No1 Prerequisite, is to reject those with air links; far better, to select a resting spot solely accessible by sea, even if the onward journey is but another hour or so onwards from your initial Greek touchdown - the ever so slight hassle of venturing further forth tends to deter the *feak* and the *weeble*, lending those harder-to-reach islands a more relaxed, conducive atmosphere for that much-needed break from normality's Daily Grind.

In Skiathos, our chosen spot was a small village near Maratha beach, far away from the bright touristic lights - or so we thought - but our bay's tranquillity was often drowned out by the noisy Banana Boats that swung in on the hour, every hour, from Koucounaries, the larger, noisier, neighbouring beach. Not best suited to such continuous cacophonous intrusion, we packed up the parasol and ventured forth in search of tavernas new.

For the following four years, we journeyed to Syros (*Siros*), in the Cyclades, a 6-hour ferry ride from Piraeus, once home to Pythagoras, later a neutral sanctuary during the C19th Greek Revolution. Nowadays, the island is more of an administrative hub than a popular holiday hotspot.

Our presence in a tiny hamlet on the island's western flank was as much of an intrigue to the locals as they were to us. Youngsters, some as wee as five, would happen, with less than subtle regularity, to be passing our way – alone, in pairs, sometimes a whole handful; the kids would sit on the wall overlooking our villa, studying us intently, and with much ill-concealed curiosity, whilst we took breakfast each morning on our sunny veranda. We'd wave, genially, beckoning them come join us, but the boys and girls would simply beam a broad smile back, gain a deep blush-red hue to their cheeks, and dash off to attend to whatever else they suddenly remembered they were supposed to be attending to just then.

With each returning visit, we became better acquainted with the Island's beauty. Our circle of Syriot friends grew likewise; invitations thence bestowed for jolly group gatherings – twenty+ people – to idyllic, secret, insider-information-only coves. The locals would rinse off their speer-fishing gear, the goal to snag some aquatically tasty fodder to then grill on the barbecue, fresh bounty to accompany the deliciously fresh salads and fresh, home-baked breads the older contingent had thoughtfully prepared that morning, and packed for us all to enjoy.

The catch, most commonly, was Red Snapper – yummy grilled over white-hot charcoals – with succulent and tasty octopus' meat a much-prized addition. Snagging an octopus on the end of one's speer takes more skill than I could ever muster, their well-camouflaged outlines being notoriously tricky to spot amongst the stony, seaweedy seabed. Those rare occasions an octopus was speared, the flesh would be smashed repeatedly against the rocks for as long as the smasher's arm could endure, the tentacles then passed on for the next person to take over - and the next, and the next – until the octopus-flesh was tenderised to perfection, and then placed onto the already smoking-hot grill. We'd all sit on the rocks, staring wistfully out to sea, our eyes ringed pink from the suction of our diving masks, a strong sea breeze blowing through our salt crusted hair, amazed at just how sublimely delicious the fresh fish and barbecued octopus tasted, enhanced with just a squirt or two of lemon, with the freshest of salads, and crustiest of fresh breads with which to mop up the juices.

At night-time, the local lads and ladesses insisted we rode pillion on their mopeds, to the local open-air cinema, a rustic, rudimentary set-up in the ruins of a dilapidated farmhouse, 5km from our small hamlet. The weekly schedule would be posted on any of the local area's suitably smooth protuberances, rudimentary paper notices pasted onto walls, electricity poles, shop windows and abandoned buildings for miles around, the previous weeks' and months' offerings flapping loosely under the more recent announcements, as the cinema's over-worked marketing bods added yet another poster to an already distinctly over-used location. Not that we really cared what was showing, in any case, the films all being old, warn reels of obscure B-movies, the names of which triggered zero flashes of recognition to us out-of-islanders.

These screenings were certainly not the latest Hollywood blockbusters, not by a long stretch, but it mattered not one jot; each film had its own individual characterful charm, and vociferously impassioned followings, repeated as they had been - over, and over, and over again - by the limited stash of reels at the poor projectionist's disposal.

Most deeply etched into distant memory banks: a 1960's colour print of *Tarzan in Egypt*, in Italian, dubbed (badly, according to the locals) into Greek, its well-worn 35mm reels hewn through a rickety projector onto a ripped, flapping, off-white screen, not quite level to the horizontal, and which rippled continuously in the gentle night air. No matter the dialogue was beyond our comprehension, the sound in any case virtually drowned out by the projector's ever-present whir and the constantly chirping cicadas, and obscured by frequent loud cheers, loud cheers that greeted each and every time Tarzan beat his chest, swung majestically from a vine, heroically fought off a wild animal, saved one of the never-ending stream of damsels in distress, or performed any number of other random, clichéd acts for which a raucous cheer was the customarily mandated response.

Hoorah for Tarzan!

The plot was barely followed in any case. Being out here was merely an excuse for the young lads and ladesses to hang out and enjoy the most convivial of evenings, far away from the disapproving, over-strict glare of the older generations.

The cinema set-up had many faults; nothing here was perfect. Nothing, remotely close to perfect.

But the cinema was perfect for us all.

****

Sunny Patmos' claim to fame is being home to *the* spot where St John is said to have plonked his exiled arse down to write the not-quite-so-sunny Book of Revelation. The island's small, yet bustling, port hives with cruise ships moored out in the bay, their skiffs ferrying thousands of excited passengers dockside for their shore excursions to visit *the* grotto where the apocalyptic scribblings allegedly took place. This *to*-ing and *fro*-ing continues regardless of the frequent inter-island ferries that regularly race, at breakneck speed, into port, honking their booming horns as they approach -'Out of My Way, Ain't Changing Course for No-One!' - before dropping anchor at just the right spot to then execute a deft 180-degree turn, reversing nonchalantly dockside, before chaotically discharging the scores of lorries, cars and pedestrians all waiting, impatiently, to alight.

If you are one of those also inclined to get ashore, you'd better get your skates on; Time, Tide, and Greek ferries wait for no man (nor woman).

You want to disembark, a frenzied swarm of locals wants to disembark, dozens of cars and lorries also want to disembark, all of you using the same, narrow, stern ramp, whilst simultaneously, and without waiting to be called forward, scores more embarking passengers and food vendors swarm up the same ramp, up onto the boat, pushing past anyone that might impede their passage without so much as a by-your-leave.

The ferries' stern ramps are no places for shrinking violets; you need sharpened elbows and gritty determination to force your way through this mêlée. Typical British manners - 'No, no, after you, I insist' - won't wash here. This is the most perfect assertiveness training, lest you want to still be aboard when the ramp rises once more.

Before sufficient time has elapsed for your quayside bearings to be established, the ferry's lines are cast, the stern ramp raised, and the engines cranked back up, the twin propellers churning the dockside waters into a mad, frothy morass. Several further booming blasts of the horn sound - 'See y'all Tomorrow, Folks!!' - as the ferry soon rounds the bay's headland, speeding off to its next island port of call.

Patmos' citadel is a picture postcard image of the typical Greek Chora, chock full of narrow alleyways and white adobe walls, with many fantastic restaurants, whose delicious food is matched by the stunning vistas their terraces afford. This is no package-holiday destination - no 'wet t-shirt' competitions, no mass bar crawls, no booming techno music until sunrise. The bars, the few that do exist, are dotted along the harbour waterfront, and round the curve of the adjacent bay. These modest establishments are strictly regulated by the monks up in the monastery: absolutely *no* dancing, *no* past-midnight closures, everyone on their best behaviour, a fiery eternal damnation awaiting your wretched soul should you have the temerity to transgress the monastery's Holy Edicts, and find yourself gyrating, inadvertently, in even a remotely rhythmic manner, to the cheesy '80s Euro-Pop played most evenings (at regulated, non-monk-ire-inducing volumes).

Patmos is home to just the one main, easily-accessible beach, reached either by road, or – far more fun – via a 30-minute fishing boat taxi ride from the harbour quay, the vessels all skippered by darkly tanned, well-weathered local fishermen who stand majestically at the helm, steering their craft nonchalantly with their feet, no matter the sea conditions the ever-present Meltemi has whipped up that day.

We all become creatures of habit, frequenting this one, same beach, day, after day, after day. The dearth of choice is no island shortcoming, adding as it does to the ease with which Routine becomes etched into one's consciousness. Choice, despite what some people will have you believe, is *not* always a Good Thing, requiring as it does decisive decision-making diligence at a time when one's mind has sunk to its lowest ebb of focus and resolve.

'So, which beach to venture to *today*?'

An unnecessary holiday dilemma.

Arrggghhh!

Brain melt.

Occasionally – only, *occasionally* - even Paradise gets too much; the urge to break free of the regimented routine can sometimes overwhelm (or, possibly, you're hoping to avoid the pretty girl you'd tried – *ineptly, embarrassingly* - to chat up the night before). For days such as this, the Round-the-Island boat cruise, with stops at an array of tiny, otherwise inaccessible, coves, provides the perfect antidote to this tiresomely wonderful monotony (or the mortification of your courting ineffectualness).

Time oozes slowly by.

The warmth of the sun is suitably soporific. After a hearty lunch of *keftedes,* or *spanakopita,* or *dolmades,* or *moussaka*, with large sides of feta-topped Greek salads bursting with fresh olives, the afternoon *siesta* is *de rigeur*, the highlight being to then awaken to the glorious wafted aromas of freshly-baked produce, aromas which could only indicate one thing: the beach café's English chef Wayne, a tattooed Diamond Geezer from London's East End - rough around the edges, but soft in the middle - has baked one of his special apple pies.

Oh, Wayne.

What *is* your secret? Why *have* you hidden yourself away in a remote outpost such as this?

Our youthful imaginations run wild, we cheeky kids competing to conjure up increasingly crazy and outlandishly eccentric suggestions:

The Long Arm of the Law following a heinous crime involving Death and Dismemberment?

A Torrid Affair with a neighbour's wife, his Heart thence cruelly broken?

Gambling debts running to £££s Millions?

A Mob hit gone wrong?

There is certainly nothing criminal about Wayne's sublime apple pie. Delightfully soft and delicate apple, generously sprinkled with cinnamon, topped with delicious, golden-brown crust pastry, accompanied by a dollop of home-made vanilla ice-cream, eaten in the café's dappled sunlit veranda overlooking the azure blue waters of the Aegean, surrounded by friends and family.

Delicious. The simple pleasures of life.

****

The Patmian regulars are an eclectic bunch drawn from wide-reaching swathes of European society. Our beach-side, backgammon and apple pie companions comprise, we learn over the years we all keep bumping into each other, a smattering of distantly-related cousins, young Dukes, Duchesses, Counts, Viscounts and Countesses, from Germany and Austria, with ties to our UK royals via a Great Aunt, or Uncle, or Grandparent. On the adjacent sun loungers, the well-healed off-spring of Greek Shipping and Petroleum magnates, whose transportation to and from Piraeus would be on the family-owned ferry; no lowly 1st Class for them, the Bridge being *their* preferred mode of travel.

Into this mix is thrown a smattering of young American Greeks, based in Switzerland, guys and gals able, in the process of one sentence, to switch seamlessly from Greek, to English, to French, and German, and back again, without batting an eyelid (although this does then render any mere mortal understanding what the hell they are on about distinctly more taxing).

This multifarious collection mixes far more completely than Oil, Greece and Water ever normally do, the only catalyst required to accelerate the reaction being an oval-shaped ball; quick-witted folk, decent conversationalists, and tough competitors on the watery American Football pitch.

Greece vs Germany vs Switzerland vs the UK vs the US; who needs the Olympics?

****

We eat out regularly in the port's open-air pizzeria, an unpretentious yet tasty diner, although language issues mean you need to stay alert and on your toes. My request one evening for a Pepperoni pizza results in my serving arriving coated with a generous portion of a mysterious green vegetable, the pizza's sole topping.

What the hell, we all wonder, is *that*?

I remind the waiter that a *Pepperoni* pizza had been the order, querying whether he has indeed brought me the correct pizza, or some other pizza by mistake.

The waiter points dramatically my serving, and at the unknown green pieces.

'Yes, yes. Peppers only,' he replies, clearly with some pride.

The waiter continues making wild gesticulations towards the pizza and the green slices atop, emphasising even more forcibly his point of having provided *exactly* that which had been ordered.

Oh dear.

Oops.

The curse of language indeed.

Unless your serving is burnt to a crisp, or your food smells rotten, it is decidedly unwise to request to return your plate of food. Chefs and kitchen staff the world over are known to sprinkle a little of their own Personal Magic into unsuspecting diners' dishes, should you be brash enough to suggest 'improvement' of what the chef considers a perfectly satisfactory plateful.

'Here,' they say, as the dish is passed around the kitchen staff, all manner of dandruff, or snot, or earwax balls (or who knows what) then seasoned into your dish, 'see how *this* improves things for you.'

A meal companion once sent back the curry he'd ordered in a Thai restaurant in London's West End – the hottest dish on the menu - on the grounds that the food he'd received was insufficiently spicy. It takes a pair of super strong *cajones* to request your dish be spiced up further, not simply because you will receive in return the most lava hot plate of food you will ever eat, or ever *attempt* to eat – 'Need more heat, eh?' the chef sniggers, as handfuls of rusty nails, broken glass, and whole chilli peppers are added to your dish – but because, by simply suggesting to a Thai chef his hottest curry might be lacking in the heat department, you are, in many ways, casting aspersions over the man's sense of masculinity, his very essence of *Self*. You might as well be insinuating that this man's wife lacks beauty, that the chef is unable to satisfy her Needs in the Bedroom, or that he might not be the only one with whom she shares her marital bed, for the insult you are unwittingly throwing the chef's way. To send a curry back in a Thai restaurant for being insufficiently spicy is, to the unaware and the uninitiated, a Declaration of War.

Back in Patmos, a pizza overladen with green peppers is not something I can guzzle down with any glee so, with fingers crossed, and with as much good grace as I can muster, I request a replacement, this time with a topping of pepperoni – sorry, *salami* - instead.

The waiter tuts his loudest tuts, *ums* and *ahs* deeply and forlornly, removing the errant plate with a theatrical flourish.

'Salami pizza, with *Special Seasoning*!' he doubtless cries, returning into the kitchens.

To be fair, our ragtag group of young renegades must be quite a let-down for this poor, beleaguered waiter. Attending to our table's previous guests had evidently been far more satisfying (and more befitting for a man of his *distinguished* service). The eagle-eyed amongst our gang had managed to grab the spot just as the previous guests were all leaving, rushing in with probably more than a *soupçon* of indecent haste, scattering chairs and bystanders aside in our desire to secure this *particular* spot. I took special care to plonk my *derrière* down in the exact same seat occupied only moments earlier by an internationally renowned pop star (who shared his surname with a classic American Hunting Knife). The seat might even have still been exuding warmth from the heat generated by this musical icon's own personal posterior.

Evidently, the eagerly anticipated creative surge from DB's residual aura has yet to be fully manifested.

Stardust be damned.

It is not entirely clear who should be contacted regarding restitutions.

****

Before 1999, the year the Euro arrived on the scene, the *drachma* was the Greek unit of currency. With the *drachma*, the cost of holidaying here in Greece for us sterling customers was more than reasonable.

Way *more than reasonable.*

A family of five could eat a hearty, 2-course lunch, of over-filled bowls of fresh Greek salads, of grilled, freshly-caught Red Snapper, of succulent *souvlaki,* and stuffed tomatoes, washed down with a bottle or two of Retsina, a bucketful of Oranginas, and as much water as the heat demanded, all this for a mere £5 equivalent.

One year, there were eighty *drachma* to the pound; the next, one hundred and fifty - at this age I am blind to the repercussions such currency devaluations have on their indigenous populations; all I knew, our spending power increased dramatically.

Greece was, therefore, a decent, low-cost, summer-sun destination.

Once, that is, you'd managed to get there.

In the late '80s, for the average youngster travelling Europe on a budget - prior to the advent of the Internet, and Low-Cost Carriers that exploited this new technology to streamline the airline business - the affordability of flying even this close to home wasn't a patch on prices today.

If your budget mandated something less eye-wateringly expensive than the standard, scheduled, flag-carrier airlines, your cut-price charter flight/ seat sale options could be found either on Ceefax Page 888, or the advertising pages of the London Evening Standard (or other, similar, local newspapers). Bagging a bargain was in no way guaranteed; the whole process was time-consuming and deeply frustrating, requiring scores of calls to these bucket shop agencies, all made from a landline phone, via a tedious, finger-slipping, rotary dialler.

One, by one, by one, by ever-so-tedious one.

Even then, you had to cross fingers and toes Lady Luck was on your side, and the dates offered matched your own specific schedule.

Were no last-minute charter flight seats available, all that remained were the scheduled airlines; British Airways or Olympic Airways.

That was pretty much that.

A monopoly.

High prices.

Pay up or shut up.

The days here in Patmos slip away. I am possessed of a Conundrum.

My old school chums have already made plans to holiday on Ios, another island in the Cyclades, a few weeks after my return from this Patmian *sojourn*.

Who wouldn't want to live a Never-Ending Summer?

The inevitable hardships of a new academic year loom large over the horizon; perpetually dank, cloud-covered days spent pouring over indecipherable Pure Mathematics textbooks, in north England's industrial heartlands, the chill of autumn slowly decaying into the dark, depressing gloom of winter, nope, none of this entices me back to the gruel of Academic slog with the slightest spring in my step.

So, no, the Summer of 1988 is not in any way over.

Not now.

Not yet.

Not by a long stretch.

But the snag, the *universal* snag as any university student will tell you, is the fiscal wherewithal to pay for such a protracted vacation. Parental support to fund the family holiday is one thing. Asking them to front up for another two-week jolly with your friends, something else entirely.

'You are more than welcome to join your friends in Ios', the parents say, 'you'll just need to find a way to get yourself there'.

That was the Deal.

That is the Conundrum.

Fortunately, I have an Ace up my sleeve.

Chapter 26

The Rag 24-Hour Hitch

Earlier that scholastic year, the first of a Pure Mathematics degree course at the **U**niversity of **S**omewhere **U**p **N**orth, I encountered the annual charity challenge creatively called, the Rag 24-Hour Hitch.

The rules were straightforward: travel the furthest from **USUN** within a 24-hour period (leaving on a specified date, start time of your choosing), without parting with any fiscal denominations for your carriage, and you will be proclaimed the Winner.

I think raising money for charity in the process was part of the deal, too.

First prize wasn't explicitly – or implicitly - stated, but the anticipated fame and kudos of winning – and I say that with tongue very firmly rammed in cheek - was draw enough for me.

Fame and kudos aside, this sounded like a cracking adventure.

Count me in.

Presented with the task of planning your own attempt at Fast & Free Travel to Far-Flung Lands, one option likely to be considered is the simple, standard, Old School approach: standing at the roadside, possibly beside a motorway on-ramp, Thumb Out in the traditional manner of the Hitch, waiting, patiently, hoping to snag a suitable ride within the shortest waiting time possible.

Option 1.

If the Old School notion of standing at the roadside, potentially for hours on end, doesn't sound overly appealing – from either a Safety, or Waiting-Time-Required, or Hoping-you-Don't-get-Rained-on perspective - or if you feel this plan relies a tad too heavily on Lady Luck to find that *one* lorry heading all the way to the Continent, you could opt, instead, to approach this challenge from a different angle: you might decide to call up an old family acquaintance, should he also happen to have connections with a large International Freight Forwarding outfit, and avail him of your requirements, namely a lorry heading anywhere across the Channel - *anywhere at all* - so long as the lorry is venturing as far away from **USUN** as possible within the stated 24-hour period, leaving Thursday morning.

Option 2.

'No problem', my contact said, after a few minutes on hold, 'get yourself to Trafford Lorry Park, by 10am on the Thursday morning, with your passport (of course, but I was a teenage student then, so, yes, Good Call), and find the Company's office. Ask for Dave.

'Dave will be expecting you.'

'Dave will be able to *hitch* you up with a suitable ride'. (So, technically, I *was* still 'hitching', yes?).

The plan worked like a charm. At the office, Dave looked down his list of imminent departures; one of the company's affiliate's lorries was, right now, about to roll out, heading all the way down to Austria.

'Any good?' Dave asked. I was more than welcome to hop aboard if so.

'You betcha' I replied, grateful for the introduction.

Geronimo.

Europe, here I come.

Well played, **Option 2**.

I was polite enough to wave at any contestants we sped past on the motorway slip-roads.

See ya! (Wouldn't want to *be* ya!)

We set off just before midday, making good time down the M6/ M25/ M2 motorways to Dover, with one brief diversion for a pickup.

We made even better time at Dover. The system may be different now, but, back then, lorries could not pre-book onto a specific ferry. You arrived at the port, checked in at the Reservations Office, and were then allocated the next available ferry departure, the time of which you displayed to the outside world by way of a foot-long white oval sign with black time digits, which you plonked in the bottom corner of your windscreen.

The time you were allocated depended on current demand.

You then waited patiently (or possibly, *impatiently*) for your crossing.

We reached Dover a little after 6pm, but when Stefan, my Austrian driver, returned from the booking office his face was a trifle glum.

We had been allocated a ferry departure more than three hours later.

Darn the long hold up, I thought; my attempt to be Furthest Traveller from **USUN** might suffer fatally if we're losing hours so soon into the Race.

Fortunately, Stefan, had other – *better* - ideas.

Waiting *patiently* was, thankfully, not one of his fortes. Over the many years of doing the run to and from the Continent, he'd presciently saved up quite the collection of time signage. With some disdain, Stefan threw the **21.45** sign to one side (not *away*, it would doubtless come in useful at some future juncture), shuffled through his not inconsiderable stack, picked out the sign reading **18.30**, and bid me hold it up for the shore crew to see.

'Let's see how *this* works', he said, as we drove nonchalantly along the lane designated for the **18.30** ferry, waved on by the shore crew, and thence straight on to the awaiting ferry, waived aboard by the boat crew.

Politely, as it seemed the right thing to do under the circumstances, I waved back.

Thank you. Thank you. Yes, thank you.

And you. And *you*.

Thank you *so much*. *Most kind* of you to let us aboard.

Yes, yes, Jolly Good Show everyone. *Thank you*.

We were the last to board, the stern doors closing right behind us.

Lines were cast. Propellers revved. Off we went.

Result.

Lady Luck was evidently shining down on me in other ways, too. It transpired our route into Austria took us past Lake Constance - the *Bodensee*, a large, beautiful body of water in the south-eastern corner of Germany – along the lake's eastern flank, not far from the School attended by one of the young (and yes, very pretty) girls I had met over the many years of our annual Patmian holiday.

'If you're ever passing my way, do drop in', she'd said, on more than one occasion.

She'd sounded like she'd meant it.

Well, it seemed *this* would be *that* occasion.

It would be a surprise. A *wonderful* surprise.

Who doesn't like surprises?

Mid-afternoon the following day, I bid farewell to Stefan, alighting the lorry at Überlingen, the closest town to my friend's school as far as I could tell from the map, using my somewhat rudimentary secondary-school German to get myself a room, with breakfast, in a basic *Gasthof* (*Ich hätte gerne ein Zimmer mit Frühstück, bitte. Wieviel kostet? Danke schoen. Bitte sehr. Danke schoen. Bitte sehr, etc, ad infinitum*).

Accommodation sorted, I took stock of my surroundings, clueless as to exactly where I now unexpectedly found myself only 24 hours after being in the grim, cold north of England, in the middle of chilly winter. To my surprise and relief, Überlingen turned out to be a cute, picture postcard Germanic township, nestled on the shores of the vast lake that is Constance; that afternoon, I wandered its quiet, narrow, cobbled streets, along the *Seestraβe* waterfront, feeling rather pleased with myself for having managed to venture so far so soon, and, strictly as per the rules, for no cash spent.

The following morning, after *Frühstücking* on *Pumpernickel*, a dense and, to my taste, unappetising bread, accompanied by an assortment of thinly-sliced smoked hams, overly-fatty salamis, and rubbery cheese slices – these Germans might, I fear, need schooling on the ideal first stomach layer of the day - I set off on foot to make the 10km journey to the School. Along quiet country lanes, amid stunning verdant farmland, I strolled, my perambulations warming me against the chill of the air, mildly trepidatious about how today's events were going to unwind.

The School and its grounds were most impressive – this was evidently an Establishment for the Better Healed amongst us. Looking back now, I am curious as to just how I was permitted entry, for I had no invitation, and nothing presumably against which my credentials might be checked; security arrangements would undoubtedly have been in place to prohibit random individuals from just sidling into the grounds willy-nilly. I can only imagine I presented myself as an honest, trustworthy individual, with a credible reason for entering, and therefore permitted entrance. I must have been pointed in the general direction of where my friend was most likely to be found - or where to find those who might know of her current whereabouts, in any case - and permitted forth to continue my quest.

Well, arriving in a distant land to see an old friend you've not seen since last summer, without any advance notice, can be the wonderful surprise you think it should be. Events can run smoothly, joy unbounded, the out-of-the-blue arrival greatly appreciated by the receiver of said surprise; much laughter and gaiety thence ensues.

On the other hand, you might encounter an unexpected hitch, or even two, events not turning out quite as anticipated, or flowing quite as smoothly as they always seem to do in the movies, when there's a team of highly-paid writers to ensure the denouement is the expected – and, being Hollywood, the *required* - Joyously Happy Finale.

My own quest hit an unforeseen snag: being Saturday, my German friend had decided to bugger off home for the weekend.

None of her friends had any idea what time she was due to return, whether today or tomorrow.

Darn and Drat.

Typical.

Without mobile phones, or the marvellous wizardry of the InterWeb, there was simply no way to contact her directly.

'Maybe', it was suggested, 'you can come back and try again tomorrow?'

Unthwarted and undaunted – well, I was here now, might as well see if she gets back on Sunday - I indeed set off again the following day.

Success!

My German friend had indeed returned by the time I reached the school just after lunch.

Surprise, surprise, surprise!!

Oh dear.

Rather than laughing about the absurdity of my happening to be in the area, it was, alas, an awkward greeting. My friend was, I sensed, less than convinced I had simply been 'passing by', feeling more this was a Romantic-if-Desperately-Lovelorn-yet-Ultimately-Futile journey across a large swathe of the European continent in order to profess my Undying Love for her.

Not necessarily an outlandish assessment based on the facts as they were presented, but in this case, an Incorrect Appraisal.

Nul Point.

I was bemused.

This wasn't the reception I had anticipated; I'd really not for a second considered any reaction to my appearance other than laughter and delight. I was unsure just how to wriggle back from this somewhat awkward, sticky situation; age had yet to armour me with the skills and wherewithal to react with sufficient style and finesse to ease my progress through this unexpected setback. I was, alas, a somewhat jejune and verecund young lad, still to fully grow into my skin, to achieve my fuller *Self*.

I was here, yet *here* I was floundering, I realised, disconcertedly.

At this juncture of this Tale's telling, it may aid somewhat to a fuller, more nuanced understanding of the situation to explain that my friend's grandmother happened to be (Duke of Edinburgh) Prince Philip's sister; my friend was (and still is), therefore, endowed with the title *Princess*. At that time, she was, I believe, nestled somewhere in the Top 40 in line to our British throne.

Whilst I tell *you* this, it must be stated that her family heritage had no bearing on anything, as far as I was concerned. To me, she was simply a more than convivial person to chat to and be around. By the time of this visit, we had been pen-pals for a couple of years, exchanging letters every few months; we'd had a fun, teasing rapport, typical of many young teenagers, during the many weeks we'd shared together over several years' encounters whilst in Patmos.

Can boys and girls ever *just* be friends?

A question as old as the hills, those snow-capped peaks off in the distance.

Maybe.

Possibly.

Sure, yes - you got me - I was hopeful our friendly banter and episcopal exchanges might eventually evolve into something more serious, somewhere down the line – who wouldn't want to date an intelligent, attractive, articulate, charming, down-to-earth, well-grounded and fun young lady? - but, well, kindly refer to the above.

There's no harm in being a Dreamer; I was also a Realist. Learning my new friend was a Princess a short time after being introduced had actually come as something of a disappointment (disappointed for *her*, not me); how the Royal Life is a Life inside a Gilded Cage; how cynical she must be to the true motives of a potential paramour, concerned that suitors might be attracted merely by the Title, in the same way rich heiresses might attract Unsavouries with a mind towards Long-Term Gain from Short-Term Romance.

In spite of my own faint hopes, that my journey had led me here to this *specific* spot at this *specific* moment *really was* down to Lady Luck and her Wondrous Machinations.

I am simply a friend who happened to be passing by, remote as that chance might seem.

You think I doth protest too much?

Hmm. There's no convincing some people, I guess.

It seemed there was no convincing her, either.

It appeared she, too, was a Cynic.

What is *wrong* with you People?

The more I tried to explain to her the nature of the 24-hour Rag Hitch, the more I tried to stress that it really *was* Coincidence I happened to be passing, the more it seemed to fall on deaf ears.

The shrug for 'whatever' needs no international translation. That she doubtless already had a boyfriend, probably a Count, or a Prince, or a Duke, who also attended this school – the *Schule Schloss Salem*, where the pupils herald from very well-connected families, and the alumni include the Duke of Edinburgh himself, Queen Sofia of Spain, and Princess Irene of Greece & Denmark – meant my presence here might be a little difficult to explain to him, or to the many gossips who'd doubtless been most intrigued by my arrival into their midst.

Just who *is* this strange British lad come a-calling all the way from Great Britain-*land*?

The school's rumour mill might have gone into overdrove. Tongue-wagging tittle-tattle isn't the sole preserve of the grungy lower classes, it should be noted. Quidnuncs exist in all walks of life.

I sensed my presence here might be lobbing a few spanners into her works, potentially upsetting her neatly ordered regime. We took tea and biscuits, as you do, for what seemed the bare minimum amount of time convention dictated, before it was suggested it might be a sensible idea to be heading back to Uberlingen before darkness fell.

I was then shown to the door.

Well, nice to see you *too*, too.

Back at my *Zimmer,* I took stock of the situation. I contemplated and dwelled on the whirlwind that had just blown through me and round me, realising my initial appraisal of my friend's reaction was probably most unfair, and certainly unkind. Sure, I don't think the visit could necessarily be classed as a *roaring success*, but then again, just what *is* the correct etiquette for greeting an out-of-the-blue arrival, from a distant land, whilst surrounded by prying, inquisitive eyes?

And just what would a *roaring success* have looked like in any case?

I hadn't called ahead. Most likely, my friend had simply been caught off-guard.

No more, no less.

Or, possibly – I had to at least ponder this alternative - she hadn't *really* meant it when she'd said to drop in if I happened to be passing by. On more than one occasion.

But why say it if you don't *really* mean it?

There may be far more to Decoding the Fairer Sex than is contained within the Pure Mathematics Curriculum textbooks I had hitherto been prescribed.

Uberlingen. Monday.

Post-stodgy breads and weird meat *Frühstück* once again – my dear Germanic *Freunden*, the Art of cereal with milk, and toast with jam, for the Breaking of the Fast, is my parting gift to you - I once again took stock of my situation.

As we'd said our Farewell but three days prior, Stefan had divulged that he was returning to the UK Tuesday, dawn departure; if I wanted a ride back home, all I needed was to get myself down to his company's depot in Bregenz, Austria, by Monday evening. I could bunk overnight in the lorry's cab.

Fortunately, another quick peek at the map revealed Bregenz to be a mere 65km from Überlingen, just the other side of the border, so I hauled ass to the train station, jumped on a train – after more fine rudimentary German skills usage (Mr Clark, *please note*) - reaching Bregenz after a passing prandial pause in the beautiful island town of Lindau. The rendezvous with Stefan worked liked a dream; we left the Austrian depot Tuesday morning, *de très bonne heure* – quite why 6am is considered a *good hour* by the French is a mystery – Dover's fine white cliffs hoving into view Wednesday, just after dawn.

At Zeebrugge, our forward progress encountered a potentially immoveable impediment. Lorry drivers are permitted the addition of a Driver's Mate to their ferry reservation, for no supplementary charge. As this system is potentially open to misuse, I was required to accompany Stefan to the check-in desk, to be paraded in front of the Reservation Clerk, so my credentials could be verified. Stefan told me, most emphatically, to not say a word - nothing, keep *totally schtum* - so when the official started throwing questions my way - The Lorry's *axle length*? The Lorry's *maximum loaded weight*? - I kept dutifully silent as Stefan answered in my place.

The official appeared most unconvinced – 'I was asking *him*!', she said, pointing at me, scowling – but the reservation was confirmed for the two of us, regardless of my inability to answer such rudimentary truck-based general knowledge.

In Dover, as the lorry required several hours to pass through customs checks prior to continuing up north, I bid Stefan a final

'Farewell & Thank You', catching the train back to the family residence in London.

The typical, long-lost student flying visit.

Hi guys!

Yes, amazing trip, thanks.

Chuck clothes in washing machine; load up the dryer; take food from fridge, gotta feed and clean a starving student after all.

Bye guys.

See y'all Soon!

I finally arrived back in Halls Thursday afternoon, a week, almost to the hour, after initially setting off.

What. A. Trip.

I had reached the German / Austrian border, a journey of more than 850 miles (in each direction), within the stipulated 24-hour period, not a single, solitary penny paid for my carriage.

Astoundingly, despite confidence in my endeavours at the very least bestowing me with the kudos of being Furthest Hitcher from **USUN**, First Prize was not mine.

Another competitor found **Option 3**, trumping my lorry connections, persuading his father, a pilot for one of the big charter airlines, to let him ride in one of their planes. They'd flown with a load of fare paying passengers down to the Canary Islands, where this guy had deplaned, taken a few steps on the tarmac, done an immediate about turn, climbed back up the steps, and flown straight back to the UK, arriving home the same day.

So, yes, *technically* this guy won, if you're playing by a strict interpretation of the rather sketchy rules.

I feel the victory was morally mine; **Option 1** adherents, I concede, might wish to argue the point further.

In any case, I'm pretty sure I'd had the better all-round experience.

Quite what my German friend made of the whole palaver I never knew, for we sadly lost contact thereafter, as happened all too easily in an age of epistolary contact, our paths not crossing that summer in Patmos, nor since.

We drifted apart, lost to the fog of time, and the absence of future online resources that have since enabled distantly geographically situated friends to stay better connected.

Were the Lady ever to Be Passing, the Lady is, of course, *more than welcome* to Drop In.

Chapter 27

Trucking Hell

London, UK.

My Patmian holiday concluded with the traditional tearful Long Goodbyes. I sometimes wonder why we choose to wind down in such great places, amongst such great company: the emotional wrench of saying *Farewell* to all and sundry undoes much of the previous three weeks' first-rate unwinding. I wonder whether, maybe, it might be simpler never to leave the confines of our own shores, to never develop a taste for such paradises, for this would be one sure-fire tactic to sidestep the inevitable melancholy a holiday conclusion habitually begets. Maybe a life of perpetual gloom, of perpetual rigid orthodoxy, of continuous nose to the grindstone, is easier and more straightforward to endure than the rollercoaster Highs of fun-filled holiday hiatuses, and the inevitable ensuing resumption of work-based hardships Lows.

I know. 1st World Problems. I seek no sympathy.

In need of a positive light inside this Tunnel of Despondency, I decide to reconnect with our friendly Freight Forwarding connection, on the off-chance he might be able to hook me up with a second lorry ride, this time all the way down to Greece.

Athens specifically.

To arrive middle of August, pretty please.

Bit of a long shot, but worth a try.

A few days later, my contact calls back. I will need to head over to the Czechoslovakian and Hungarian Embassies, to avail myself of the requisite Transit Visas - these cannot be issued at the respective borders, unlike those for East Germany and Yugoslavia - but, yes, he has an Athens-bound departure, setting out from Battersea Park in just under a fortnight's time.

Be there week on Monday, no later than 2pm.

I scurry excitedly around central London, to the respective Embassies, returning with the necessary Transit Visas duly stamped inside my passport, all ready for the adventure to begin.

I have no idea.

The driver's name is Milngavie Monroe (this is not his real name, for reasons that will shortly become all too apparent). Monroe hails from Scotland, from a wee village just to the north of Glasgow, a place pronounced *Mull-guy* (the non-obvious pronunciation isn't a problem if the place-name only comes up in conversation).

Pronouncing place names in a manner totally disparate to their phonetic spelling (at least, to the average (wo)man on the street) is a cunning ruse locals employ all over the UK, to swiftly delineate between Friend and Foe, to deftly weed the Also-Ran-Undesirables out from the (S)He's-Alright-Jack In-Group.

'See 'im,' the Locals will say – conspiratorially, whisperingly - at your butchering of their village's moniker, ''e's Not From these Parts be...'

Best to get out of Dodge. Fast.

Even were you an obvious outsider, breezing into, say, Frome, having established in advance that this fine town is, in fact, pronounced *Froom* – other such urban linguistic traps include Fowey = *Foy*; or Cholmondeley = *Chumley* - will grant you a markedly more genial welcoming party, than if you'd rocked up from the Big Smoke, whizzing in like a bloody Knight Rider in your glitzy, gas-guzzling Chelsea Tractor – You, and your fancy *Big City Ways* - and then butchered their cherished village's name.

Me, I hail from the south of England, a quiet, leafy suburb of SW London. My enunciation and pronunciation are therefore Home Counties. Those with a habit of dropping their *t's* and losing their *h's*, who believe *glottal stops* are devices with which dentists wedge rotten gums wide apart, might even say *posh*.

By contrast, Monroe's accent is broader than the Moray Firth, and deeper than the darkest depths of Loch Ness. Making out even 10% of what he is saying as he greets me that morning is therefore something of a challenge.

Of course, you'd have to ask *him* what percentage of *my* utterings he is able to decipher.

Our shared British values of politeness and civility mean we smile and grin at each other, despite our obvious differences.

This trip, I have a feeling, will be interesting.

Monroe shows me inside his smart Scania cab. Up front: two large, extremely comfortable spring-loaded seats - driver on the left, passenger on the right, despite the UK plates - separated by a large flat surface (which in a car would usually be taken up by the gear lever and the handbrake).

Back of the cab, behind these two seats, a set of bunked beds, sleeping arrangements far more restful than their first viewing suggests. Curtains can be drawn, creating perfect blackout conditions for a restful night's slumber.

Food provisions: stored in a compartment half-way down the outside of the truck's first (of 2) container set up (same overall length as a regular single container set up, just with an additional pivot point separating the two containers). We have quite the hoard, Monroe shows me, sufficient food for a fortnight, he says, not the anticipated 4 - 5 days I have been told this trip will most likely require.

All in all, a most amenable set-up.

****

Perusing a map of the European Continent, you might on first glance conclude, as did I, that the best route between England and Greece takes you down through France, across the top of Italy, thence around and down through the Balkan states, that, in 1988, were still the single entity *Yugoslavia*, but are now (in the 2020s) their own separate countries: Slovenia; Croatia; Serbia; Montenegro; Macedonia; Kosovo; and Bosnia.

For us and our 40-ton lorry, however, this itinerary has serious drawbacks, hindrances in the shape of the not insignificant mountain ranges, the flanks of the Alps, that provide a not insubstantial barrier to the smooth non-mountainous passage a bulky, freight-loaded lorry demands.

Monroe's route, instead, takes us across the channel to Belgium, through West Germany, into East Germany, down through Czechoslovakia, Hungary, and Yugoslavia, before finally heading through Thessaloniki, in northern Greece, thence to Athens, a little more than 2,000 road miles later.

Our route takes us close to Berlin; around the ring-roads of Prague and Budapest.

Behind the Iron Curtain.

Another World, as far as I am concerned.

Unbeknownst to us all, the Fall of the Berlin Wall is less than a year away. A dramatic, long-awaited event which, almost comically, will be inadvertently set in motion, a poorly-prepared Official giving out incorrect Procedural Information at a hastily convened press conference, a briefing intended to *quell* rumours that permanent Exit Passes might available, rather than add to the quickly swelling numbers then heading towards the main checkpoints.

Thence, the restoration of Germany as one Single Entity.

A domino of Capitulations across other similarly constrained Eastern European Countries.

Thence, the removal of heavily-militarised borders between East and West Europe;

And so, the end of 40+ years of oppressive and brutal Totalitarian Regimes.

Joy and happiness unbound, therefore, for all those trapped inside this Authoritarian Hell, although to off-set this joy and happiness somewhat, David Hasselhoff will then decide to rock up for his Moment in the Spotlight.

So, yeh, even in these joyous, epoch-defining moments, there will still be some serious hurdles for the poor, put-upon Communist Citizens to overcome.

'*Looking for Freedom*?' the Hasselhoff will warble.

If you had the misfortune to be living behind this Curtain of Iron, with few Basic Liberties, scant Freedom of Speech, under the Constant Glare of rather different sets of Spotlights, Disappeared at Will, the answer might be something along the lines of whether Bears prefer to Poop in Densely Arboreal Topographical Regions.

The timing of our Trip would therefore prove most aleatoric; a last chance to sneak a peek at the ravaging effects of Communism, for as the Wall came crashing down, the European Continent was forever changed.

****

Lorry drivers are contracted by Freight Forwarding companies for each load they ship. Rather than being paid by the hour, or by the day, they are simply paid a one-off fee to transport a load from A to B.

The driver has complete autonomy over his (or her) decision-making processes.

The driver chooses the route.

The driver decides how many days the trip will take them (whilst keeping to a deadline).

The driver pays their own fuel and other associated costs.

Obviously, the fewer days each run requires, the more loads a driver can accept each month; the more each driver will subsequently earn.

To counter the risk of lorry drivers spending more hours at the wheel than is considered physically or mentally safe, all (legally running) lorries must be fitted with a tachometer. These tachometers record the lorry's speed and driving hours onto a paper disk that sits behind the dashboard speedometer (the technology has since gone digital). A lorry's tachometer disc must be surrendered on demand should a police officer request. These discs must also be filed by the driver after each trip, for a period of several years, in case their tachometer records are required by their Government for auditing purposes.

These discs are therefore designed to ensure each lorry driver adheres rigidly to the Rules.

No more than nine hours' daily driving duration, although for two days a week this can be extended to ten.

No more than 56 mph on the speedometer.

Rules. Rules.

Pesky Rules.

According to my connection, Milngavie Monroe was a legend amongst the UK Trucking Community, regularly completing the London-Tehran run in a mere ten days, quite the feat for a 3,500-mile journey, across a dozen or so frontier crossings and border/customs checks, a journey for which most drivers required a fortnight, or more.

Under normal circumstance, and strictly by the Rules, the London-Athens run requires a week to be completed, my connection says.

Monroe, he informs me, will most likely cover the distance in just four days.

I am, needless to say, intrigued.

****

Introductions complete, tyres kicked, load checked and secured, passports and visas at the ready, we set off for Dover, for the ferry across the English Channel to Zeebrugge, fresh in the excitement of such a long road trip, to pastures new and sights unknown.

Well, I, for one, am excited.

Hard to tell with deadpan, poker-faced Monroe.

At the port, I learn Good News: lorry drivers and their Drivers' Mates are provided with a complimentary berth on the ferry.

I say, *Good News*.

As it turns out, whilst free accommodation may be a welcome addition to the comfort of the 5-hour night crossing, one needs to then consider the fact that your new cabin roomies could be as many as seven total strangers, total strangers in the shape of truckers – most likely of a conspicuously corpulent nature – truckers whose personal hygiene regimes might be politely described as *somewhat suspect* at best, and whose unhealthy guts, being rocked incessantly by the relentless churn of the mid-Channel swell, will, more than likely erupt - at either end - with predictably objectionable results.

That evening, we are presented with a mere Force-5, south-westerly breeze, creating a moderately dynamic sea swell. Gale force winds these most definitely are not, yet despite this relatively calm sea state, all night long terrifyingly guttural sounds can be heard emanating from the men's Heads, disturbing sounds not best suited to soporific goals, sounds echoing continuously along the lower deck corridors, sounds only punctuated by the frequent crashes of heavy, unlatched doors slamming shut, over, and over, and over, and over.

Boom!

Boom!

Boom!

Boom!

Inside the cabin, the truckers' continuous grunting and farting creates an agricultural pungency difficult to ignore. The density of these noxious gases forces them to sink groundward, coagulating at just the wrong height for those of us on the lower bunks to then have clean, fresh, oxygenated air at our disposal for the fundamental requirement of breathing.

There appears no escape.

Seeking respite under the bed covers risks suffocation; remaining head above the sheets risks gradual poisoning.

I am left to stew in this windowless, subterranean vault, relentlessly counting sheep, chalking off never-ending minutes, tugging on that imaginary rope pulling the ship fathom by fathom port-wards without ever seeming to bring our destination any closer.

For five of the longest hours, sleep is impossible to find.

So, no, not the most restful crossing ever.

Chapter 28

Adroit, or *à Droite*?

Our lorry departs the port of Zeebrugge.

Monroe and I immediately approach our first Continental road junction together.

This is a deeply symbolic moment, for this is the first of what will doubtless be thousands of such junctions before we eventually reach Athens, more than 3,000km away.

Here we go.

Our options?

To the right: the sign announces, *Toutes Directions*;

To the left: *Centre Ville*.

I imagine this a beginner's level Decision for Monroe to make.

We are now turning left.

Hmm.

OK.

Interesting.

I ponder whether to query out loud the inherent wisdom of this decision, but consider it far too early in our relationship to be questioning Monroe about his choice of route, about whether he's clued up sufficiently on the direction we're supposed to be taking.

'Just *who* is this cocky kid who thinks he knows the route better than me?' I imagine him thinking.

It is our first junction together, after all.

Casting aspersions on my new buddy's sense of direction from the Get-Go is almost certainly *not* the Done Thing.

In any case, we may be turning right again before too long; Monroe may, for all I know, have a cunning short cut in mind.

Alas, no.

Faster than you can say 'Should've-turned-right-Old-Pal' – *Toutes Directions* being the optimal choice, after all – we and our lorry of not-inconsiderable dimensions have reached Bruges town centre.

Beautiful, medieval Bruges.

Narrow, 12th century cobbled streets.

17m, 40-ton, articulated road-train.

In an ideal world, the two should never become acquainted.

Sure enough, before we've had time to register the potential ramifications of our current situation, we reach a tight, narrow, 90-degree bend in the road. The truck can proceed no further, forward progress blocked by the requirement to utilise both sides of the road to effect this sharp turn, and the oncoming traffic now blocking our way needing to reverse fifty metres, or more, for this manoeuvre to possess even a remote chance of success.

In a flash, Stalemate has been achieved.

So, what to do?

Monroe shrugs, a deep sigh emitting from his person.

Quite what this deep sigh means is a mystery. Did he mean to turn left; or has he only just awoken to the error of his ways? I sense that asking too many probing questions right now might not be the most constructive of ideas.

From our perspective, backing up is Out of the Question, given both the volume of traffic that has quickly built up behind us, and the difficulties of reversing an articulated, two-container truck in any case (simply reversing in a straight line requires a great deal of skill, the front container causing the rear to veer off course at even the tiniest off-line deviation).

The tailback of cars now blocking our path seems to have no desire to reorganise themselves either, to enable us all to simply get on again with our days, with minimal delay from this unexpected turn of events.

Stalemate indeed.

Given our collective intransigence, the traffic has now come to a complete standstill, in both directions, the tailbacks building up fast.

All too predictably, after less than a minute, the Automobile Birdsong begins, dozens of car horns blaring angrily, with ever-increasing frequency, as if one *beeped* call is a response to another in this Sea of Song, majestic yet mysterious interactions between this flock of two-ton chunks of steel.

Toot!

Toot!

Honk!

Toot toot!

Honk! Honk!

Toot toot toot!

Quite what these peculiar calls signify, or what purpose they serve, Scientists have yet to decipher, despite many years of focused, in-depth research. In the midst of this curious cacophony, dozens of drivers then leave their vehicles, embarking upon a series of unchoreographed, bizarre dance movements, movements incorporating elevated sound projections and wild, arhythmic bodily gesticulations – a tad heavy on the arms, hands and digits, particularly the middle- and fore-fingers, not enough with the legs, if you asked me – movements all seemingly directed towards us inside our lorry.

All the while, the Automobile Birdsong continues its Merry Tune.

For these drivers, these bodily gesticulations must serve a deeper, hidden purpose, given the absolute zero impact on easing the current deadlocked situation they appear to possess. The movements don't seem to be making them any happier, in any case, such are the deep frowns etched upon the multitude of faces now staring intently our way, at the two of us, ensconced, safely – for now - inside our cab.

'Sure, shout, and holler, and throw hand-gestured insults our way,' I feel like shouting, 'but *none of us* is going *anywhere* if you lot don't sort yourselves out, soon'.

Instead, I slink down in my seat, feeling rather overwhelmed and embarrassed by the whole affair, and far too visible and exposed due to the cab's double-heighted windscreen.

All the while, the Automobile Birdsong continues its Merry Tune.

The arm-waving and hand gestures persist.

An age seemingly passes before the Police finally deign to arrive - two in cars, two on motorbikes, lights flashing, sirens blaring - to attend to this Major Incident caused by this wee foul-up, our unintentional misreading of a simple road sign.

My youthful embarrassment only increases with the Police's presence; just what have I got myself into?

The officers quickly take control of the situation, blowing their whistles officiously and shrilly at all and sundry, forcing the drivers back into their vehicles, pointing at each car in turn, ordering them to move to one side, or to reverse into a more out of the way spot, until, ten minutes later, all the cars have been suitably repositioned. The road then opens up for us to set off once again, this time a Police Escort leading the way, until we have crossed the town limits, no longer a grave menace to the peaceful *Bürgers* of Bruges.

See. That wasn't so hard, was it?

Quite why these supposedly mature drivers couldn't have worked that all out for themselves is a mystery.

Still, not quite the start to our journey I had been expecting.

As we continue on our way, Monroe says nothing about his wee error.

I decide to follow his lead, and take the Not Mentioning It option, too.

****

We continue on through Belgium. Outside, light rain falls; it is a decidedly grey morning. Inside the cab, the mood is equally grey. Silence masks a sense of unease at why what just occurred actually transpired. Monroe has driven this route scores of times previously, or so I believe.

He can't be making this up as he goes along, can he?

I am still trying to process our Bruges debacle when, an hour or so later, we turn off the autoroute at a random, nondescript junction, passing through narrow residential streets of nondescript, grey, pebble-dashed bungalows, in a nowhere village you surmised would have looked no less bleak even were the drizzle not to have been falling persistently as it was, the type of drizzle that appears harmless to the uninitiated, but has you soaked in just a few minutes nonetheless.

Torrential drizzle.

Trust me. It exists.

I glance across at Monroe, who must have sensed my unspoken question.

'Fuel', he says.

I nod.

This proves to be one of the better Monroe conversations; one word spoken; one word understood.

100% ratio. Should probably quit whilst we're ahead; it can only be downhill from here.

Our detour destination hoves into view, an unassuming fuel depot, whose gates are, it appears from the heavy chain and over-sized padlock, firmly locked. There is no one around to greet us and grant us access.

Despite our unscheduled town centre stop, it is still early morning. The day has yet to really get going.

Monroe honks the truck's horn. A minute or two passes before a glabrous, mid- to late-fifties guy sporting a superior level of embonpoint emerges from out of nowhere, waddling over to unlock the gates for us, his shiny pate glistening brilliantly in the drizzle.

We drive inside the compound. Given the weather, I decide to stay in the cab whilst Monroe gets down to speak with this man. The two shake hands heartily, grinning at each other like long-lost friends. Formalities concluded, our fuel depot buddy then points to a spot beside one of the fuel containers, a railway carriage-sized cylindrical metal container with a range of Hazchem signs adorning its side, up to which Monroe then slowly manoeuvres the truck.

I am advised to decamp whilst the tanks are now filled.

Can't have me being blown to smithereens should the truck decide to explode courtesy of an errant spark somehow overcoming the incessant drizzle, permeating the highly flammable fuel.

We're not just filling the main tanks, Monroe tells me, but also the Reserves.

I learn the first of Monroe's many bugbears when he points out, with, I sense, deep-seated annoyance, that Continental lorry drivers visiting the UK usually rely on their own Reserves for the entirety of their visit to our fine motorway network, thereby avoiding paying into the UK tax coffers for the use of *our* roads.

Fuel in the UK has high levies added to cover the cost of road network upkeep (unlike countries where fuel is cheaper, and the cost of usage is covered by Motorway Tolls, or *Vignette* purchase).

Not paying for their UK motorway usage gives European truckers an unfair advantage, or so Monroe feels.

Mad, angry Monroe of Milngavie.

Something, Monroe says, needs to be done.

I don't know enough about the issue to comment either way.

What I do know enough about is drizzle; I know I am now completely soaked through.

See. Told you.

Chapter 29

Sneaking a Peek Behind the Curtain

The Belgian autoroutes soon give way to the smooth *Autobahn* of West Germany. We are pottering along the inside lane at a sloth-like 56mph, some terrible late-'80s European Rock blearing out of the crackly radio, whilst an array of finest West German industrial innovation speeds past us at 160kph+, disappearing off into the distance in a blur of fuzzy light.

Mercedes. BMW. VW.

Glitzy, shiny, expensive specimens of Advanced Mechanical Engineering.

Vorsprung durch Technik, or so used to be said.

The *Technik* whizzes past before I've had time to blink.

Our own *Vorsprung*, by contrast, is far more sedate.

We continue our march onwards, ever onwards, our snail-like progress allowing me to study in minute detail the finest roadside architecture and motorway intersection layouts Europe has to offer, until, after several hours of driving, the first large rectangular signs appear at the roadside, announcing our proximity to this section's conclusion.

The border slowly looms large, the crossing into East Germany at *Herleshausen/ Wartha*, one of three *autobahn* Border Checkpoints.

Slowly, but emphatically, the Curtain is closing in.

The *Iron* Curtain.

Just saying those words evokes a weird sense.

Rushes of excitement and nervous anticipation course through my veins, a sense like nothing I, at my young age, have hitherto experienced: all the Tragic Tales, all the Sad Stories, all the Hype, the Mystery, the Other-Worldliness surrounding the mere mention of Communism and Totalitarianism.

I am nervously excited to soon witness this Land of Horror through my own eyes.

Something forever an *abstract* Reality, soon to become a *tangible, material* Reality.

Sure, you can read scores of books, watch dozens of TV documentaries, study any number of photographs, but these all lack a *certain something*; there's simply no substitute for experiencing a place such as this - this *Place* in this *Unique Moment in Time* - up close, in person, in oh-so *Real Time*.

No substitute for being able to step inside the scene your mind has conjured up, from information gleaned over the better part of a decade.

How, you wonder, does the reality compare to your own, most likely inexact, interpretations formed from these information sources, interpretations limited by your own somewhat narrow, definitely blinkered, dearth of life experience?

The traffic going this way thins out dramatically as we approach the frontier.

We have arrived.

There is no turning back.

Time to peek behind the Curtain.

The West German exit formalities are passed through swiftly, without hassle nor sideways glance; no, 'Why would you want to go *that* way?' glares.

An unexpectedly straightforward process.

Auf Wiedersehen, West Germany.

Slowly, we drive through the eerie No-Man's-Land between West and East, until we reach the next frontier marker, a vast – *Deutsche Demokratische Republik* – sign, writ large in bold, Gothic-Germanic-Blackletter-font – a foreboding stylistic format that lends even the sweetest of love sonnets a creepy, sinister air. We are surrounded by double-lined, 12-foot high barbed wire topped metal fencing, as far as the eye can see in either direction, fencing punctuated at regular intervals with elevated, turreted spotlights and watchtowers.

Ubiquitous, ominous signage announces *'Halt!'*, *'Verboten'*, *'Achtung!'*.

The thought 'Or else?' never for a millisecond enters your mind.

We have, it would appear, entered a place where Things are *Very Serious*.

This Place exudes the aura that *Bad Things* have occurred here; *Bad Things* will certainly occur here *again* if you don't watch your step, Sonny Boy.

This Place shouts loudly, I am not a Place you should mistakenly enter, the result of a misjudged wrong turn, or a spur of the moment whim.

This Place is neither *Centre Ville,* nor *Toutes Directions*.

This is Place is *Eine Richtung*.

Proudly, openly, and to my mind conceitedly, the signs emit a sense that you may not like where this road leads, but you'd be mistaken for not taking this Place *Very Seriously Indeed*.

I am wondering what happens next, whilst we round a 90-degree bend in the road, a slip road now leading us behind and parallel to the endless lines of high-security fencing. Despite it being daytime and a less-than-dull day, a spotlight appears to target us, illuminating unnecessarily our slow progress along the access road.

We roll forwards at a deliberate, sloth-like pace, slowly towards a large canopied arena about half a mile down the road. As we near, and the scene comes better into focus, I make out a building that for all the world resembles many a city's vast central train terminals – high-vaulted, canopied ceiling, supported by a skeleton of knobbly metallic struts - except for the distinct lack of tracks running beneath this canopy.

Trackless this Place may be, but awaiting our arrival is an array of over-sized, 5-truck-length platforms, standing there in expectation of our manoeuvring alongside, given the platforms appear to be just the right for us to be able to step straight from lorry onto the grey, concrete-slabbed surfaces.

We approach the underside of the canopy; as we enter its shadow, on the platform, fanning out rapidly and with military precision, are twenty or so uniformed, rifle-armed soldiers.

Bright ceiling lights are switched on, dazzling brighter than the daylight outside.

Yikes.

Now, we are being directed to park alongside this soldier-hewn platform.

As we manoeuvre into position, the soldiers perform another coordinated scamper.

Now, we are being completely surrounded.

By the time we have parked to the satisfaction of the soldier guiding us in, and the engine has shut down, the lorry's position is completely covered by the *Grenztrüppen*; the sight of these men just a tad menacing when viewed from inside the cab.

I take stock of our new surroundings.

Now, another squad of twenty well-armed soldiers is congregating on the platform, in addition to the twenty now surrounding the truck. Their exaggerated machinations and manoeuvring create a deeply daunting, and genuinely foreboding, sight to my young eyes.

I feel the Commanders could possibly be accused of employing a slightly excessive Show of Force against our solitary truck – accused from a suitable distance of course, out of earshot; yet who knows what horrors they have previously encountered, what threats they currently face.

Monroe and I could hardly look less like an Invading Force if we tried, but what do I know.

We may be *exactly* what an Invading Force chooses to look like.

Double, triple *secret* bluff, with sprinkles.

I evidently lack their years of military expertise, and extensive military intelligence. I fear we may have unwittingly driven ourselves into another fine, yet far more serious, mess.

There may be no Police escort to save us from this situation; no whistles nor sirens to extricate us from this particular pickle.

Monroe and I sit motionless in the cab, a little unsure what to do next.

One of the soldiers waves at us, gun now aimed in more than just our *general* direction – rather more *at* us, than *towards* us, if you asked me - grabbing our undivided attention, beckoning us to exit the cab, pointing then towards a screened partition over in the middle of the platform, repeatedly, any ambiguity as to what is now required of us most definitely removed.

Us - partition; us – partition; us – partition.

Us over to Partition.

Right you are, old chap.

Just be a sec.

We both step down onto the platform through Monroe's side of the cab and are duly escorted over to the screen in the middle of the platform, some thirty or so metres from the lorry.

'Wait here', we are told, 'don't move'.

Here behind the screen is the Place we should Stay, not anywhere else, *Verstehen Sie, ja?*

Dutifully, as one would when surrounded by a small platoon of menacing, well-armed soldiers, we comply without hesitation, very much being in a state of Total *Verstehen*.

Monroe and I stand there in silence.

Minutes pass.

I look Monroe; Monroe looks at me.

I stare at the floor, the ceiling, the soldiers' rifles, my fingernails.

As my gaze relocates from floor to ceiling, it momentarily coincides with of one of the soldier's head turning motions.

For a fleeting micro-second, my eyes lock with his.

Oh shit.

I smile that pathetic smile you effect when finding yourself in an awkward situation and you've absolutely no idea how to respond.

The soldier doesn't return the acknowledgment.

I look back at my fingernails with increased scrutiny.

I hope I've not overstepped an invisible line.

I hope smiling is not *Verboten* here.

I hope the soldier's not thinking of shooting me for my impudence.

I am now a tense bundles of nerves.

There is no bench for us to rest our rumps on, so Monroe and I are forced to stand, for what seems an age, shifting our weight from one leg to the other, and back again.

An Age become an Eternity.

From the other side of the screen I can hear dogs barking – Alsatians – sniffer dogs used to detect the presence of stowaways who might, for whatever reason, be trying to get into East Germany.

I suggest to Monroe that surely the more pressing threat would be the tens of thousands trying to get *out*, but, again, what do I know?

Monroe shrugs.

He appears dulled to the commotion.

He's totally unfazed, having seen this all dozens of times previously.

An Eternity becomes an Epoch.

A whole fifteen minutes. Twenty, maybe.

Longer, possibly.

Just like that, on the other side of the partition noise is suddenly noticeable by its absence.

The sounds of bustle, of voices issuing instruction, of doors slamming open and shut, of dogs barking, of feet marching forcibly along the platform, of purposeful and directed activity of any description emanating from the other side of this partition, all appear to have now ceased.

For no reason I can think of, I decide to take the opportunity this lull in proceedings permits to poke my head out from our hidden position behind the screen and assess the current State of Play.

Mistake.

Big, big mistake.

One of the Alsatians catches sight of me, immediately transforming into a dog exhibiting signs of extreme agitation, even to the most un-canine-cognisant. The beast is tugging belligerently on its leash, sharp fangs bared, with a sense of growled urgency, an urgency thankfully thwarted by the soldier's firm grip on its lead.

I recoil in shock, doubtful as I am that the dog's sudden urge to rush over is merely for the purpose of cuddles and belly rubs.

This canine commotion is then joined by loud, unintelligible yet most definitely angry shouts emanating from the soldiers standing either side of the man holding Cujo's leash.

The men all point at me – You! Yes, You, Laddie! - with some urgency, their gestures most definitively requesting me to Shoo the Hell Away, and to Shoo the Hell Away now.

I am not fully fluent in standard East German military hand signals by any means, but I am pretty sure their manual motionings mean, 'If you don't want to be ravaged by a wild, rabid Alsatian, Fuck Off back behind the screen, and Fuck Off back behind the screen NOW!'

Monroe grabs me by the scruff, duly pulling me back behind the screen.

'I wouldn'ae do tha' a-gin, boy,' he says, sagely, although, to be honest, the penny has by now already dropped.

Not looking around the screen. Gotcha.

Another twenty or so minutes pass.

The soldiers and their dogs have, one would presume by now, been inside and around the entirety of the cab and its two trailers. It would appear the *Grenztrüppen* are satisfied we are not transporting any stowaways, nor other clandestine or illegal merchandise inside the truck, nor concealed on our person.

We are, the Head Honcho finally informs us, free to continue our journey to Passport Check.

We climb back aboard, thanking the soldiers for their time, as you do if you are British and brainwashed into politeness, and set off, having successfully navigated Passport and Documentation Control, out into East Germany proper.

We are now *behind* the Iron Curtain.

I need to kick myself to check if this is all real.

We are now behind the f-ing Iron Curtain!

We've driven only about five or ten minutes on from the border when, for no real reason I can think of, I decide to remove my simple Point-and-Press holiday-snaps camera from its resting place under my seat. I'm not entirely sure what I intend to do with it, but now seems as good a time as any to fiddle around with the camera, to check it is still fully functioning.

Monroe looks across at me, then at the camera, his face in a flash draining of all colour.

'You have a camera?' he asks,

'Er, yes', I say, holding it up for him to see in better detail, even though I'm guessing this was more of a rhetorical question.

'Shit, shit, shittetty-shit,' comes the reply from the other side of the cab.

'Is that a problem?' I ask. I have no idea what the issue might be.

'Well, ye'see', Monroe replies, 'I hav tae reet doon a leest ona peece'o peyper all te el-lek-tronik ee-quip-ment we're brin'in in we'us'.

(At this juncture, I wish to apologise profusely for my piss-poor attempt to replicate Monroe's broad Scottish accent and his idiomatic peculiarities. I have is no desire to cause offence. Believe me when I say that my attempts are a very rough approximation, that were I able to phonetically transcribe his vernacular verbatim the result would look most odd indeed).

My camera. His list.

Ah. The penny drops again.

'So, it's nae prob-lem tae hev one, bu'it'll be whin thee chick t'list on tae way oot. What we hav has'tae mutch ex-ootly. If there's a cam'ra here whin there were nae cam'ra a-fore, ooh, there'll be troo-ble for oos. A' bes', they'll mek me dreev o'er i'wit me trook. Tae croosh it. At wors', weell...'

The ante has, inadvertently, been raised.

DefCon 3.

Condition Amber.

With the full innocence and naivety of youth, I remain blissfully blasé about the whole issue, unlike Monroe, who, true to his word, becomes somewhat jittery at each of the subsequent Inner Line border crossings we make.

Thankfully – obviously, given I am writing this here now, not locked up somewhere cold and dark, penning this sad tale via a medium of bodily excretions writ upon scraps of scavenged (used) toilet paper - my now illicit camera is not detected.

The *Hohenschönhausen* can wait. It may have been a close-run thing, but, well, who can honestly say?

****

There are numerous unique and exciting new sights to take in now we've entered East Germany, but what first catches my attention is not visual but aural.

The billiard table smoothness of the West German *autobahn* has been replaced by a constant, incessant, *da-dum, da-dum, da-dum, da-dum* emanating from somewhere beneath us.

Is something, I wonder, wrong with the truck?

Nope. The issue is not with the lorry.

With its government strapped for cash, East German motorways consist merely of one long strip of concrete, which when initially laid and hardened is then set upon by Line Punching machines, creating narrow breaks into the solid strip's surface, at regular 50m intervals, breaks into which a freeze-resistant, rubber-like material is then poured.

The pouring levels are inexact, alas, creating small mounds of rubber overspill, at regular 50m intervals, all the way along the motorway.

Da-dum, da-dum, da-dum, da-dum, da-dum.

There is absolutely no getting away from it.

Da-dum, da-dum, da-dum, da-dum, da-dum.

In an attempt to blank out this unwelcome background soundtrack, I avert my gaze to the other vehicles sharing the motorway with us. The road is sparsely populated; vehicular volume roughly 70% down on the West.

Gone are the shiny, brightly coloured, state-of-the-art (for the time, at least) West German Beemers and Mercedes.

In their place, a motley assortment of dull, pastel-hewed, rickety, run-down cars, a collection of beat-up Ladas, Skodas and Trabants, odd-looking vehicles for all the world resembling the bastard offspring of a drunken, late-night, behind-the-bike-sheds knee-trembler between a Morris Hillman and a Robin Reliant.

Dark greys, light browns, dirty creams, faded ochres; an achromatic assortment that could never be accused of exuding fun, happiness, nor any sense of *joi de vivre*.

Colour, gaiety - and quite possibly Happiness – it would appear, have been roundly banished from this Place.

Totalitarian regimes, it seems, need to (re)emphasise the point that they are seriously *Serious Places*.

Colour *ist Verboten*.

Alles ist Verboten.

Perhaps, even *Verboten* is *Verboten,* too.

Every now and then, the outside lane fills as a convoy of shiny, black Mercedes races past, a dozen cars or more, packed nose to bumper in tight formation, presumably transporting dozens of High-Ranked, Slightly-More-Equal-than-the-lowly-Hoi-Polloi Officials to their vitally important, *Annual Farming Production Output* conferences, their, *Low-Cost, High-Efficiency Methods of Information Extraction from Unwilling & Unwitting Interrogation Subjects* pow-wow, or possibly simply *en route* to their lavish pads in the countryside, where their nubile young mistresses patiently await - under pain of being carted off to the Camps should they have the temerity to complain – primed to sooth away the Unbearable Stresses of running a Totalitarian Regime.

'Darling, it's Murder out there'.

Well, exactly.

Chapter 30

Short Cut to Heaven?

Monroe brings me up to speed on his driving strategy. His first point – underlined, highlighted in yellow, written in CAPITALS, flashing lights, too, in case the emphasis is not yet sufficient - is that he never, *ever* exceeds the speed limit.

Rule One.

Rule Two, he demonstrates as he reaches the end of what would normally be today's permissible 9-hour driving stint, is to replace the paper tachometer from behind the dashboard with that belonging to his 'brother'. He writes the new name in pencil on the fresh, unmarked circular tachometer, and onwards we speed (but not speeding), unencumbered by neither Rules nor Regulations.

What Rules, Rules, pesky Rules?

Monroe is, I am informed, a married man. **Rule Three** states that our overnight stops are not, alas, going to be in the vicinity of the many notorious truck stops dotting our route.

I don't really want to frequent one of these Dens of Iniquity in any case, Monroe says, populated as they are by overly soused, rough and ready truckers, and scores of brazen women of ill-repute, renowned for their moralistic lapses and worrisomely lascivious appetites.

Well....

No, seriously, these truck stops do, indeed, sound *dreadful* Dens of Iniquity.

Can't imagine *anywhere worse* to drink a beer.

Or two. Or three.

On the other hand, these are places of such infamous legend you feel a just one visit, for just one hour - or two, or possibly three - would be a highly educational endeavour.

In a purely Socio-Psycho-Anthropological sense of course.

After all, Knowledge is Power.

****

Day Two.

We've left East Germany. The border exit formalities were a markedly more laid-back affair than the heavily militarised shenanigans of the previous crossing, Monroe's camera stresses notwithstanding.

Of course, we are still behind the Curtain, still under the constant gaze of Who Knows Who?.

Nothing has changed in this regard.

Next up: Czechoslovakia.

I am not sad to see East Germany in our rear-view mirrors; not an ounce of regret that we have said *goodbye* to the incessant motorway-induced, mind-meltingly repetitious *da-dum, da-dum, da-dum, da-dum*. My brain can once again rest easy, no longer requiring the erasure of this sound from the other, more interesting, sensory inputs being sent my way.

We are once again cruising merrily along, at a strict 56mph, on an A-road, the scenery no longer one of empty vistas and grey, concrete monoliths, but lush, verdant, rolling hills, cultivated small-holding farmland, blink-and-you've-missed-them hamlets. More people are outside milling about, more people standing on the roadside, many with their thumbs out in the universal Language of the Hitch.

These hitchers are a mixed bag. Whilst most are well-presented, there are those who might wish to consider making a bit more of an effort, who might benefit from putting the boot on the other foot, from wondering, were they to see a muddy-from-head-to-toe individual holding a pig under one arm at the roadside, with his thumb out (the individual, that is, not the pig), would they *really* stop to give that person a lift?

Well, maybe the pig. Not so sure about the hitcher.

Most of these roadside thumb-waggers are youngsters, teenage girls predominantly, who have no qualms, it appears, in seeking a lift to the next town or village from whoever may be passing that way. We stop and give a few of them rides - a couple of girls, one young guy - each going ten or fifteen miles down the road, and having not a care in the world, or so it seemed, about getting up into a truck cab with two unknown men whose motives for offering them a ride might have been less than innocent.

It is, for sure, a more trusting landscape than that back at home.

We endeavour to engage the young lad and laddesses in conversation, but a triumvirate of a Czech trying to speak English, a Scotsman trying to speak English, and an Englishman trying to make heads or tails of both, whilst providing very rudimentary sign-language subtitles to his own dialogue, doesn't make for the most in-depth analysis of, 'Quality of Life and Prospects for the Average Teenager in 1980's Czechoslovakia'.

On a more positive note, I learn that Czech women, whose compatriots I had only ever previously studied on the telly once every four years, are not all endowed with the full-figured physique and rough-yet-homely visage of Olympic shot-putters.

Quite the revelation, in fact.

We drive tantalisingly close to Prague, the ring-road being the only view of that beautiful city I am afforded.

Budapest receives similar, brush-off treatment.

Oh, for there to have been time to spend an hour or two meandering these cities' cobbled streets, soaking up their atmospheres.

But this voyage, alas, is no sight-seeing trip.

Sure, OK, we have already taken in *one* medieval city-centre side trip.

Monroe is not, it seems, inclined to repeat *that* unintended excursion.

****

Day Three. Hungary.

We are currently approaching a motorway junction along an A-road we've been following the last few hours.

We reach the junction, then suddenly bear left.

We are now driving up, onto the motorway.

I am sure, however, that this section of road is in fact the Off-Ramp.

A car passes us in the opposite direction, lights flashing wildly.

Yup. This *is,* as I feared, the Off-Ramp.

What the…?

We are now on the motorway proper. We are now driving *into* the direction of traffic.

Sweet Mother of Mary.

Emboldened from the time spent with Monroe, this being our 697th junction together, I suggest, aloud, that there's maybe a wee possibility we might have just taken a second wrong turn.

'No, no', Monroe says. 'Short Cut'.

This is unlike any Short Cut I have ever previously taken.

Maybe it is a *Short Cut* to Heaven.

Monroe selects the right-hand of the two lanes, the one adjacent to the central barrier. We are on the left-hand side of the two-carriageway motorway, the two main carriageways separated by a continuous waist-high metal fence, the type designed to absorb the impact of any out of control vehicle attempting to break through to the wrong side of the motorway, into the oncoming traffic.

Had we suddenly been teleported back to the UK (or Thailand, or South Africa, or Japan, or Malta, or Australia, or India, or New Zealand) our position would have rendered us in the correct carriageway to be occupying. Alas, for us, we are not right now in any of those fine countries. Not being in any of those fine countries, right now, as far as I can tell anyway, we are currently heading straight into the oncoming traffic, with all the implications that driving on the wrong side of the motorway straight into oncoming traffic usually brings.

Bugger.

This brand of crazy, arse-about-face shenanigans doesn't usually end well.

In our favour, the road is not as densely packed as the M25 (London Orbital) during rush hour, or even the M25 during one of its less rush-houry moments.

What few evenly spaced cars there are currently heading straight for us have ample time to flash their lights, angrily, before changing lanes so as to pass by on our left-hand side, thereby avoiding an horrific, head-on collision.

'You're on the wrong side of the road, you idiots!!' their flashing lights seem to say.

'Yes, *we know*! *So* kind of you to move out of the way,' we reply, in headlight Morse.

We continue onwards, forwards, continuously hooted and flashed at by whoever we happen to encounter. Monroe remains serenely undeterred by the obvious ire being shown our way.

'Might is right' or so the saying goes: if you've got the bigger rig, it's a pretty safe bet others will be the ones to ensure what needs to be done to avoid a collision is *indeed* done, lest *they* come off decidedly second best.

'What', I ask Monroe, '*are we doing?*'

Monroe tells me he has a Plan.

He has a Plan!

Thank the Lord.

Were he making this all up on the spot, we'd both be in serious trouble.

The Plan, he divulges, is for us to simply keep driving along on the wrong side of the carriageway, until such time as we encounter a gap in the continuous central reservation.

Monroe will then stop the lorry.

I, then, will be required to jump out, and pull apart the bollards purposefully placed in such gaps to stop crazy lorry drivers from using them for shortcuts, and suchlike.

I, then, will need to create a gap of sufficient space and width for us to then shimmy the 40-ton lorry through this newly created gap, enter the right - correct - side of the road, and thence be on our merry way.

Simple.

I wonder why I hadn't thought of that myself.

Some Plan.

How, *exactly,* did we get ourselves into this fine mess?

How, *on earth*, does Munroe think this route is a suitable short cut, no matter how many miles it might shave off the overall journey?

Sure enough, after about five more minutes of this mad malarkey, with yet more cars flashing and honking their horns manically at us, we encounter the first suitable shimmy-through gap. Good to his word, Monroe stops the truck in the fast lane of the motorway, oblivious, it seems, to the increased danger that this has placed him – us - in.

To mitigate the danger, the *Hazards* are illuminated.

So, that's alright, then. *Totally* safe now.

Quickly, I jump down from the cab, scurry over to the bollards, and survey the scene, to evaluate just what this 'pulling the bollards to one side' job actually entails.

The bollards, it appears, are in fact neck-high metal poles, embedded into waist-high tubs of concrete, each one I'm guessing weighing the better part of 200kgs+.

I set about budging the first bollard in the line.

Darn.

Nope, light and easy to budge it most definitely is not.

I pull with all my might, I push with all my weight, but this bugger of a bollard really does not want to shift. The concrete-on-concrete action of the bollard against the carriageway is too much friction-induced inertia for me to shift.

'Get a move on!' shouts Monroe.

'I'm trying!' I reply.

Less than a minute later, his patience expires in a puff of smoke.

Monroe leaps down from his side of the cab into the fast lane of the motorway – Danger? What danger? - walking slowly around the front of the lorry to join me in my endeavour. He quickly learns that, whilst I might not be the world's strongest man, it's not entirely my weediness that is causing my ineptness.

What we have here is a Krypton Factor test: shift a half-dozen, 200kg+ concrete bollards, in the shortest time possible, no prize for winning, the consolation prize for failing simply to remain on the incorrect side of this carriageway, for all Eternity.

We try pushing the bollard together simultaneously.

Nope.

We try pulling simultaneously.

Nope.

Simultaneously, we rock the bollard forwards, and backwards, and - ah, lightbulb moment – yes, we have found the solution.

Once we've shifted this bollard onto its base rim, together we are able to roll it, carefully, manoeuvring the chunk of concrete to one side.

Bingo. Lift off.

Having figured out the solution to this wee problem, we roll the second, the third, the fourth, the fifth, and finally the sixth bollard, out to one side, working as quickly as we can whilst simultaneously trying to ensure that each bollard is rolled in a straight line, and not out into the road, as the circular base is want to do, or over our feet, as did occur.

More Haste, Less Speed. A damn fine motto.

Shimmying-gap created, job all done, we climb back up into the cab, perform our wee shimmy through this newly-created gap, quickly checking there is no oncoming traffic on our right-hand side – got to be *careful* after all, *don't want to cause an accident* - and we are now back on the right – and *right* - side of the road.

Simple

'Seaved oos for-tea mile, tha' di',' Monroe informs me.

Events have unfurled so rapidly, I wasn't able to spot whether there had, in fact, been an available on-ramp at that last junction. I guess I have no other choice than to take Monroe's word at face value.

It occurs to me, suddenly, that this cannot be the first time Monroe has performed this manoeuvre.

I wonder how many times previously he's used this mad system, or just when it occurred to him the option existed.

My mind boggles.

In any case, what happens in Hungary, stays in Hungary.

His secret is safe. For now.

****

Time on the road does not fly by, despite all the intriguing sights greeting us alongside our route.

Indeed, at a cool 56mph, very little flies by.

I feel a tad sorry for Monroe, for I am not currently the most engaging of conversationalists; I am not providing him with a boredom busting output of quick wit and roadside repartee. I am still working through that awkward phase of teenage development, a stage that comes with being one of life's introverts, I guess.

The maturation of age has yet to seep deep into my bones.

Being able to confidently express thoughts and insights with just anyone is a skill yet to be fully harnessed.

There is so much to ponder in these formative years, so many hurdles to overcome, those tiny yet not-insignificant questions - 'Who *am* I?'; 'What do I Want to *Do* with My Life?' - requiring urgent (over)analysis.

Youth is not the best of times for we introverts; too many crises to deal with inside our constantly churning, over-thinking minds, too much over-analysis from the never-ending stream of internal dialogue.

Damn those extroverts, with their lack of internal dialogue, ruling the roost of the teenage years, the most fun at parties, their empty, internal echo chambers requiring constant external stimulus.

These are the guys all the girls swoon over.

That shy, socially awkward introvert in the corner currently having an interesting debate inside his own head. Not so much.

Unfortunately, Monroe's attempts at conversation don't lead to much either. My response to the majority of what he imparts being, 'Eh?', or 'Sorry, didn't catch that', such is the depth and breadth of his accent.

Subtitles have, alas, yet to be invented.

Most times Monroe makes forth an utterance, it is a fair assumption he's simply requesting another brew, yet another cup of tea or coffee, a process that involves placing the gas cannister and burner onto the flat, central space on the front dash, in between our two seats, sparking up the gas, and placing a small, rather beat up metal pot filled with one mug's worth of water atop of the flame. The water is thus heated whilst we continually bounce along.

Safe?

Not so much.

Fire risk?

More than likely.

Risk of scalding?

Most definitely.

But, out here, we are beyond the remit of pesky Health and Safety oversight.

In any case, the brew must go on.

****

Early morning, Day Four.

Yugoslavia, modern day Macedonia, just south of its capital Skopje.

Finally, the sun is shining.

Glorious pine forests are all around, their sweet scents wafting most welcomingly into the cab. This fresh pine scent is most welcome because, after three long days on the road, our personal hygiene routines have, I am ashamed to now admit, been rather lax. For my part - a teenage lad - this laxity might, tragically, be nothing out the ordinary; even in more normal circumstances, two showers a week are more than sufficient to remove deep layers of grime and grease from a teenager's person, are they not?

No, you say? Interesting insight...

The fresh pine scent inside the cab is a wonderful *pot pourri*, an olfactory feast invading the nasal passages, hitting the right frontal cortex at the sweetest of spots to thence cheer the soul somewhat after long, tiring days spent in the saddle (and I've not even been doing the driving).

We are rolling along, as has become the new norm, eyes flickering on the road ahead, and the scenery off to our side, my own mind off and away on some random daydream, when we suddenly encounter an army-fatigued man, carrying a machine gun strapped loosely over one shoulder.

This man stands at the entrance to a lay-by, currently motioning for us to pull in.

Monroe slows, ready to comply with the soldier's arm-gestured orders.

Well, you would, too: The Man has a Gun!

On the other hand: 'Keep Going! The *Man has a Gun!*'

Once stationary inside the lay-by, the soldier moseys over towards us, standing at the cab's side, beneath Monroe's door, notepad in one hand, pen poised in the other, evidently about to write us out a ticket for some unknown and currently unspecified misdemeanour.

The soldier spends several minutes engrossed in the minute detail of the form, glancing up at our licence plate, checking his watch for time and/ or date, before climbing up to the footplate for better access to the cab, making his head now level with Monroe's.

Monroe lowers the window, enabling face-to-face communication.

The soldier points at the dashboard, a gesture that Monroe understands immediately.

Monroe pulls out the paper tachometer, handing it to the soldier.

'Watch this,' Monroe whispers over to me.

I smile the smile of someone who hasn't yet fully cottoned on to what, exactly, is occurring.

The soldier's facial figurement suddenly morphs from one of cheery, happy *Gotcha!* glee to a dark, angry *Bugger, no I don't* frown.

The soldier takes a second look at the tachometer, just to double check he's not actually seeing things, before handing the disc back to Monroe, stepping down from the footplate, tearing his ticket up with rough, angry, frustrated strokes.

Dejectedly, without further glance in our direction, the soldier waves us be on our merry way.

'**Rule One**,' says Monroe, gleefully, as he pulls out onto the road again. 'Gits 'em e'ry teem.'

Now I think might be a good time to broach a different topic, for offering up a suggestion for a new Rule - **Rule Four** - you know, something along the lines of Not Driving on the Wrong Side of the Motorway into Oncoming Traffic.

I decide to bite my tongue. My dry sense of humour is often misconstrued.

The Yugoslavian motorway network is virtually deserted. Our only occasional, brief companions are yet more fleets of nose-to-bumper black Mercedes, racing up or down the road to more high-level meetings, or military pow-wows, the merits of which would have been lost on the average citizen whose basic standard of living these bigwigs were spectacularly failing to improve.

Up at Mercedes Head Office accounts department, hands are, however, rubbing in glee at the latest sales figures just reported.

By mid-afternoon, we pass into Greece, just to the north of Thessaloniki. The mountain-side pine trees thin out leaving barren hillsides for us to traverse.

We re-enter the West, free from the yoke of tyrannical anti-democratic regimes, or so it would superficially seem.

The Greek governmental system of the '80s is not exactly the free and open arrangement one might associate with a normal Democratic society. Ruled by the Far Left, with a surfeit of (allegedly) corrupt government officials, by most standard measures of success its economy in tatters, Greece is, at the time, considered by many economists a basket-case of a country, its Millennia of History and Cradle of Civilisation notwithstanding.

Cash rules business, nobody but mugs completes their accounts electronically, as, well, don't be so stupid - that would mean you might have to actually *pay* tax.

Paying tax. Therein lies the rub.

According to the many Greeks with whom this issue has been discussed, over many years, the average person's reluctance to pay their full, socially responsible, tax increments is not because the average Greek is a tax-dodging crook - not that anyone admits to being one, anyway - but because any money that *is* sent to the Central Coffers is, they fear, certain to be misappropriated, doled out, untendered, to Ministerial lackies and close business associates, or sweated away in the form of corrupt handouts and decidedly dodgy dealings.

Corporation tax levels are but a tiny percentage of the total tax revenue. The State, currently, is 'run' by an unnecessarily bloated surfeit of Officials, all of whom have jobs for life, and who are bestowed with sky-rocketing State pensions, being able as they are to retire at little over fifty years of age, to continue enjoying many years of this good life without having to bear the tedious brunt of actually having to go into the office and work for their unsustainably swollen salaries.

Needlesstosay, when 1999 arrives, Greece's entry to the Euro is fudged, and approved; the Common Currency always being more of a political decision than one based on fiscally reasoned suppositions.

It is late, just after midnight, when we reach our final destination. Monroe takes us around Athens city centre, down into Piraeus, the main port area, where we park up for a few hours' *Z*, before my dawn ferry departure to Ios.

All of a sudden, *this is it*.

The, at the time, Never-Ending journey is now pretty much done.

What an eye-opener of a Trip this has been.

Certainly, I have yet to fully digest all I have just witnessed; quite some time will be required to fully comprehend the implications of all this new knowledge.

Like our bovine friends, I will need to find somewhere quiet to repose, somewhere to regurgitate the sensory overload I have just ingested, and ruminate on all the details, extracting as much experiential nutrient as can be extracted.

The island of Ios, from what I have heard of its wild reputation, might not be the best place for this process to successfully occur.

Instead, I am now eager for the next stage of the trip to commence, keen to meet up, once again, with my friends.

Hopefully, meet up with my friends, that is.

The pre-mobile phone, pre-Internet era is still upon us.

Hooking up with someone, at a pre-arranged time and place, is never, ever, a foregone conclusion.

Stuff happens. Life throws curveballs into your path.

Delays mean keeping to schedule is not always possible, despite your best intentions.

And young lads have terrible memories, and an almost pathological inability to keep to any previously agreed schedule.

Returning through Piraeus from Patmos a few weeks earlier, I had presciently checked up on the ferry times down to Ios. From what I'd been informed of our expected journey time down to Athens, I had told my friends that - assuming all goes to Plan - I would be rocking up on one of three ferries; and Monroe and I have arrived in time for me to catch the third of these three ferries.

My friends, assuming they really *are* my friends, will therefore *definitely* be there dockside to greet me, to lead me to our lodgings, where no doubt several cool ales will have been lined up to celebrate my successful arrival.

At least, they all darn well *better* be there.

Dawn has barely risen when I bid my Farewells to Monroe, thanking him for his kind hospitality, for putting up with my dour company, for getting me this far, crazy side trips and excursions onto the wrong side of the motorway notwithstanding.

The ferry docks at Ios a short seven hours later.

I scour the quayside for signs of familiar life, for a friendly face, for *two* friendly faces, even.

Nope. Nothing. Not a sausage.

I disembark, standing like a prize lemon all alone on the shore, taking stock of where I am, where there might be signs of habitation, trying to evaluate in which direction, left or right, it would be best to commence walking.

There is suitable signage: no *Toutes Directions*; no *Centre Ville*.

I have no idea of the island's layout. I have no idea where the main accommodation area might be, where might exist the greatest likelihood of finding my now so-called friends.

Having covered more than 2,000 miles, this endeavour might be about to fail at the final hurdle.

Darn.

I set forth, somewhat dejectedly, in my new mission.

Suddenly, out of the silence, I hear my name being shouted out.

'Whoo hoo!! Over here, Darling!! Whoo hoo!!'

I turn in the direction of the sounds, spying my (evidently one and only) good friend, Alicia, currently waving her hands frantically above her head, whilst running like a mad dervish across the quayside, scattering innocent bystanders and freight caskets in her wake.

'Whoo hoo!! Over here!!' she shouts again.

Well Met, that lass.

Bless her.

Chapter 31

Ios

The holiday, in earnest.

I feel no urge to go into too great a detail, here; I believe what thence transpired is still bound under the strict, exacting terms of the Official Secrets Act, and not due for public consumption for at least another 30+ years.

Were I to elaborate, I would be describing thousands of identical teenage holidays, whose participants behaved in an identical manner, identical, indeed, to that of a gamut of adolescents on their first summer sojourns *sans* the full-beamed glare of parental oversight.

Surely, you are already more than familiar with the crazy chaos that is the typical Teenage Summer Break without Grown-Ups:

Beach rarely achieved before midday;

The consumption of Mexico's GDP-boosting volumes of Tequila;

A cluster of stupidly Daft Antics and Pranks;

Embarrassingly awkward Dalliances with the opposite sex;

Museum and Art Galleries conspicuously lacking from the daily schedules.

Culture, bless it, can wait.

We had our own, unique, culture requiring of our getting to grips.

I introduce to you - the original **Ios Tequila Slammer**:

Having downed the Tequila, Tia Maria and lemonade slammer, you are then required to don a much-battered crash helmet.

The bar owner will then smack you over the head with a mallet, with quite considerable force.

You will become light-headed. Decidedly discombobulated.

Everyone in the bar will then clap loudly, for some unknown reason.

You have paid good money for this process to be performed.

May I also present: The **Tequila Stuntman**:

Here, the salt is coerced into short lines, and ingested via the nasal cavities (it will stick to the nostril lining, causing your nose to stream, copiously, or so I am informed).

The Tequila is then downed.

For the *finale,* the lemon will be squirted into your eyes.

Quite why anyone would *choose* go through such an ordeal, I have no idea, whatsoever.

Not *me*. Never.

But I have witnessed such an endeavour: guys High-Fiving each other having been (hopefully) temporarily blinded from the citrus acid just squirted into their eyes.

It really does take all sorts, this planet.

Australians, mostly.

Finally, I present to you, the **Tequila Body Slammer**.

This Fulsome Fun-Filled loveliness requires the participation of a Nubile and Willing female.

A fully naked, lying horizontally, supine, Nubile and Willing female.

The salt is applied around the nipples; the Tequila, poured into her belly button; the lemon, slotted in where the sun doesn't shine.

And I don't mean Margate on Bank Holiday Monday.

I trust I can leave you to figure out how *that* Fulsome Fun-ness all plays out?

OK. I'm sensing you're now going to tell me that this exuberant excess bears all the trappings of a Misspent Youth.

If so, we'll have to agree to disagree.

Go on, Live a little.

Youth passes all too quickly. If you can't get this type of exuberance out of your system during these few fleeting formative years, then, well, in all likelihood, it'll remain pent up for many years still to come.

I would humbly suggest studying the events at Mt St Helens for the potentially explosive upshot of excessively pent up pressure.

Pretty, the results, they ain't.

Surely, it's far better for the Youth of Today to be letting rip in such manners, than for them to be letting rip – indeed, to be *exploding* - in manners more worrying, more terminal to those around them.

In any case, before you know it, Responsibility is thrust our way. Maturity duly beckons,

Childish Behaviours all too soon considered consigned to the eternal dust heap, never to be revisited, all presuming these behaviours have been suitably expunged.

Best to grab what you can, when you can.

Enjoy *Then,* as and *When*, for there'll be no **Then** again.

Island life also passes all too quickly.

Whether a week, ten days, or a fortnight were spent, I cannot, hand on heart, recall.

What I can, hand on heart, state is that friendships were cemented, life-long friendships that continue to this day, thirty+ years later.

True to habit, my friends' are still rarely, if ever, on time.

The Bastards.

Chapter 32

Homeward Bound, How I Wish I Were...

Homeward Bound.

Except, hmm, I realise I have not a Scooby as to exactly how the vast distance back to the UK is now going to be covered.

It appears that, in my rush to get down to Greece, I have failed to apply due consideration to the getting-back-home-again requirement.

I am, it would appear, currently in deficit to the tune of one carefully constructed and structurally-sound Exit Strategy.

(This lack of forward planning, whilst an obvious Schoolboy Error on my part, is, over the forthcoming decades, a deficit mirrored by many Governmental Regimes, a fact that soothes me no end).

I have no contact with Monroe. He could be anywhere, most likely far-and-away in some far-distant land. The Monroe option is definitely out of the equation.

In my favour within this new Conundrum, my stepfather has presciently given me the key to an apartment belonging to an American colleague of his, a base strategically situated in the centre of Athens, just off Kolonaki Square. I decide the best course of action will be to make my way there from Piraeus, and take stock of what options might lurk, currently unseen, on the table.

The apartment turns out not to be a pokey, one-room flat, but an entire, 3-floored dwelling, with a large, open-plan, First Floor living area, very well maintained, and plushily furnished. (**Important note to my American friends**: the sequence goes: Ground Floor/ First Floor/ Second Floor, *etc*).

Not a bad pad at all. Great location, too, being but a short walk from the Lycabettus, Athens' second hill, a peak which affords fantastic views over the Parthenon, and Athens as a whole.

OK, so the Conundrum is already slightly less of an Overwhelming Dilemma.

I call home.

Options are discussed.

I am told to contact AlexisT, another well-connected business associate of my stepfather's, whose Head Office is not far from Kolonaki, and who will be able to assist with the funds for the purchase of one homeward-bound air ticket. Those damn awkward Grecian currency controls mean wiring cash to me from the UK is Out.

The following day, I go over to AlexisT's Head Office. His secretary kindly shows me in without much delay, thanks, I presume, to my stepfather calling ahead and letting them know I would be stopping by. AT is, from the luxuriant trappings of his personal office space, not doing too badly for himself; he has, he tells me, quite the array of large-scale business ventures currently ongoing.

I am in safe hands here, I feel. Having explained my predicament, AT suggests I visit a nearby travel agency, and ascertain the cost of a one-way ticket back to Heathrow.

At the Agency, it transpire the price of a ticket is not just affected by current availability.

No, no, no. Far too simple.

Also to be factored into the equation is the means with which the ticket will be paid, whether a Withdrawal/ Exchange receipt for the cash will be provided, or not.

Talk about making things unnecessarily difficult.

I explain to the Agent that, sadly, I am unable to provide such a receipt.

She *Ums* and *Ahs* – I've evidently thrown a potential spanner into the works, here - looking pensively at her computer screen for some minutes, before picking up the phone to call Pan Am.

Success.

The Pan Am departure to Heathrow the day after tomorrow is a tad more costly than the BA or Olympic options, but does not require that annoying cash receipt.

Oh, these crazy Currency Controls.

Back at AT's office, his secretary arranges for funds to be made available, so by mid-afternoon I am back in the Kolonaki Square apartment, airplane ticket in hand, all set to go in a little over 36 hours.

So, how to pass a day and a half in Athens?

Just then, the apartment phone rings.

Thinking it might be my stepfather checking up on my progress, I pick up.

'Hi?' I say.

'Hello?' says a male voice, with a distinctively Far-West-of the Atlantic twang. '*Hello*? Just *who* is *this*? And what the **** are *you* doing in *my* house?'

The voice sounds rather angry.

Oh dear.

My stepfather's Business Associate, who evidently hasn't been cc'd in on the Memo detailing my potential temporary requirement of his fine abode.

Oh dear. Nobody told *me* the Communication was Bad Round here.

I do my best to explain my credentials, and how I now come to be inside his fine abode. This appears to placate the Man a little, although I guess the fact that he is 10,000+km away, somewhere in the US, whilst I am in his Athenian apartment, there isn't really much he could do (Call the Police? Possibly, but I guess I must have convinced sufficiently to avoid a Raid).

The Man tells me he was actually expecting his Son to answer.

His Son, it seems, is due to arrive here at the apartment *any time now*.

Awkward. *Super* awkward.

I tell the Man I will pass on his message, and ask his Son to call him back as and when he arrives.

An hour or so later, I hear the front door latch open, and someone heavy-footedly stomping up the stairs.

'Hello!', I call out, to lessen the shock of his reaching the top of the stairs and being confronted by a totally random, and completely unexpected, stranger.

'Hello?' replies the voice, also with a distinctive Far-Far-West-of the Atlantic accent, as the man reaches the top of the stairs.

I allow the man time to put down his over-sized bags and catch his breath for a few seconds, before offering my hand in greeting. It is a rather odd feeling, to be greeting someone for the first time from the inside of their own pad. The overwhelming sensation is one of my being out of place, as if I shouldn't really be here; that I am, most definitely, intruding on someone's personal, private space.

Once again, I explain my situation.

Fortunately, the man is an American of the super-chilled variety, rather than one of those more uptight versions you sometimes encounter.

Late twenties, I guess.

Californian, hence the chilled vibe.

Ostentatiously hispid, with bushy facial furniture.

Just in town for a few days, part of a Europe-wide trip.

We chat for a while, before I sense it would be best if I headed out to see some of the town and allow this obviously weary fellow his own space in which to relax after his recent journey.

Athens is a mighty fine city in which to spend time pottering about. Ancient sites abound; stunning hilltop views; verdant, shaded residential squares where weathered octogenarians sit in their dozens, drinking ouzo, and playing intensely focused games of dominoes. These squares' dappled sunlight provides the perfect spots in which to catch your breath during the heat of the midday sun whilst people-watching, whilst the world percolates slowly around, whilst time passes slowly, yet also in the blink-of-an-eye.

I return to the Kolonaki pad early evening, to find my Californian buddy sofa-bound (he might call this piece of furniture a *couch*, but, well, Americans have been known to bodge the English language periodically), engrossed in deep conversation with a young lady roughly his own age.

I am introduced to his new companion. The two of them, it transpires, just met at the American Express office, not an hour ago, when he popped in to collect his mail. It transpires, too, that they used to be an Item back home, and haven't seen each other for far too many years; drifting apart is all too easy, even from those with whom you'd really rather keep in touch.

The two of them have taken this random re-encounter to be a Sign, a Portent that their romance requires immediate rekindling, that the Universe has Spoken, that this Love is Meant to Be.

Suddenly, I feel even greener and hairier, even more of a spare wheel, a random stranger now here in this house, with these two Eyes-Only-for-Each-Other lovebirds.

My presence might even be putting a dampener on the advancement of their ardour.

As things transpire, I needn't have worried.

Our collective paths don't cross again until early next evening. This time, when I return from my city-wide explorations, they are once again cosied up together on the sofa.

Californian Man is clutching a whisky bottle close to his chest; a 1/3rd full bottle of Scotch.

'Hey man!' he calls out, as I hove into view. 'What's up?'

I detect a definite slur to his speech, a definite narrowing of his eyes.

That bottle's been hit, and hit hard, I think. That bottle may even have been full when play first commenced.

'Good, good', I reply. 'Seeing the sights. Hitting the heights.'

The lady and I acknowledge one another. I notice she is holding what looks like a large sewing needle in one hand, readying herself for some serious needle poking action.

Californian Man takes another swig from his bottle, necking quite a gulp.

'Having my ears pierced', he says, his voice definitely more than a little slurred. 'Shared pain,' he continues. 'A bonding exercise. The pain brings us closer.'

Sure.

Whatever you say, Man. Whatever Floats your Boat.

I know which side of this equation I'd rather be on.

The lady advances the needle towards the fleshy part of one lobe. Californian Man winces, then yowls in pain as the pin is pushed straight through the soft flesh of his left-side lobe.

'Man! Holy Wow!' he shrieks.

The lady laughs.

Might she be enjoying administering the pain punishment a tad too much?

No matter. California Man laughs, too.

Inside the laughter, they embrace. Then, they kiss.

It is something of an overly wet, full-on slobbery, full-tongue, Extended Play, Ariston - and on, and on - of a kiss.

Ah, bless'em.

'Say,' California Man asks, pulling away from the slobber, 'you fancy joining us this evening? We're hitting a concert. Santana. At the Lycabettus.'

At this stage of my young, hardly lived life, I have yet to hear of the entity that is *Santana*.

I have no idea quite what a Santana concert might entail, so I politely decline. It is hard to tell if the request was being made simply out of courtesy, in any case.

Obviously, hindsight has shown declining this invitation to be a *Spectacularly* Bad Decision, up there in the Top 10 of Bad Decisions ever made (I shan't bore you with my other nine).

Carlos Santana, Live in Concert, in the awesome setting of the Lycabettus.

What a seriously good addition to the nostalgia memory banks *that* would have been.

On that bum note, this incredible adventure comes to a rather anticlimactic conclusion. The weary traveller arrives back at Heathrow the following day, with no further to-do, no fanfare nor bunting at the airport to herald his safe return.

Back to Reality, as people are want to say.

Well, one form of Reality.

I set off to finding a suitable spot in which to lie, for contemplative consideration and revered rumination.

Reality has provided me recently with much worthy of deeper consideration.

Chapter 33

Egg on Face

Two years have elapsed since my London - Athens road trip.

AlexisT's 18-year-old son, Dimitri, has joined us on our annual family skiing holiday in the French Alps. He and I are out hitting the slopes, now sharing a 12-minute gondola ride back up the mountain, our four-man *Egg* completed by a young couple, who face us in the tight, enclosed and, what is to many, claustrophobic space.

Dimitri and I alternate between chatting quietly, facing each other so we can keep the volume of our chatter down, and staring out of the *Egg*, down at the *pistes* a short distance beneath us, in contemplative silence, selecting the next fun run to take back down the mountain. The enclosed, compact environment makes looking in the other couple's general direction, and running the risk of making eye contact even for a micro-second, a definite No-No.

For there are *Rules* to Riding inside a Cramped Gondola.

These Rules are similar to those governing the Riding of a Packed Tube Train, unspoken and unwritten Conventions dictating that, as your own personal space has been seriously impinged upon, you must pretend the other people sitting, or standing, only centimetres away from your person, simply do not exist.

The Conventions dictate everyone adheres to these same Regulations: the Absolute, Definitive, Cast-Iron Prohibition of entering into conversation, or even make eye contact, with someone in your close proximity, some random stranger desperately trying to endure this squished-in-like-sardines ride without exploding from the claustrophobia, someone anxious to get home from their shitty day at work, without having to put up with the ordeal of making polite chit-chat with someone like you, you who, for all they know, might be a Complete Loony.

Trying to engage your new Tube neighbours in conversation is an unforgiveable social *faux pas*, marking you out, instantly and irrevocably, as a Loathsome Social Reprobate.

Should these Conventions be ignored, should you choose to Cock a Snoop their way, should you decide to Thumb your Nose up in their general direction, then, well, whatever Chaos thence ensues, the Courts, in their Infinite Wisdom, will conclude, in a fraction of a micro second, you *most definitely* had it coming your way.

'Your Honour, the Accused attempted conversation with a Stranger inside a packed Tube during Rush Hour.'

Guilty!

Send Him DOWN!

Next!

As we rise up high, into the clouds, out of the corner of my eye I notice that the couple has become rather engrossed in their own personal conversation, their body positions more tightly pressed together than the already cramped conditions perforce require. His mitt-less digits are now stroking her face, her chin, her shoulders, and her, *hmm*, bumpy lower down bits (no, *not* her knees).

The volume of their chit-chat increases to a level hard to ignore. The two are conversing in a language I immediately recognise as 'Greek'. The pair of lovebirds seem oblivious to our presence – which, correct, is one section of the Convention - having not a care in the world that we can hear their every word, and can tell exactly what they are up to in a physical regard, even though we are both most definitely *not* looking their way.

Getting Excessively Fresh with your Partner is most definitely *not* condoned within the Rules.

We rise even higher, up through the clouds, out into the bright sunlight, Dimitri making that flicky, sideways motion eye-shift towards the couple – eye motions clearly articulating, 'Can you *believe* this?'.

By now, the couple has reached a state of totally inappropriate over-touchy-feely-ness and over-amorous-ness, their mouths firmly pressed to one another's, all sorts of slobber flying out;

they are also making no effort whatsoever to keep their voices – and moans and groans - even remotely hushed.

Maintaining the illusion that this couple is not currently sitting less than a foot away from us is now a complete impossibility.

Their overly touchy-feely-ness is one thing to pretend is not currently occurring.

Their rapid, overtly salacious verbal – and non-verbal - communications, another altogether.

Dimitri keeps turning his head to look out of the window, or towards me, trying desperately to suppress a smirk, trying desperately *not* to burst out laughing. I get the impression whatever this couple is saying - blissfully unaware every utterance is being understood this side of the Egg - is of an excessively fragrant and fulsomely fruity nature.

Oh, to have a running translation fed directly into my ear.

Oh, to have rolling subtitles to be able to read.

Finally, the gondola reaches the top station.

Dimitri and I exit the Egg first, closely followed by the Overly Amorous Lovebirds.

Dimitri and I step to one side, allowing them to pass, more out of an urgent desperation to know what the couple have been saying to each other than politeness on my part. Before I can grab Dimitri's attention, however, he meanders calmly up to the two love-crazed loons and utters something to them.

Something, *obviously*, in Greek.

The look on their faces: Priceless.

Oh, to have had a camera to capture this sublime shock, for the abject horror etched into their features is one for the centuries. The two both suddenly turn a deep, fiery red, their cheeks glowing hot, their brows frowned and deeply pensive, a look of utter embarrassment and total bemusement etched into the very depths of their souls.

OK, it appears they're not hanging around for the Encore, for they suddenly take flight.

In a flash, they're off, accelerating away in a mad rush to leave the scene of their humiliation, their poles dangling haphazardly from their arms, their skis dragging awkwardly along the floor behind them, other skiers bumped and banged dispassionately as they dash to the perceived sanctity of the mountain outside.

We wave a sarcastic *Farewell* as the couple zooms off, a trail of bruised torsos left in their wake.

So Long!

Thanks for the Ride!

Guess you Enjoyed the Ride, too!

Poor people.

Or Silly Buggers?

It is hard to feel much sympathy for their plight.

For if you choose, wilfully, to ignore the fundamental Rules of the Gondola, you only have yourselves to blame should things then take an unexpected, 1-in-a-Million, leftfield turn.

For what were the chances of them sharing a ski lift, in France, with the only other person fluent in Greek, within a 100+ mile radius?

PART FIVE

Chapter 34

What Were the Odds of That?

September 1993.

Dahab, on the Sinai Peninsula of Egypt.

The end of my year's Voyage of Discovery is fast approaching.

I decide to share a taxi with a young English couple, to Santa Katarina, the starting point for the in-darkness ascent of Mt Sinai, to witness the spectacular sunrise from its summit (an endeavour heartily recommended, current geo-political situation permitting).

I am due to fly home in a couple of weeks, to attend my sister's wedding, one of those life events you simply cannot miss (and if you do No-Show, you'd better not show your face again for a decade, *minimum*).

It transpires this English couple are also about to head home; they are scheduled to leave Dahab a week ahead of me.

Back to London, as am I.

The dreaded day arrives. Heathrow beckons. The Trip is *Now Over*.

I've been back in London for a few days, at a loose end, somewhat ambivalent about being back Home.

Sure, it's great to see friends and family after such a long time apart; having had to call Time on my voyage around this amazing World of Possibilities and Wondrous Marvel, not so much.

On a whim, I decide to head up to central London, catching a Piccadilly Line tube from Hammersmith, up to Leicester Square.

I am off and away in my head, as you do when travelling the Tube.

Remember: There are Rules when Riding the Tube.

No Eye Contact.

You most certainly don't spark up a conversation with the random person beside you, an alien concept after being free of such introspection for so long. I have become used to sparking up conversations with all and sundry, for, I have learned, people each have their own fascinating Tales; all *you* have to do is ask.

Real life; so much more wondrous than anything even a writer with the wildest imagination can conger up.

The Tales are all true; this stuff *happened* (and if they do embellish, well, that's for their consciences to resolve).

The stations progress, slowly:

Baron's Court;

Earl's Court (change for the District Line);

Gloucester Road;

South Ken (for the Museums);

Knightsbridge (for Harrods & Harvey Nicks);

Hyde Park Corner;

Green Park;

Piccadilly Circus (for Regent Street).

Next stop, **Leicester Square**.

The train fast approaches the station, so in preparation for a speedy exit, I rise, ready to alight - like any *true* Londoner - placing myself bang in front of the sliding doors.

The train comes to a halt.

The doors open.

I step off the train, onto the platform.

Wait. *What*?

What *is* this I am seeing?

Who *is* this now stepping onto the Tube at this *exact same* carriage, at this *exact same* door, at this *exact same* moment?

None other than this *exact same* English couple from Dahab.

Holy Moley!!

Our motions, me stepping down onto the platform, them stepping up into the carriage, are but a whisker apart.

As we pass, my eyes fix on them both - first her, then him, then her - my face etched in wild excitement at the bizarreness of it all. At least, I hope *wild excitement* is the expression my face is currently displaying.

Her face: wide smile, Joyful Wonder.

His face: furrowed brow, Doubtful Reticence.

She and I both thinking: 'What are the chances? How *amazing*?!?'

Him likely thinking: 'What are the chances? You *following* us or what?'

All of this communication is conveyed in the mere blink of an eye, a mere fraction of a second, for I find myself now standing on the platform, the two of them now standing inside the Tube carriage, before I've even had a chance to react, to turn myself around, to proclaim, 'Wow there, dear Universe, *Time Out!*'.

Before I've even had the chance to think my next thought, the Tube doors slide shut in front of them, cutting us both off.

Before I've even had the chance to register a suitable response to this crazy, 1-in-a-Million situation, to utter anything of note their way, to accomplish anything that could even vaguely be described as *Communication*, the Tube is already slowly pulling out of the station.

Just like that, in a flash, the train enters the tunnel at the end of the platform.

The couple is gone.

Gone For good.

I am left there, alone on the platform, wondering whether what just went down, actually, really, just went down.

Just what, dear Universe, were the odds of *that*?

PART SIX

Chapter 35

The Unbearable Randomness of Being

Good Things should *only* happen to Good People.

Bad Things, *only* to Bad People.

Right?

Lest, well, where's the Fairness in *that*?

I met this lady. Let's call her Sofia.

Back in 2003, Sofia travelled around South America – Peru, Bolivia and Ecuador – before deciding to then head up to the Caribbean coastline of Colombia. The Caribbean coastline was at the time, I believe, a region of Colombia deemed *Safe* by the UK Foreign Office, and most people in general (*Safety*, like many things related to the World of Travel, is, of course, a relative concept).

For Sofia, her main reason for travelling to the coast was to make the trip to *La Ciudad Perdida* - the Lost City - ruined remains said to predate Machu Picchu by 650 years, located deep in the jungle, a tough, 4-day, 45kms (round-trip) hike from the coastal town of Santa Marta.

Touring *La Cuidad Perdida* was considered a safe endeavour; tours large and *ad hoc* had been running for many years without incident. It is unclear whether or not Paramilitaries were known to be operating in the area. Some reports exist of payments being made by the larger tour operators to these Paramilitaries, to ensure the tours' smooth and safe operations.

Either way, trekking out to the Lost City was not, by and large, considered to be running any *real* risk, over and above overcoming the not-inconsiderable physical effort required to traverse rough jungle terrain teeming with creepy crawlies of the 4-legged variety, both large and small, in swelteringly hot, humid conditions.

Preferring a more *ad hoc* approach, Sofia procured the services of a local guide, a cook, plus some donkeys to carry the load, setting off in excited anticipation of a brief jungle adventure.

Alas for Sofia, her visit to *La Cuidad Perdida* would prove the Exception (did it then prove the Rule?).

Early morning of 12 September 2003, heavily armed Guerrillas raided the two huts the amalgamation of large tour and *ad hoc* travellers were all sleeping in, under the pretext that two individuals had been killed further down the road, and the foreigners needed to be led out to safety. This explanation sounded not unreasonable; in any case, resistance was not an option, given the ubiquity of arms the Guerrillas were brandishing. The travellers were hurriedly collated, then divided into those who were fit and mobile, and those who weren't; those the Guerrillas deemed commercially or politically viable, and those who weren't; those who were romantically attached, and those who weren't.

The Guerrillas sought to assuage the travellers' fears during this separation routine.

Don't worry, they were told, the two groups will all meet up again *soon*.

The definition of 'soon' being employed by the Guerrillas was, it would transpire, not the standard definition you or I would recognise.

Once the initial dust had settled, Sofia found herself in a group totalling eight people, the lone female amongst those the Guerrillas had selected suitable for kidnap.

Sofia's group comprised a pair of Brits, four Israelis, a German (her), and a Spanish/ Basque national. Four nationalities amongst eight people isn't quite as wide a range of nationalities as might otherwise have been hewn from the options at hand; the Guerrillas' whittling process could be viewed as *flawed* at best, as *distinctly haphazard* if you were less inclined to be so magnanimous.

The two guides were tied up. Shortly after the Guerrillas departed with their new captives, one of the guides managed to wriggle free of the ropes with which he had been bound. He then completed the 2-day journey back to Santa Marta, to raise the alarm, in just one day – whilst barefoot, the Guerrillas having relieved him of his shoes (despite this Herculean effort, that the guide had not been taken hostage raised eyebrows with the Authorities, the poor man then spending many weeks having to prove he had played no part in the kidnapping).

On the first day of their ordeal, as the hostages were being led along a ridgeline deeper into the jungle, one of the Brits made a daring escape, throwing himself down a ravine, and not only evading the gunshots fired in his direction (although the shots fired were more in the air than *at* him, to alert the other Guerrillas that something serious had occurred, spread out as they all were along the ridgeline), but managing to find his way out from the jungle to the safety of civilisation a full twelve days later.

Quite a feat for someone with presumably no jungle survival training. So much for the Guerrillas' belief that there was no point chasing after him: the Brit, they boasted, would surely be consumed by the many man-eating jaguar and cougar known to roam this region of the Colombian jungle.

For the remaining seven travellers, the forthcoming days would be a torrid time. They were marched deeper, deeper into the jungle, for ten days and nights, with little rest, fifteen to twenty hours a day.

It was only on day five that the Guerrillas formally told their captives they were being held hostage.

The 'Why' would not emerge until later.

Sofia told a tale of constant fear, fear for what could happen at any given moment, from any of the guards, for the day-to-day hostage security has been bestowed upon a ragtag group of illiterate teenage lads with whom it was impossible to hold a conversation, let alone attempt to reason.

Twitchy. Itchy.

Loving the power holding an automatic rifle bestows.

Scary. Scary. Times.

****

Bolivia, early Noughties.

I met a man who'd just taken a Tour of the San Pedro prison in La Paz, a prison run not by the guards but by the inmates, a set up that, back in 2000, was probably less official than it might be today. Unbeknownst to the prisoners conducting that day's Tour, a Government Official had decided to perform an unannounced Inspection Visit that day, too. Fearing the Tour my friend was on would be uncovered, with who-knows-what repercussions, the prisoners told my friend he would have to be locked inside a cell whilst the Government Official made his rounds. My buddy was obviously not overly-enthused about the prospect of being locked inside a prison cell, in the notorious San Pedro prison, for *any* length of time, not even five seconds, given no one else currently knew his whereabouts, and his lack of a mobile phone with which to communicate with the outside world should something untoward occur.

His protestations were, however, in vain.

He was bundled into a cell.

The door slammed shut.

The key turned inside the lock.

And that, very suddenly, was that.

The words, 'Don't worry, it'll probably only be for an hour, or so,' hung in the air as this poor man found himself locked, in solitary, in a prison cell in deepest, darkest South America.

Surely, most people's sweaty, heart-pounding-rapidly, No1 Nightmare Scenario.

'An hour. *Or so.*'

The 'Or so' created the deepest dread, he told me.

Thankfully, my buddy was let out just over an hour later, once the Official had completed his rounds.

Those 70 minutes were the longest 70 minutes of his life, he said.

Not knowing for how long you are doomed to be held captive is just one of the many mental tortures a hostage must endure.

You have no idea for how long you must mentally plan, how long you will have to withstand this horror, just how distant the light at the end of the tunnel might be (presuming you are able to see the faint glimmer of *any* light in the first place).

So, you do what you can, what you *must*, to survive.

Rule 1 of being a Kidnap Victim: get your kidnappers to see you as a person, rather than a mere commodity.

If you can get them to *like* you, even better.

If, say, your kidnappers suggest you pose for photos with them, holding an AK47, proudly, just as they are – as happened to Sofia - you don't then question their motives, nor try to resist.

'Come closer, so we can all get into the shot.'

'Hold the rifle a little higher.'

'Say *Cheese!*'

You don't question, or negotiate.

You comply.

Happily. Smilingly.

Anything to get to the next hour, the next day, the next week, and so on, forever onwards.

This compliance, tragically, would come back to haunt Sofia.

Over time, some of the strict conditions the hostages were subjected to on a daily basis were relaxed. They could take care of their bodily functions without having a guard standing over them; they could wash in the river without having a guard observing their every move. The atmosphere between the captives and their captors became more peaceful, friendlier even, a small change which to you or I might seem negligible, but to those under the yoke of a gun was as precious as anything could ever be.

The Israelis were, however, being uncooperative victims, which is somewhat predictable given their standard background in military service, and these lads' general antagonism towards authority; whilst you or I might meekly accede to the captors' requests, for the Israelis, having been trained to handle firearms, to be resourceful and adaptive in combat scenarios, playing the role of 'compliant hostages' was not high on their To Do list.

This lack of cooperation pissed the kidnappers off no end.

In an attempt to minimise the Israeli resistance, the group was divided in two, putting Sofia with two of the Israelis, for three days, but this split failed to have any discernible effect on the Israelis' disposition to their current captivity, or their attempts to remove themselves from this state of incarceration.

Several times, the Israelis attempted escape; on one occasion, their attempt at absconding was successful.

Alas, their freedom lasted just one hour.

The consequences of this botched attempt for the remaining three were, Sofia told me, 'Horrible'.

Horrible, is, of course, masterful understatement.

Convinced she and the Brit had helped the Israelis escape and/ or knew their current whereabouts, the guards dragged Sofia outside, making her and the Spanish national watch as two rifles were trained at the head of the Brit, who'd been positioned on the ground on all fours, like a dog.

Sofia was certain they were going to be made to watch the Brit being shot dead, right there in front of them.

The guards then changed tack, turning their attention to Sofia, roughing her up, pointing their guns at *her* head, at *her* body

('We'll shoot you in the leg to make you talk, see how *you* like *that*!'), the tension being ratcheted to maximum in an attempt to squeeze out of her information she simply did not possess.

Then, four shots rang out from close by inside the jungle.

Sofia was convinced the four shots signalled a tragic end to the Israelis' prison break.

Thankfully, the four guys emerged soon afterwards, having been recaptured only a short distance from the camp.

Basic Procedures in the Kidnappers' Playbook state: 'No Failed Prison Break can go Unpunished'.

The Israelis were bound and thoroughly beaten for the trouble they had caused. Sofia said their unremitting moaning and groaning throughout that night were some of the most haunting sounds she has ever experienced.

The Israelis' dash for freedom did little to improve inter-hostage relations. Rather than be apologetic for the retaliations meted out to the others, the Israelis' proclaimed their short burst of freedom to have been a wonderful experience, their Best Moment Ever.

The debate as to the required role a hostage should inhabit is an Existential one:

Compliant Captive, waiting for events to unfold as they will?

Or *Belligerent Hostage*, never allowing the kidnappers an easy ride, always seeking to exploit potential security lapses, always looking to disrupt the smooth flow of daily Kidnapper-Hostage interactions?

Who are we on the outside to judge which role should be employed, which role conveys more moral superiority, or which role is more likely to ultimately result in survival?

As a result of the breakout, all previous Peeing-without-Being-Guarded, and Washing-without-Being-Guarded, privileges were retracted, leading to the worsening of the in-camp mood.

Sofia had her torch (with a compass) and a precious watch confiscated. Conditions overall deteriorated drastically as a result of this failed bid for freedom. But, despite the increased hardships, playing cards with seven is ultimately more enjoyable than with just two others, so, over time, the inter-hostage rift was healed.

Better to save your angst for those who truly merited it, they all thought.

A week or so later, the group was once again fragmented. Sofia was separated from the rest of the hostages, held alone, in a dark, dreadful, dingy hut, that festered with a panoply of creepy, crawly bugs, her only company three equally creepy, crawly kidnappers, and their automatic rifles.

Time inched forward, slowly.

So slowly.

Days became weeks; weeks became months.

The protracted suffering is unimaginable.

Then, out of the blue, Sofia was reunited with the Spanish national.

By now, three months had passed. To her surprise, that was the morning a helicopter hove into view, a standard, military-style, green-liveried helicopter, with a Red Cross emblem adorning its sides.

Behind the scenes, the Catholic Church had been negotiating for the release of both the Spanish national and Sofia. A deal had been struck: two workers from the United Nations, whose remit was to investigate the Sierra Nevada region for Human Rights atrocities being allegedly perpetrated by paramilitaries on the indigenous tribespeople, were brought in to take their places. Whilst a car had initially been planned for the release, the kidnappers insisted a helicopter be used for their safety. Sofia and the Spanish national, under the guise of the Red Cross, were, finally, removed from their captivity.

The ordeal was now over. Or so Sofia thought.

I know not what Sofia did in those first days and weeks after her release. One can only imagine the mental scars in need of gentle massaging; the process required to heal from such a harrowing ordeal.

A difficult period for sure.

With scant regard to her mental scars, or her recovery, only two weeks after the joy of her release, the German Government decided to lob a metaphorical hand grenade into Sofia's midst.

She was sent an Invoice.

One Helicopter Rescue: €12,640.05, *bitte schoen*.

Payment: Standard 30-day period.

Don't forget those all-important five cents.

Sofia was, naturally, somewhat taken aback by this request. She was, of course, and would be eternally, grateful that behind the scenes plans had been enacted to facilitate her release. Her gratitude towards those who had strived so ardently to assist her could not be stated in monetary terms. However, the better part of €13,000 is not the sort of cash most people have sitting around in their bank accounts, especially a youngster who's been travelling for the better part of a year. Even were she to have that sort of money lying around, the merits of the request were dubious at best.

The German Government's reasons for enforcing this invoice were twofold: they wanted to make a Point, they stated; and, more importantly, they wanted to change the Law.

Sofia's would be a Test Case, in the creation of this new Law: that any German national who finds themselves in a kidnap situation can be asked to repay Government expenses.

Of course, Government spin fed all this to the Press rather differently: firstly, that Sofia had, by travelling to this region, by ignoring the advice of the German Foreign Office, put herself in clear and present danger, so it was only Right and Proper she should pay for her release; secondly, that Sofia, by *choosing* to handle an automatic rifle, and *deigning* to pose for photographs with her captors, had become *too pally* with the kidnappers.

And *smiling* in the photographs.

'Yes', the Press wanted to know, 'why on *earth* was she *smiling*?'

It is hard to fathom the logic or reasoning here.

The German Government were, to put it bluntly, simply being bloody-minded, wielding their immense statutory powers simply because they could.

'We'll teach you a Lesson,' they thought.

That no other German national has since had to pay any Government expenses following their release from kidnap (the cost of return plane tickets excepted) does make the teachings of this particular Lesson a tad hard to fathom.

Sofia challenged the Invoice in the German Courts: *joy* as the decision went her way.

All over?

No such luck.

On the last possible day, the German Government appealed this decision. The Government then took the case to the Higher Courts, which they also won.

This time, Sofia appealed the decision. And lost.

Sofia considered whether to take her case higher, to the European Courts, but by that time the toll of challenging this outrageous invoice had become too great.

To continue was pointless.

€12,649.05 had by now swelled by another €8,000, after legal and court fees were included, and whilst there was the faintest glimmer of good grace from the Government in that the repayments could be spread over several years, this debt was still quite the financial burden for someone trying to rebuild their home life, and attempting a return to 'normality'.

Whilst all this was transpiring, the remaining hostages were, thankfully, all released, a month after Sofia's liberation, the result of the publication of the UN report into the alleged atrocities.

One of the hostages - the Brit (Mark) – happens to be a TV and film producer. During their captivity, he had nurtured a recurring thought to compile, at some point in their rather difficult-to-know future, a documentary of their ordeal, ever hopeful their outcome would be positive.

After their release, Mark, Sophia and the other hostages kept in regular contact with one another. What Mark really needed for his documentary film, for the full 360-degree perspective, was contact with the Guerrillas: a year after their release, and totally out of the blue, Sofia received a Facebook Friend Request from two of the kidnappers.

Crazy!

In fact, this couple were not the kidnappers themselves, but the Guerrillas' Social Workers

Yes, Guerrillas have Social Workers. Even crazier!

This couple had visited the camp from time to time, the only friendly faces the captives experienced throughout the duration of their ordeal.

(Later on, the couple would even invite Sofia and Mark to their wedding. Crazier still!

The invitation was obviously declined - Sofia wondered what she and Mark would have said to the other guests when asked: 'So, how do *you* know the Bride and Groom?')

As Sofia had established a positive rapport (of sorts) with this couple, accepting this Friend Request was easy. Sofia then forwarded the couple's details to Mark. This channel of communication would be vital to exploring the Guerrillas' underlying motives, to understanding more fully the reasoning behind the poor victims' capture.

'How could the Guerrillas justify taking away the hostages' Human Rights simply to highlight the loss of Human Rights of another group?'

'Do the Ends always justify the Means?'

'And would an Apology for the distress and turmoil caused be out of the question?'

Communications between the two sides continued sporadically for many months.

Some years then passed.

Finally, in 2009, the couple agreed to meet with Mark and Sofia, in Panama. As a cathartic process, a means to bring the nightmare to full circular completion, Mark had managed to follow through with his idea to produce a film documentary of the group's terrible ordeal. The interview with this couple was to be the mainstay of this film.

Sofia and Mark met up with the couple, Antonio and Camilla, in Panama, as arranged. The pair had belonged, it transpired, to the ELN – *Ejército de Liberación Nacional* - the National Liberation Army. The motivation behind the kidnapping, Antonio and Camilla stated, was the need to highlight the plight of indigenous communities within Colombia, communities who were being attacked and disappeared by right-wing Paramilitaries with alleged ties to the Colombian government.

To highlight the loss of *one group's* Rights and Liberties, yes, it was necessary to remove the Rights and Liberties of *another group*.

Somewhat ironic, possibly hypocritical, hardly fair, but then again, any belief that the world should *be* fair is surely misplaced, and a total waste of our energies in trying to maintain.

Bad Things befall Good People.

No, Life really *isn't* Fair.

Deal with It.

As part of the deal to release the hostages, the kidnapping - as the Guerrillas had initially intended - resulted in an International Team investigating these alleged crimes. Contained within the report was confirmation that Human Rights *were indeed* being violated, in horrific, unimaginable ways, with whole villages being brutally murdered.

That it took this kidnapping to highlight these atrocities is as much of a scandal as the kidnapping itself.

There were other questions regarding their ordeal that Sofia needed answering.

Why hadn't they been properly fed? – 'The area had been closed off by the military, there was simply no food to give the hostages';

Whether they would have shot the Israelis the night of their attempted escape – 'It was close';

Would they have shot *her* had a rescue attempt been enacted? – 'Yes, they would'.

The apology had been a pipedream, a hope, wishful thinking, rather than a realistic expectation, so it was a truly wondrous moment for Sofia when Antonio and Camilla offered her a sincere and honest apology, on camera.

A burdensome weight was lifted from her shoulders. It was a huge and most welcome relief.

Sofia, Mark and two of other of the hostages returned to *La Ciudad Perdida*, the final part of their cathartic undertaking, the end of a long and painful journey to expunge the horrors of what they had endured.

The film gained a release, under the title of 'My Kidnapper'. It comes highly recommended.

The Moral?

Life is Random, and Uncontrollable,

For all that Sofia's plight was a case of, 'There but for the Grace of God go I', there was one aspect she divulged that made the event even more traumatic, at least to my eyes.

As anyone who has experienced or studied the effects of Trauma will tell you, there are Stages to the Recovery Process, Stages of Grief, another journey that must be made: from Anger and Denial, to Acceptance and Moving on, the timing of each transition into the following Stage specific to the individual griever.

The Process can take months. It can also take years. There are no rights and wrongs, no 'normal' or 'abnormal', when it comes to the timing of this journey.

The 'Why me?' question would have certainly irked for some time.

Wrong person, wrong place, wrong time, that's for sure. But what would have sent me over the edge, possibly into a downward cognitive spiral, was learning that these Guerrillas had intended to kidnap the group of travellers the previous Full Moon before Sofia's ordeal, that on the way to the Lost City the kidnappers had *themselves* got lost.

Getting *Lost* on the way to the *Lost* City.

Oh, the irony of it.

Delicious, if not so tragically serious.

'So, if you Nitwits could read a bloody map, if you had been even the slightest bit organised, I would not have had to endure what you Nitwits put me through'.

Although the word *Nitwits* might need to be replaced with something just a tad stronger.

'If you Nitwits could read a bloody map, I would not have had to suffer the Agony of being held captive';

'If you Nitwits could read a bloody map, I would not have had to suffer the Agony of having to endure, too, the recovery process';

'If you Nitwits could read a bloody map, I would not have had to endure the repercussions of my release, the financial imposition, the many years of legal wrangling, the stress that this brought on'.

'If you Nitwits could read a bloody map, I would not now be suffering ongoing physical pain brought on from my time in captivity.'

If only you Nitwits could read a bloody map…

There is another group of travellers, at *La Ciudad Perdida* a month prior to this event, all blissfully unaware at just how lucky they were, how lucky they *are*, how lucky that *they* were not the ones so ensnared.

Not through judgment, nor skill, nor situational awareness.

Just luck. *Sheer* luck.

The Fates had not seen to include this little ordeal into these people's Futures.

This was not what the Universe had in store for Them.

Karma spoke, and she spoke in Their Favour.

We might believe our life's direction is controlled - or if not *controlled,* at least *highly influenced* - by the sound decision-making paradigms we employ.

Life's big decisions - and there are many - require deep thought and experiential wisdom to ensure the correct choices are made.

Virtually no heed is afforded to life's supposedly *small* decisions. With so much energy focused on those so-called Big Decisions, life's small decisions are simply left to take care of themselves.

Yet, for all the effort we might put into any of our decision-making paradigms - big decision or small - our Future might simply hang on the simple issue of whether a bunch of guys strolling down a jungle track can read a map, or not.

At the next Junction, Bear left, you daft idiots.

No, not right. Left!

At this bifurcation, therein lies your Destiny.

See, the Fates have already decided *our* course. *We* will only ever end up at the destination to which we were intended, when our Path was originally laid out.

Maybe, my Indian compatriots have indeed figured out the true Nature of the Universe.

Chapter 36

You Lucky Cow!

Guatemala, Central America. 1996.

The year for many ever-hopeful England fans football was *definitely* Coming Home, at least until our team was dumped out of the European Championships semi-finals by the Germans, courtesy of, all too predictably, a penalty shoot-out.

Our nation's hopes and dreams snuffed out by one poorly taken spot kick.

A few weeks after watching the disappointment unfold in a remote jungle outpost (with, yes, a German the only other non-Guatemalan watching the large screen), I bumped into another Brit whilst journeying by bus back up to Antigua, a man with quite the Tale to tell.

My attention was first drawn to what looked like a tatty piece of metal sheeting sticking out from his pack.

'What', I wondered aloud, 'are you doing carrying a piece of tatty metal sheeting around in your pack?'

'This?' he asks, pointing at the metal sheeting. 'This is a section of plane'.

'A piece of a plane?' I reply, intrigued. 'And you're carrying a section of plane in your rucksack because...?'

He then proceeds to share his Crazy Tale with me.

In the northern Guatemala rainforest, not far from the border with Belize, sits the ancient Mayan site of Tikal. Anyone slightly Star Wars geeky will recognise the temples that tower above the forest canopy as the watchtowers over which the TIE fighters rise as they set off to destroy the Death Star in Episode IV. If you're in the area (Tikal, not the Death Star), I recommend stopping in for a day or two.

Travelling directly between Tikal and Guatemala City, you have two options.

A 12-hour, overnight bus journey along roads of dubious quality, squashed into an overloaded bus with the not-so-great and the more-than-likely unwashed. The real Hardcore Traveller option: rough going, knackering, but economical (getting you from A to B, whilst also saving the cost of a night's accommodation).

If this doesn't sound overly appealing, you could splurge out roughly $100 (or more nowadays) for a 1-hour ride in a single-prop, 8-seater plane, a fine solution for those fortunate enough to be operating on a less constrained budget.

The distance between Tikal and Guatemala City is only 300km, as the crow flies, but the bus is required to take an L-shaped route, north-east as if you were heading to Livingstone on the Caribbean coast, and then north-west to Tikal, a two-sided route adding more than 200kms to the poor crow's wearily flapping wings, a route necessary thanks to the presence of *La Sierra de las Minas,* a gnarly mountain range, peaking at over 3,000m, running east-west across Guatemala.

My British friend was on his way back to Guatemala City, with a full load of other travellers, in such a single-prop plane. They were about half-way into their flight, cruising serenely in the cloudless sky, the mountain range way down below them, marvelling at the stunning views in all directions, when the incessant racket of the propeller's unceasing gyrations suddenly disappeared.

His first thought? 'Thank God that awful noise has stopped.'

A quick look around the cabin confirmed that the rest of the passengers were also pleased the unruly racket had been replaced by the soft swishing of air as it passed over and around the plane's fuselage.

Almost immediately, the penny dropped.

That god-awful noise the propeller makes is there for a very good reason.

Its presence is to be cherished.

It is a harbinger that all is well with the aerodynamically induced lift holding them, and the plane, almost four miles up in the air.

Up front in the cockpit, the pilot commenced frantic communication with person, or persons, at the other end of the radio (in Spanish, of course, which neither my new buddy nor any of the other travellers understood), whilst simultaneously pushing and pulling an array of knobs and dials on the control panel, all with no discernible positive effect.

The passengers all stared at one another, desperate for a sign that whatever the fault was, it wasn't going to be terminal.

A small hiccup. A temporary glitch.

'Ha! Ha! Had you worried there for a second.'

No such reassurance was forthcoming.

This was, they quickly realised, not one of those issues overcome simply by pressing *Off* then *On* again.

The plane, now devoid of any forward propellant, began to slowly tilt its nose downwards, ominously, commencing a gradual glide towards the ground - or more specifically the twisted, jagged mountain range - still thankfully 20,000 feet below them.

The pilot's voice became more frantic, his attempts with the dials and levers ever more frenetic, but the plane simply continued its powerless glide downwards, downwards, until 20,000 feet became only 8,000. Then, they were almost level with the mountain tops; now, below the peaks, gliding downwards, following the path of a valley, a valley with just the faintest blue, curvy line of what could be a stream or river beneath them.

Abruptly, the pilot's radio comms ceased. His attempts to restart the engine also ended.

The pilot then turned to his passengers, uttered just the one word, in English - 'Crash' - suggesting with the aid of visual demonstration a suitable position the passengers should employ to minimise the impact of this imminent collision with *terra firma*, as if adopting the brace position would help in the slightest with the impending high-speed collision with a cliff face, a jagged peak, or whatever else Fate had in store for them in a few - Oh-God-This-Really-**IS**-It - minutes' time.

The plane continued its glided descent.

The valley bottom rapidly grew closer.

And closer.

The faint blue line morphed into a stream, then into more of a river than a stream, as their glide brought them down to just a few hundred feet above its fast-flowing waters.

Then, in the middle of the river a short distance ahead of them, a small, relatively flat, island hove into view.

Could this island be their Saviour?

The plane was definitely coming down now.

Here.

Wherever they were going to be in fewer than twenty seconds, *there* they were going to land.

The island rapidly grew larger in the plane's windscreen.

They were almost on top of it now.

On the island, the form of a cow - standing there, munching grass as cows the world over are want to do - came into focus.

A cow.

A large, innocently-minding-her-own-business cow.

And then, Impact.

The plane hit the island's soft muddy ground, wheels first, turning ever so slightly to port after impact, the side fuselage then immediately smacking into this innocently grass-munching cow, sending the poor bovine away from the sanctuary of planet earth, 30, 40 feet into the air in quite the arced trajectory.

The plane, its momentum slowed sufficiently by its brush with the cow, bounced off its original line like a cue ball hitting the black (and in this case, brown), completed a full 360-degree spin, then coming to an abrupt halt, nose down, wheels down, passengers shaken sideways.

Inside, everyone looked at everyone else; then at themselves; then at the ground; then back at everyone else.

By the love of all things Shaped-Like-A-Cow, they were Alive!

And, it would appear, all unhurt.

Did this group of Blessed Passengers then exit the plane, kissing the ground in relief, throwing a few Hail Mary's into the mix as they so did?

Did they all hug each other firmly, expressing tearfully profound emotions of Love and Compassion for their Fellow Brethren, and Humankind as a whole?

Did they choose to all take a minute or two to centre themselves in Meditation, offering heartfelt prayers to their preferred Deities?

Did they heck.

As I am sure 99% of us would do if presented with the same situation, the passengers all rapidly de-planed, forcing open the hold, rummaging around for their bags, and retrieving their cameras, for the *absolutely first thing* you must do having survived a plane crash is to take a photo of yourself, or have one taken for you, standing next to said recently crashed plane.

The cow, meanwhile, having finished its own unplanned and totally unexpected flight, landed with a neatly executed barrel roll, finishing in the standing position – a *non-supine bovine*, if you will - just as she had been a few seconds before this Thing from Out of Nowhere had rudely interrupted her lunch (or breakfast, or supper, or tea). Seemingly lacking any inclination that what had just occurred was in any way Out of the Ordinary and worthy of further, deeper consideration, the cow dropped her head, sought out the nearest clump of juicy green grass, and carried on snacking.

It is unknown whether the cow told this tale to her other cow buddies to while away those cold, dark Guatemalan nights, and whether they believed her if she did.

A cow jumping over the moon?

No problem.

A cow describing a beautiful arc through the air, the result of impact with a light aircraft?

Pull the udder one (cows, as I am sure you are already aware, are well known for their appreciation of dodgy Dad puns).

For this group of lucky travellers, rescue was but a few hours away. Helicopters arrived to transport them all back to Guatemala City, the first group to have survived such a plane crash that year (it was June), light aircraft crashes in this part of the world happening with all too predictable frequency, and mountain ranges not usually being the most ideal locations to bring your plane down for an emergency landing, presuming you all want to still be alive post-touchdown.

Back in the Big Smoke, the other passengers chose to return to their home countries, doubtless to spend thousands of Pounds or Euros on many years' worth of Trauma Therapy.

All passengers except one.

My acquaintance was offered a free flight back to the UK but had respectfully declined the kind offer.

He was here, he contested, he still had a trip to complete, and what were the chances of anything else on this trip going wrong to such a scale after that? (I was going to point out that this wasn't quite how statistical probabilities worked in practice, but figured this information, most likely, wouldn't add to the poor man's overall Sense of Knowing).

The salvaged piece of plane was now his Totem of Good Fortune. So long as he carried it with him, he said, he felt impervious to any further negative vibes the Universe might wish to throw his way.

As our paths diverged, I wished the man all the best for the Future.

Karma had evidently been strong inside the plane that day.

Karma chose to send this Island and this Cow, by way of the Fates.

The more I think about it, maybe Indian Karmic Fatalism does indeed have much to say.

Chapter 37

A Sinking Feeling

Before the likes of Facebook enabled us to instantly create long-lasting links with those we meet in the course of our lives, and on our travels, there'd be many occasions where you'd part company with someone with whom you'd established a good rapport, and then never hear from, or about, that person ever again. Handing out your home phone number was never quite on the same level of continued contact as being able to follow a friend's life progress around the world, from half-way around the world yourself, would turn out to be.

'What ever happened to (*insert name here*)?' you'd catch yourself wondering, from time to time, over the ensuing years.

Tanzania, 2004.

I climbed Kilimanjaro, then headed over to Pemba for a week of diving its outer reefs. I'd nearly not made it over to the island, having been required to dash frantically down the airstrip in order to stop my flight from leaving without me (the young lads at the bus terminal in Arusha had assured me the trip to the airport would only take six hours - *Yes Sir, honest*! - rather than the nine it had in fact required.

Lesson learnt: always take the first available bus, no matter what the locals tell you, no matter if it departs at some ungodly hour of the morning.

The greeting on arrival at the Diving Outfit was convivial, although some rather concerning information was imparted at this time.

'You should', I was told, 'have been here *last* week. *Last week*, there was a bevy of nine nubile Swedish Ladies diving with us here.'

Well, darn, drat and double darn.

This is not the sort of information a young, unattached lad wants to learn.

No good can come from knowing this information.

Oh, how I wished the imparter had kept this information to himself.

But the cat was now out of the bag. The damage was done.

You can't Unknow what you now Know (amnesia aside).

Sometimes, no Good comes from Knowing.

Sometimes, Knowledge can be a Cursed Entity.

Nevertheless, I'd had a pleasant week's diving on Pemba. Neil, the Dive Master, was a cool and sociable man, his cool demeanour probably helped no end by the fact that one of the nubile Swedish ladies had hung around for a second week, and was providing him with frequent back rubs, shoulder rubs, and who-knows-where-else rubs.

Together, they appeared a fine pair, a perfect couple.

Good luck to them both, I thought.

When life throws you apples, it's best to grab'em with both hands. And the apples.

We'd dived the southwestern reefs over the course of the first few days; the north-western reefs the latter part of the week. There had been some worrying bleaching to the coral even back then. The only other issue of remark were the currents in the southwestern reef area. At one point during one of our dives we – my buddy, myself and the Dive Leader – had had to hold on to a coral outcrop in order to maintain our positions, such was the force of the tidal stream. Swimming against the current, even to remain in the same spot, might have been possible, but barely for 20 seconds, such was the power of the flow.

At the end of the week, I said my farewells to the Team, sad to once again be moving on. After a quick flit through Zanzibar and Dar es Salaam, I flew back home, to a life more *ordinaire*, the memory of my new buddies stored in the holiday memory banks, hopeful that Fate would ensure we crossed paths again, hopefully sometime in the not-too-distant future.

Out of the blue, less than a year later, I received notification from a separate source there had been a terrible diving accident on Pemba.

A Dive Master and the four people he had been leading had disappeared during the course of a dive.

The initial news was a little sketchy, and subject to confirmation, but reports seemed to indicate that Neil had been acting as Dive Buddy for one young Danish lad, whilst a Danish mother had buddied up with her two sons, the five then forming one group for the dive. There had been two dive groups in the boat that day out to the southwestern reefs; the groups had separated at the start of the dive, yet had crossed paths, as planned, at about 12m depth halfway through the anticipated 30 or so minutes the dive had been planned to take.

At the end of the full 30 minutes, the second group emerged back by the dive boat. Neil's group were, alas, nowhere to be seen, having failed to meet up with the second group at a second, agreed spot during the dive.

Rapidly, the situation had been escalated, with extra boats and a couple of light aircraft swiftly dispatched to aid with the search. Over the coming days, further rescue resources were added, yet after three long, frantic days, tragically no sighting of the missing divers had been made. A discarded BCD buoyancy aid and some other diving paraphernalia were discovered on a reef in the northern part of the island, proof that the divers, or at least one of the divers, had surfaced, as a BCD doesn't come off on its own accord. It would be presumed that the diver removed this to aid swimming to a suitable point of safety; if they had been too far from land to make swimming a viable option, the buoyancy provided by a BCD would aid flotation for several days in the warm waters of the Indian Ocean.

It is mystery never solved, as far as I can tell.

No bodies were ever recovered. It is a terribly sad tragedy that will have profoundly affected the many close friends and family of those who went missing.

My thoughts are with all those affected.

So, you wonder how Time treats the people you meet Along the Way. When you then learn of the terrible Fate that awaited them, you rather wish you'd *not* learnt just what *had* happened.

Sometimes, no Good comes from Knowing.

Sometimes, Knowledge can indeed be a Cursed Entity.

RIP Neil.

Dessert

Daft Pudding

May 2007.

Having enjoyed the wondrous magnificence of the 50-hour train ride from Chicago to Seattle, across the great States of Minnesota, North Dakota, Montana, Idaho and Washington, I now find myself at the Green Tortoise Hostel, a cool, well-run establishment right in the centre of the city, just across the road from the famous Pike Place Fish Market.

Tonight is 'Open Mic' Night, and as the hostel runs a cheap bar in addition to offering organised entertainment, the place is packed.

The first three participants at the microphone are decent enough performances, if somewhat unremarkable, and totally unmemorable. Even moments later, I cannot for the life of me recall what they were. The seated audience watched on in a respectful hush, chit chat kept to a bare minimum.

The fourth act is a Scandiwegian lady. She has seen fit to entertain us with some Traditional Scandiwegian Folk songs. Songs for us to marvel and delight at, or so, I guess, she thinks.

Alas, the lady is not a great tune holder, although I may be doing her a disservice. She may in fact be recreating the melodies note perfect; it's just that the melodies themselves may leave a lot to be desired, devoid as they are with both harmony and concordant keys.

She, and the songs, go on.

Ariston. And on...and on...

The chit chat grows louder.

And Louder...AND LOUDER...

After what seems like an eternity, but was probably only ten minutes, the lady finally finishes, to a polite ripple of applause.

The audible sigh of relief that she has finally finished drowns out the applause, which cannot be a Good Thing.

We all give each other *that* Look: 'Phew! Glad *that's* all over'.

So, when the lady then announces she is going to bestow us with the gift of one final Scandiwegian Folk Song, the groan everyone tries to repress – unsuccessfully - is embarrassingly loud.

Nooooooooo!!!!

Lady. With the greatest of respect, but if there's one thing you need to learn, it is that it's *always* better to leave your audience wanting more.

Always.

And with Scandiwegian Folk Songs, it might be better to leave your audience never having suffered them in the first place (no offence to all my fine Scandiwegian friends out there).

Scandiwegian Ladies are evidently made of stern stuff, and, it would appear, not easily put off by an increasingly hostile crowd.

The Show must go on.

And so, on she goes, on with the Tune, noting that I use that word most advisably.

On. And on. And on.

By now, the general hubbub in the bar is far louder than the volume originating from the stage: partly because no one is really interested in what the lady is singing, none of us even the slightest bit conversant in Scandiwegian, so therefore unable to understand a word of, or revel at, the lyrics; partly because the tune actually sounds like a whale trying to purge a particular baleful dose of trapped wind - the more noise that could be made to drown out this ear-splicing torture, the better.

But mostly because the audience is by now bored, and restless, and is therefore drinking far faster than they otherwise might, had we really been paying attention to the on-stage activities, which we most certainly, by now, are not.

By the time the lady finished – to be fair, I don't remember when she exited stage left and was replaced by the next Act - the crowd have quite evidently stopped caring about Open Mic Night; we're all having a great time chatting, swapping travelling Tales, cracking jokes, exchanging sightseeing tips, and generally mucking about.

The next Act, had we been paying attention, looked quite Serious: Serious in what he had chosen to wear - a *cool* sheepskin jacket, a *cool* Trilby hat - his two-week beard growth and long matted hair completing the get-up of an Artist who was here to Perform; and Serious in what he was going to Perform, such was the manner in which he held his guitar and maintained his Rockstar-postured gait.

Had we been paying attention, we would have noticed he clearly meant Business.

Had we been paying attention.

But, alas, for the Act, we are not now even in the teeniest sense paying any attention.

The first song begins, not that anyone is *still* paying any attention, for if we were we might have noticed the young man's mounting irritation, as the song progresses, at the lack of audience consideration or positive feedback, or any small nugget of appreciation whatsoever for his evidently substantive Creative Offering.

Song One ends, with again a light, polite ripple of applause, presumably originating from the two or three people still engaged with the evening's original purpose.

Song Two starts without the lad pausing for breath.

Were we paying attention, which we weren't, we would have noticed the young lad's irritation now intensifying towards Peak Dyspepsia, for halfway through **Song Two** - maybe, possibly, I don't know, I wasn't really *paying attention* - the young lad suddenly stops playing, smashes his guitar with some force against the floor, multiple times - Bam, Bam, Bam, Bam - until the guitar is now a shadow of its former self, given that its neck is broken, its body holed, and its strings pointing hither and thither, and not in the direction generally countenanced of a properly constructed or still-functioning guitar.

Well, that certainly did the Trick.

That Shut us all the hell Up.

All heads in the room turn to face the young lad, standing motionless, yet still Postured, up on stage. The silence is quite something to behold, given the unholy ruckus just a few seconds earlier.

We sit there, motionless, not daring to move or utter even the slightest sound.

We wait, nervously, excitedly, expectantly, for what might happen next.

This might just turn out to be the best Open Mic Night, **EVER**.

Time drags, slowly, so slowly.

People awkwardly look at their feet, the floor, the ceiling, all around, darting their eyes from one spot to the next, not wanting to make eye contact with anyone else, such is the uncertainty as to what, really, is currently going down.

Is the poor lad having a Mental (slash) Nervous breakdown?

What have we missed?

Finally, the Performer breaks the silence. He speaks into the Mic.

'This', he says, 'is a **Serious** Song about **War**', deadpan, anger - oh so deep anger - resonating through the speakers.

The young lad then flips the whole room the Bird.

And on that sanctimonious note, he hurriedly leaves the stage, dashing out via the nearest exit, maybe never to be seen again.

We all look at one another, wondering how long etiquette requires us to suppress the laughter we are all currently barely containing, mindful of not being insensitive towards the man's potentially fragile mental state.

But, well, Bugger *that*, *this* is Funny.

Uncontained Laughter suddenly fills the room.

The following morning, whilst making my way out for the day, I stop in at the front desk to check a few details about harbour ferry times with the man on Front Desk duty.

I wonder, aloud, whether he has heard about the Events at last night's Open Mic session?

He has not.

So, I explain.

And as I explain the evening's shenanigans my head turns slightly to the right, enabling me to see through an open door to the side of the reception office, and into a shelved storage room. Atop one shelf I espy the remnants of said guitar. Sitting there, sad and forlornly.

Still, obviously, in pieces.

'Oh, look,' I say to reception man, pointing into the room at the now ex-guitar, 'there's the remains of the guitar.

The man peers into the room.

His face drops. His complexion suddenly gains a deathly, ashen-white hue.

'Fuck Me,' the man says.

'FUCK! ME!'

'That's **MY** guitar. I leant that Fucker **MY** guitar!'

I stand there, facing reception man, in silence, not knowing quite what to say.

No ideas on how to reframe this sad episode are currently leaping into my mind, nothing that I suspect will, in any way, improve this sorry situation.

Hmm. OK. So, how to politely extricate myself from this awkward situation?

The time.

The *Time*!

I look at my watch.

'Ah, well, gotta dash. Ferry to catch.'

And with that, I am gone.

Epilogue

The '90s was a Different Era for the World of Travel.

You may be sufficiently well-ripened to remember a Time even before that.

You may nostalgically lament how radically the World of Travel had changed even by the time the '90s poked its fresh-faced mugshot into view.

Either way, compared with today, the early 2020s, the '90s were a Different Era; a Different Age; a Different sense of Sophistication; a Different of set of International Threats; a Different level of Technological Advancement.

In the '90s, the Internet had yet to be rolled out for the masses, connecting the furthest flung corners of the world, and pretty much all spaces in between; pocket-sized Mobile Phones were more than a decade away (sure, the military possessed 'mobile' interpersonal communicators, the size of large suitcases); ATMs were yet to be globally accessible; and Credit Card purchases still required carbon-copy Click-Clack machines, and telephonic authorisation.

No, *You Are Here* real-time phone-based maps.

No, Online, in the Moment, Translation capabilities.

No, Online Hotel Reservations, nor Travel Booking systems.

No, Skype-based local or international calls.

No, *I'll Just Google That* informational access.

No, Constant News Updates from the World Back Home, and At Large.

No Facebook/ Instagram/ TikTok/ Twitter (thankfully, where's the Delete button for that lot?)

The Result?

Travelling was hard work.

Really, it *was* Hard Work.

Sure, not as challenging as performing life-saving surgery on sick children, nor fighting wildfires, nor striving for decades to find a cure for cancer, or a vaccine to end a novel virus pandemic, nor establishing a lasting solution to World Peace, I grant you.

But still, tough enough.

The many difficulties weeded out the meek and foppish from even considering Venturing Forth.

For those with the *cajones* to firmly grasp the nettle, saying 'Goodbye' to your friends and family, 'See you in a year', really did mean, 'Goodbye', *'Adios'*, *'Auf Wiedersehen'*.

You stepped onto the aircraft, and then disappeared off the grid. Completely.

You were now On Your Lonesome.

Yikes. Scary Stuff.

You learnt to be Resourceful and Adaptable, and to Plan well Ahead.

You learnt to be Confident and Assertive (whilst also learning some Humility, too).

You learnt who you could Trust, and when you were being Hoodwinked (often, the hard way).

You were forced to Grow (up) as a Person.

If you couldn't resolve a problem *yourself*, someone heroically riding in to save the day was wishful thinking.

As a result, inter-traveller communication became your Go-To safety net. The Travelling Community became, not simply friends, but your new sense of family, essential not just for information about where to go, what to see, where to stay, but also for the all-important verbal communication and inter-personal connections we all need to mitigate the sense of isolation that being a solitary figure in a strange land thousands of miles from home can occasionally engender.

Chat between random Travellers - in bars, in restaurants, on buses, on beaches, anywhere and everywhere - was perfectly normal; sparking up conversation with a random stranger you'd only just met, Quite the Done Thing.

If you weren't entirely confident in yourself when it came to starting up conversations with random travellers you were forced to learn, forced to face your insecurities, forced to adapt to your inadequacies.

There's no greater learning environment than Total Immersion, with No Easy Cop Out.

Sadly, nowadays, should you have the temerity to spark up conversation with a fellow traveller, or add your tuppence-worth to an easily overheard discussion, you are more likely to receive merely a disdainful look, a look akin to your having just admitted possessing a penchant for unsavoury activities with livestock.

People: if you don't want to chat to other travellers, Stay Home, Ride the Tube.

As you alighted from a bus in some middle-of-nowhere outpost, a group would naturally form, all of you with the same mission, to find lodgings for the night. Your collective mission automatically brought you all together – a new Team.

Sometimes, you might find yourself walking down a random street and espy another Westerner way up ahead of you, a hundred yards away or more; they then espy you. Immediately, you both turn and gravitate towards each other's position, eager to swap Tales about the Craziness of the World around you.

This (ever so slightly) Grumpy Old Man's rant is my Lament to the passing of that Era.

For The Team; The Community; The Family – it is *no more.*

The ubiquity of free Wi-Fi provided across this vast globe, from the most out-of-the-way roadside food shack in Tanzania, to the ramshackle, rickety, end-of-the-line beach café in Cambodia, to the tiny village nestled high in the Andes, means most Travellers now just sit in isolation, staring gormlessly down at their phones, checking in with whatever rubbish their friends have just posted, rather than taking the opportunity to converse with those sitting right there next to them, those now moving amongst them.

They're *Here*, but none of them are *really* Here.

Total Immersion is a joke of a concept for many of today's long-term holiday makers.

The world might seem better connected through this InterWeb contraption; yet the technology also seems to be driving us further apart.

Over the years, I have gathered more interesting perspectives from talking *directly* to people from all corners of the globe than I care count, gleaning information from other travellers on a vast range of topics in a manner such that the information hasn't been tainted by the bias from which it might suffer when gleaned through the prism of our Home Media Network.

Of course, if the people you chat to only collate *their* information through the prism of their HMN, you'll become similarly infected should you choose to not take everything you're told at face value. No researcher worth his/ her salt would ever countenance relying on anything less than multiple sources, from a 360-degree perspective, before committing to a position, before having the audacity to consider their comprehension of a topic sufficiently extensive to be even vaguely definitive.

That's the Trick: To Keep an Open Mind.

Surely, if Travel teaches us *anything*, it is to Keep an Open Mind.

****

Grumpy *After Eight*

This is the Issue.

People now communicate with others, people worldwide, all without having to leave the safety and comfort of their messy bedrooms.

Why, they ask, do I need to travel to find out that which can already be gleaned through the Internet?

I am already made Wise by the Information I have learnt via Google, or so they say.

Ah. Wise, possibly. In a purely theoretical sense.

But not *Worldly* Wise.

Picture Robin Williams, sitting on a bench, telling Matt Damon's Will Hunting *savant* the simple facts, that no matter how much think you have learnt from Books, or have gleaned from the Internet, or how well your Teachers taught you in College, there's no substitute for First Hand *Out There* Experience.

No matter how Smart you think you are, the World *Out There* will teach you a Lifetime of Knowledge, first-hand, real time, up *real* close and *very* personal.

Instead, we choose, now, to immerse ourselves inside a World mirroring our own ever-narrowing World View, our views reinforced perpetually without challenge or exposure to Alternative Ideologies, our opinions calcifying to a point of being unbreakable, even were pertinent information to come our way, information that would, under less rigid circumstances, shatter this specific Viewpoint, or even an entire Ideology.

If we only converse with those in our Social Media Echo Chamber, our views will doubtless be reinforced, become entrenched, our stance on any issue solidifying as each person we meet agrees with that stance. The true strength of any viewpoint is only really established when pitted against the most opposing of arguments.

Over time, if we're not careful, our Views and Opinions become personalised; they become encapsulated into our Identity, into how we want Others to perceive *us* (other people's opinions of us are *very* important).

The chance of being swayed to alter our Opinion should a new perspective or convincing argument be heard becomes more and more remote; the effort required to change our whole outlook, our Identity, too great.

But cracks will soon start to appear, for internalising and holding conflicting, illogical, hypocritical or plainly incorrect Opinions whilst simultaneously maintaining our mental equilibrium is quite the (impossible) Challenge.

The only Challenge we *should* be facing should come from others, Challenging our views, rather than attempting to grow resistant to the concept of *being* Challenged.

For what if the Views were hold *are* incorrect?

What if we *do* want to change our stance?

What if that Viewpoint *pivotal* to our self-image is shown to be *manifestly* incorrect?

What then?

****

Cognitive Dissonance explains much of the Online Outrage and city-wide Mob Violence we sadly see today: when presented by two opposing or contradictory Cognitions or Behaviours, or two seemingly incongruous Beliefs or Attitudes, Dissonance is created, an uncomfortable sensation, the frisson of two unstoppable Attitudinal forces clashing for superiority.

For instance:

Support Minority Rights. Islam is a Minority (in the West).

Support Women's Rights. Islam does *not* support Women's Rights.

How to Support both Women's Rights *and* the Rights of Islam?

Equally:

Support Minority Rights. People of Indian Heritage are a Minority (in the UK).

Oppose (Historical) Slavery. (Some) People of Indian Heritage are aiding Modern Day Slavery (in the UK).

How to both oppose Modern Day Slavery *and* maintain this pro-Minority Stance?

Or try this:

Support Minority Rights. Native Americans are a Minority.

Support Migrant Rights. Anyone who is anti-Migrant is immediately labelled a Racist.

(Some) Native American tribes were decidedly anti-European Settler. By the preceding logic, this would make those Native Americans racists (which is clearly not the case).

Conflict of Beliefs and Attitudes - Dissonance, frisson, outrage.

Changing our Belief system, adapting to the conflicting stances, is the only true way to reduce the Dissonance. But this is a Challenge that requires effort.

Indeed, the sheer weight and effort required to adapt to and internalise this new Cognition simply overwhelms, in a flash creating instead internalised conflict, conflict that in turn invokes Anger in the individual experiencing the Dissonance.

This Anger could be directed inwards, but usually - *more easily* - it finds its expression outwardly.

The greater the Anger, the more the individual expressing the Anger is suffering from the Dissonance of their Cognitions.

Constant Debate, constant Challenge, constant refinement of our Views, constant reshaping of our Beliefs, this is only way to stops ourselves from identifying to others simply through a set of poorly formed (and formulated) Beliefs.

In conditions of ever-increasing Tribalisation, the likelihood for Groupthink is magnified. Extreme positions become more prevalent. People self-select to only socialise or debate those who agree with their World View; suddenly, the world is being split into smaller and smaller groups of people who, holding opposing views on specific topics, can no longer mingle and be in each other's company.

'I could never be friends with someone who believes...' seems to have become a recurring theme.

Sure, there are always going to be a few dealbreakers for who we socialise with, but these should be reserved for serious matters - violent criminal behaviours, extreme rudeness to strangers, or *actual* racist or misogynist behaviours, rather than how people define *racist* or *misogynistic* behaviours nowadays.

Just when did Debate and Opposing Viewpoints become such dirty words?

For those who choose to Travel, this can be a golden opportunity to place yourself outside your comfort zone, to establish a greater perspective on Worldwide Reality, rather than purely theoretical stance gleaned from a life lived solely inside the confined shores of your life sphere, from knowledge gleaned *solely* from second-hand sources.

Why Travel, though, if simply to remain in your Safety Bubble, doing nothing more 'noteworthy' than posting countless selfies of you posing in the exact same well-known spot thousands - no, tens of 1000s - of others have posed before?

This is not Travelling – this is what is commonly known as a Holiday.

Even a 6-month trip is still a Holiday if you're not continuously Challenging your Belief Systems.

Opposing perspectives, opposing viewpoints, *these* are what make the World Go Round.

Despite what you might believe, none of us is *Normal* – *our* Opinions, *our* Behaviours, are not the *one and only* Normal.

There is a *vast world* of difference Out There, just waiting to be discovered.

And whilst Travelling, there's a new concept I would heartily suggest trying out.

Silence.

Simple Silence.

It is in these quiet moments we might be lucky enough to experience the Epiphany we did not know we were seeking; we might experience one of those Eureka moments of comprehension and understanding of the deeper meanings within our own Personal Existence.

A-Ha.

We *don't* always have to be doing something.

We *don't* always have to have our faces fixed onto our screens.

It really *is* OK occasionally to daydream, to stare, transfixed, out of the window of a moving bus or train, for hour, upon hour, upon hour.

It really *is* OK, occasionally, to drift off and allow our minds to wander.

It really *is* OK to cut ourselves off from everything we ever knew, or thought we knew, for if we never truly *leave* Home – mentally - we never truly *arrive* in our Destination.

And to those loudly and obtrusively recording yourselves into your phones for you latest Blog Episode, whilst the rest of us try to savour the beauty of a Gobi Sunset, *no one cares.*

Really. *No One.*

****

OK. I apologise.   *Way* too much Grumpy Old Man diatribe.

I may already be preaching to the converted, in any case. If so, I can only apologise once again. Kudos to you, dear Seasoned Traveller.

I need to conclude on a high note, on a more positive vibe.

A Happy Ending.

Who *doesn't* like a Happy Ending?

I would like to offer out some heartfelt thanks to a few people – names un(*never*)known - for their kind help, their vital assistance in getting me out of tough scrape, or five.

There really are some amazingly selfless and altruistic people in this World of ours, people who don't hesitate in putting themselves out to assist a total stranger in their Time of Need.

These people were (*are*) the Best.

The South-African Dude: Who drove me an hour each way, at 1am, from East London to the nearest hospital (no taxis/ no ambulance), when my thumb was badly sliced open, and who waited at least an hour whilst the cut was attended to, before driving me back to East London.

To the Mexican Dudes: Who translated for me at the Police Station, when my bag was stolen in Oaxaca (you *do* remember how to pronounce that, yes?).

To the German Lady: Who also translated for me at the Police Station, when my bag was stolen, this time in La Paz (obviously, *not* the *same* bag).

To the Random Lady in the Queue: For giving me €5 for the bus from Geneva into France, the (unexpected) Rail Replacement Bus Service - and its extremely surly French driver - not accepting card payment, nor the Swiss ATMs giving out Euros.

To the Random Taxi Driver in Fez: Who appeared out the blue, at sunset, when there wasn't another taxi for miles around, at the most perfect moment, given that I was, at the time, being pursued by four young Moroccan lads, lads who had expressed a keen interest in rearranging the current layout of my limbs, kneecaps and/ or facial features.

And to the hundreds of Fellow Voyagers who've showed me kindness, consideration, and compassion; who've told decent Tales, or funny jokes, or simply lightened the mood; who've taken the time to enlighten me and further my knowledge on a whole host of topics – Thank You.

You People Make the World Go Round.

Printed in Great Britain
by Amazon